THE HANDBOOK OF
FOREIGN BIRDS
IN COLOUR

VOLUME ONE

Their Care in Cage and Aviary

By A. RUTGERS

English Edition
edited by K. A. Norris

BLANDFORD PRESS

POOLE   DORSET

First published 1964
Second (revised) edition 1968
Third edition 1972
Reprinted 1970
Fourth (revised) edition 1977

ISBN 0 7137 0815 8

From material in
Tropische Volière Vogels
by A. Rutgers, published by
Littera Scripta Manet, Joppe, Holland.

Colour printed by Ebenezer Baylis & Son Ltd., The Trinity Press, Worcester
Text printed and books bound
in Great Britain by Richard Clay (The Chaucer Press), Ltd.,
Bungay, Suffolk

CONTENTS

ACKNOWLEDGMENTS

Most of the colour photographs were taken by Mr. Jeremy N. McCabe, by arrangement with The Zoological Gardens, Regent's Park, London; Bleak Hall Bird Farm, Woburn, Beds.; Mr. Drury, "Oakfields", Stapleford Abbotts, Essex; and the late Mr. K. A. Norris, former President of the Foreign Birds League.

Other acknowledgments for colour illustrations are as follows:

> Dennis Avon and Tony Tilford—Wildlife Studies Ltd. for Nos. 69, 73, 103, 142.
> Anthony J. Mobbs for Nos. 126, 128, 131.
> Colorbank for Nos. 47, 61, 63, 64, 71, 72.
> F. Collet/Ardea Photographics for No. 29.
> Horst Bielfeld for Nos. 6, 35, 74.
> Thomas Brosset for No. 77.
> Malcolm McGregor for No. 91.
> Horst Müller-Schmidz for Nos. 14, 24, 68, 93, 96, 104, 109.
> Plazikowski for Nos. 26, 36, 78, 94.
> P. Ramaekers for Nos. 27, 49, 52–56, 59, 60, 65, 81, 132.

A special acknowledgment is made to the late Mr. K. A. Norris, the editor of the original editions, for preparing the book for the English reader, and writing additional descriptions.

INTRODUCTION

Man has always found interest and pleasure in domestic pets. Birds have proved an especial source of delight to many people. As long ago as 284 B.C., Kallixenus describes in the *Chronicles of Alexandria* how parrots were carried in processions, and Alexander the Great had the distinction of being the first to import Indian Ring-necked Parrakeets (*Psittacula krameri manillensis*) into Europe. He saw them in India and took them back to Greece.

Today there are a vast number of bird keepers and fanciers all over the world. Fortunately bird keeping is now carried out under much happier conditions with spacious aviaries largely replacing restricted cages. The Zoological Gardens show the birds under excellent conditions, where they are kept healthy and with safeguards against disease, and where they are able to fly freely and live in natural conditions, supplied with the right food and enjoying sunlight and air. These are necessities which must be provided by everyone who keeps these delightful creatures.

In nature, the more intimate details of bird life are unseen, and only the most persistent bird watcher is able to obtain a glimpse of them. But in a well-arranged cage or aviary everyone can see and study the habits of the birds.

Most of the birds described in this book are kept in pairs, possibly with other different species, but always in such a way that their natural life can be developed to the full—so that nests can be built and families raised. Others may be kept solely because they make such excellent pets. In these cases less emphasis is laid on the bird life than on the bird companionship.

The more experienced bird fancier will miss certain species from this book, but it is written mainly for those whose knowledge is elementary and who need a guide to the care of the birds so that the risk of losses, which otherwise may be considerable, is reduced to a minimum. Unnecessary disappointments might well bring to a premature end a 'hobby' which was started with enthusiasm.

Shows held annually all over the country not only arouse and stimulate interest in the hobby, but also provide an opportunity to study the birds and obtain information regarding the best methods of housing and treatment. The breeding of new colour varieties and types is also encouraged.

As in all hobbies, personal taste plays a large part in the setting up and furnishing of a cage or aviary. It is possible to employ experts, but a great satisfaction lies in the 'do it yourself' making of cages and aviaries. Some designs which have proved satisfactory are outlined.

Nomenclature is difficult. In the basic scientific nomenclature (generally Latin, sometimes Greek) and occasionally in native names, continual research necessitates frequent changes. Hence names which are correct today may change by tomorrow. Throughout this book the scientific name has been used, together with the English name in common use. This should help to avoid confusion, and many synonyms have also been included.

1. ACCOMMODATION

The Outside Flight

As it is not easy to provide suitable accommodation for many birds indoors, most varieties are housed in the garden. This is best for the birds, if precautions are taken to protect them from cold winds and a shelter is provided which can, when necessary, be heated in winter.

An aviary can be built as a lean-to extension to the house and a full view of it obtained from indoors. Some aviaries take up the whole of the garden, and it is a glorious sight to watch the birds flying in full freedom, nesting perhaps in the ivy covering the fence, and with young life in bush and shrub. The birds will be perfectly safe, for all over the flight wires are stretched to keep out cats and other predators. Flights which take up all the garden are, of course, exceptional, but the sunny side of a small back garden may be turned into an aviary.

The size and design of the aviary will depend on the garden, and it may be planned imaginatively, taking care to ensure that it is practical and safe. It is a good plan to build against a wall facing south; if the wall is overgrown the birds will appreciate it for nesting purposes.

FIG 1 *Garden aviary, with safety entrance*

Here is a simple two-compartment aviary (Fig. 1). Planted with shrubs and climbers, it can be made most attractive.

The shelter has doors at the back and can, if necessary, have a connecting door to the flight. If it is desired to enter the shelter, the trap to the aviary should be closed, and the birds shut outside. Most people like a larger shelter and it is advisable to add a wire netting-covered porch (as illustrated) through which entry can be effected. Only with such a safety passage can one be certain that the birds cannot escape.

The birds will enter the shelter only if there is sufficient light, so large windows at the top, front, and side are necessary. On the inside of the windows should be fitted a wire-mesh-covered frame which can be fastened in position with bolts or buttons; the windows must be cleaned on the inside so the frame should be readily detachable. The mesh prevents accident caused by birds taking fright and flying against the glass, and prevents the birds escaping if the glass is broken.

The bob hole between the shelter and flight should be sufficiently large, as some birds will never become accustomed to a small entrance. It is wise to have the door constructed so that it can be operated from outside; it may be necessary to close it on cold winter nights.

The flights themselves can be covered on top, wholly or partially, by glass or a double thickness of polythene. The whole of the back wall, if it faces north or east, should also be covered.

Houses which have a bay window, a loggia, or a small lean-to conservatory offer excellent possibilities. A door and window with leaded glass make an attractive partition between the living-room and the birds' home.

It is essential that the sun is able to penetrate as long as possible during the day, and the north wind must be excluded. As a roofing material, use may be made of plexiglass or a double thickness of clear polythene, which admit the sun and keep out rain and wind.

Older houses have balconies which are no longer used. These make ideal sites; the shelter is there and only the flight has to be provided. Basements can also be used as shelters, provided sunlight can be admitted. As a rule they are frost-proof and can accommodate several types of foreign birds.

Another likely place is a loft. This can make a very suitable home, and a small flight can be built out from the dormer window.

FIG 2 *Small flight built out from loft*

Fig. 3 shows an outside aviary with several partitions which can easily be made. On the right it can be seen how the mesh is carried below the ground and then folded outwards. A brick wall may be substituted for the poles laid on the ground. Fig. 4 is the plan of Fig. 3. An enclosed shelter at the back can be especially useful in winter.

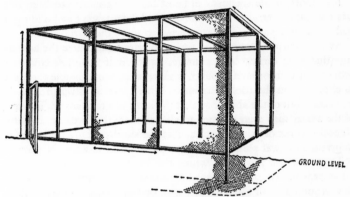

GROUND LEVEL

FIG 3 *Outdoor aviary, showing method of extending wire under ground to prevent vermin burrowing into the flight*

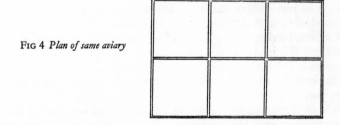

FIG 4 *Plan of same aviary*

Such a shelter needs large windows facing south. There should be a sliding door at the bottom and a higher flap door to serve as entrances for the birds, the lower door being used by ground birds such as quail or pheasants. It is wise to have the shelter higher than the outside flight as birds seek the highest place to roost and so will be encouraged to use it.

The outside aviary should have an entrance lobby or double door to prevent the birds escaping when the aviary is entered—although this may not be necessary if the aviary is very large.

If different species of birds are to be kept apart for breeding purposes, it is best to build a range of aviaries side by side.

White river sand can be used as a floor covering.

The floors of the shelters can be of brick or concrete to keep out rats and other vermin. There are many different ways of building a shelter; often a shed can be converted to serve the purpose.

Aviaries entirely covered on top with wired glass have the advantage that a cat can do little damage, especially if this glass covering projects an inch or so all round, which makes it impossible for a cat to climb up on the roof. Personally I like a narrow strip projecting from the front of the shelter so that the birds can take cover. The rest of the aviary may then be open to all weathers; the birds often enjoy a good shower of rain and it benefits the shrubs. Many birds prefer to go into the wet shrubs for a bath instead of into a pan of water.

There are many ways in which the aviary and the birds can be safeguarded from cats, besides using wired glass. It is usually possible to surround a small town garden with ordinary chicken wire of 2 in. mesh, the top part of which can be bent inwards or outwards. This wire can often be fastened on to an existing fence. Overhanging branches of a tree which would allow a cat to climb on to the aviary should be removed, or the tree made unclimbable by hammering in a round of nails. A double layer of wire netting may be put around the aviary, leaving a couple of inches between the inner and outer layer, but this is usually too costly and the look of the aviary is not improved. The home cat can be trained to become accustomed to the birds; it is the stray cats which cause most trouble and have to be kept out.

The chief enemies are, of course, rats, mice, and weasels and these must be destroyed. Mice are small enough to slip through ordinary $\frac{1}{2}$-in. mesh wire. Not only do they eat and foul the seed, but they may also cause great damage when they disturb a nest or frighten brooding birds away from the nest at night when they would have difficulty finding their way back in the dark.

Never lay poison in the aviary or shelter, not even in places which are difficult for birds to reach, as mice have a habit of dragging the

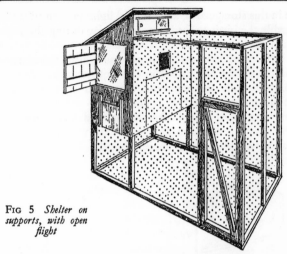

FIG 5 *Shelter on supports, with open flight*

poison into the open. Traps are forbidden inside the aviary. Feeding troughs should be placed where mice cannot get at them.

If a covered feeding place is made in the outside aviary, the birds will use it most of the time. It should preferably be close to the door which gives access to the entrance lobby so that it can be supplied without entering the aviary and disturbing the birds. The shelter also should have some arrangement for feeding and drinking. A good way is to suspend the feeding table on two chains, within reach of the entrance.

In addition to permanent aviaries, portable models are also made. Their advantage is that they can be moved to fresh ground when the grass is soiled and no longer suitable. Care must be taken to see that the surface on which the aviary is to be placed is perfectly level, otherwise birds will escape and vermin may gain access.

In a large shelter it is advisable to reserve a part in which to place breeding cages and to store such requisites as food bins and cleaning utensils. The breeding cages should be several feet above the ground and shelves should be built below on which to store feeding stuffs, medicines, and utensils of all kinds. Partitions can be made by a wire-covered screen which will prevent loss of light. In the winter the heating apparatus can also be placed here, since no birds will be flying loose in this storage area, and artificial lighting is an advantage as it will enable the birds to feed later in the day during the winter months, when the hours of daylight are so short.

A net is indispensable, especially when young birds have become independent and need to be placed in other quarters. Troublesome fighting males must also be removed. A large butterfly net, with a deep bag of fine mosquito netting, is best.

Special trapping cages (Fig. 6) can also be used. They work well and cause little disturbance. The chasing of birds with a net must be avoided in an aviary where birds are breeding.

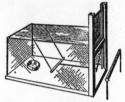

FIG 6
Trapping cage

For an aviary to hold a mixed collection, as much space as possible is needed. If only a few pairs are kept for breeding, it is best to supply each pair with its own enclosure; then the birds get used to one another and there will be no disturbing element.

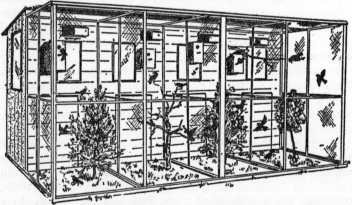

FIG 7 *A very suitable design of aviary to provide separate breeding accommodation for 4 pairs of birds. The aviary is entered by a main door at rear of shelters, and there is a low connecting door between each shelter and flight*

Cages

Song birds are usually kept in a roomy cage in the living-room indoors. Many fanciers place their breeding cages in a small separate room, where the birds soon settle down contentedly.

A cage with fine mesh is preferable to one with bars, and certainly to a glass cage, which is necessary only for birds so delicate as to require a temperature thermostatically controlled—humming birds, for example. The cage should be covered with wire on all sides, and have glass or wire on top so as to admit both daylight and artificial light. The front should be of mesh and doors should be made at each end; one should be large, with a smaller one at the opposite end. One or two holes about 2 in. wide are needed in the wire, and the nesting boxes can be attached to the outside with the entrances over these holes, giving the advantage of easy nest control. If possible, the bath should be attached outside so that no flying space inside is lost.

If the mesh is painted green or dark brown, it will be much less conspicuous and do away with any annoying 'shine'. Perches should be fixed at various heights. The food and drinking bowls can be put inside through a small door and a small rack for green stuff must be easy of access. The large door should be opened only when alterations have to be made, when birds have to be caught, or when a big clean out is necessary.

One or two metal trays, $\frac{1}{2}$ to 1 in. deep, should be placed on the floor. Dry bird sand can then be sprinkled on these; good clean river sand, sterilized by heating on a stove, is recommended. Sawdust is sometimes used instead of sand, but this material is unnatural, and the fact that it blows about a great deal makes it undesirable. Moreover, sand contains traces of many beneficial minerals, valuable to digestion. The greater absorptive property of sawdust might make its use more desirable with fruit-eating—or nectar feeding—birds, which seldom pick anything up off the floor, but even with these it would be preferable to use a layer of peat dust. As an alternative the trays may be covered with blotting paper or newspaper which should be changed regularly. The trays should have handles so that they can be withdrawn easily, and the fronts concealed by a hinged wooden flap.

A glass plate, 4–6 in. high, fitted round the bottom of the cage will prevent sand, feathers, and seed husks getting into the room as the birds fly about.

The minimum measurements of the cage should be 2 ft long by 16 in. deep by 20 in. high. It is essential to provide adequate space for exercise if small foreign birds are to be kept in perfect health, so smaller sizes should be avoided.

My indoor cages for 4 or 5 pairs of Waxbills are 4 ft long by 2 ft deep by 40 in. high. They are placed one on top of the other. The top one is raised on legs so that the lower cage can be illuminated properly from above. The whole unit is mounted on wheels so that if the sun is not in a favourable position the cages may be turned with a slight touch of the hand. A hanging feeding tray is placed in the top cage as the birds cannot be seen if they feed on the floor. These cages can be made at home.

The barred cage has one advantage which must be mentioned. Some birds are apt to overgrow their claws, and these may get caught in the mesh with unfortunate results. All birds should be inspected from time to time and claws cut when necessary, but the barred cage presents far less risk of their getting caught up.

Punch-bar cages can also be made, but are much more difficult. Fronts can be bought ready-made, but they are not cheap. These fronts are usually fitted with doors and excellent cages can be constructed with them.

The so-called French aviary with a roof is beautiful and decorative. The furnishing is usually very practical—doors at various heights, trays, provision for attaching baths, drinking fountains, and even nest boxes.

The cages must, of course, be light and sited where the sun can reach them. A lean-to conservatory, or a bay window facing south, is ideal. The birds must be able to find shade in the cage as they do not always want to be exposed to the sun. A disadvantage of 'all wire' cages is that the birds are not sheltered from the draught, to which they are susceptible, and the consequences may be disastrous. Windows are sometimes opened wide with the result that a blast of cold air causes the temperature to drop considerably, and some birds quickly fall ill. In the wooden cage this danger is greatly reduced and the birds feel safer.

A cage in front of the window is best; the birds face the light and the room seems darker, so do not take fright when approached. If the cage is against the wall opposite the window, and someone enters the room between the birds and the light, the situation is reversed and the birds take fright at every movement. But they feel happy when the lights are on in their cages during the evening and the light in the room is out. It is then possible to approach close to the cages without disturbing the birds, as they see little outside their own light orbit. A living picture may be made in this way, or it might be possible to arrange, as an experiment, an exhibition where the birds are in illuminated cages, without netting or bars to disturb the view as the visitors pass by in the dark. This has been done successfully at Antwerp and other zoos.

Sometimes people try to brighten a dark corner with an illuminated glass show-case but this is absolutely wrong and bad for the birds.

It is important to provide height where birds can fly if something frightens them. At night, also, they look for the highest spot to roost; this is usually also the warmest spot in the cage.

Nesting boxes should be hung high up on the back wall so that they cannot be easily interfered with, especially by children.

As the birds must be caught now and again, there should not be too many branches, which also limit the amount of flying space. Catch the birds by hand or by a net or trap cage. (Fig. 6.)

A small bamboo cage is sometimes used for a single singing bird. It should be as large as possible, and the bird will become reconciled to its abode and sing merrily, especially if allowed out occasionally to fly round the room. Doors must be provided and the bath—which no bird must be without—should be hung on the outside. A cage with a large bird should not be hung up, for its movements will cause the cage to sway and birds do not like this. They are happiest if their cage is at eye level or a little higher. A tame parrakeet or canary which is allowed to fly freely for a couple of hours a day does not require elaborate accommodation. Such a bird looks to its owner for companionship, perches on the shoulder or hand, and comes to the table for titbits. Birds, when kept singly, learn very rapidly what is expected of them and it is never necessary to catch or chase them. They will return to their cage of their own volition.

The Bird Room

An ideal home for birds can be constructed in a room, conservatory, or large bay window facing south. It is much better for them than cages.

The walls must be painted in light washable paint, so as to make cleaning easy. A thick layer of sharp river sand should cover the floor. The windows need wired frames so that if broken the birds cannot escape. Wired frames should be made removable for washing the windows.

The design will depend on the needs of the occupants. Plants in troughs or pots can only be put in if there are no parrots or parrakeets flying around. As a rule only foreign finches or small insect-eaters will be the fortunate inhabitants of the room. In that case a wide choice of plants can be made and this greatly adds to the appearance.

A set of cages can be hung along one wall where fighters can be confined, or pairs separated to breed in peace. Breeding results are usually much more satisfactory in such large spaces than in cages, but harmony must exist between the occupants. It is essential to watch the birds and segregate the troublemakers.

The furnishings should follow the plan of an aviary. The room must be heated and have a system of thermostatic control to maintain an even temperature.

Lighting shortens the long winter nights and its use until 8 p.m. and again at 6 or 7 a.m. will be sufficient. Most of the birds will still be found at the feeding table in the evening.

2. THE FURNISHING OF CAGE AND AVIARY

Perches

A bird in captivity has many restrictions to contend with, and its living conditions should therefore be made as natural as possible. Metal perches should never be used. It is true that they are more hygienic, will not harbour lice or mites, and are easy to keep clean, but they are absolutely unsuitable.

An outside aviary with a shelter needs an adequate number of branches of varying thicknesses; these should also be supplied under the covered-in part and some must be arranged as high as possible.

The birds will prefer the latter for roosting, and each bird will have its own sleeping perch and defend it against all comers.

In a cage, fresh branches or rounded perches of wood of various sizes should be used. If only thin perches are used, the birds' claws will grow too long. With thick perches the birds keep their claws trimmed by rubbing, and the sand on the floor is also a help.

Branches with the bark on are best. They retain their natural resilience for a long time and they help to keep the birds' legs in good condition. Soiled perches must be changed regularly. Branches under the sleeping perches become very soiled, and should be removed, except during breeding when the aviary or cage should not be disturbed.

Most birds prefer thin branches for roosting; and these should be placed in the highest spots.

In a small cage, perches should be placed so that as much uninterrupted flying space as possible remains. Too many branches will obstruct the flight. For birds with long tails it is essential to have perches arranged so that the tails can hang down freely, and they must also be sufficiently far away from the wall to permit freedom of movement otherwise the tail will soon be ruined.

In small cages, particularly, perches should be attached to the bars by means of hooks or clamps at one end only at various heights. They will then be springy and more closely resemble natural branches and twigs.

Nesting Facilities

Small finches like to use nest boxes filled with hay, hemp teasings, and feathers. Such boxes should be supplied at breeding time (although many birds prefer to build in the shrubs) and hung at varying heights. Some birds select hidden spots; these can be provided by tying up bundles of heather and hanging them close together with nest boxes in between. Pine branches, bundles of reeds, and broom, can also be used to provide seclusion. Part of the wall may be covered with tree bark, and if any of the pieces stand away from the wall, the space may be filled with hay, thus making suitable nesting cavities for which some birds will show a preference.

The well-known beech and poplar log nests can be obtained in all

B

sizes, but small finches should be provided with a choice of breeding sites and nest boxes.

A small hole should be drilled in the side wall of nest boxes to allow air to penetrate, as the parent birds may sit for hours in the opening and consequently very little fresh air can reach the youngsters.

Coconuts provide the handyman with a means of making more natural-looking nests. Only a small amount of drilling and sawing is necessary. The size of the entrance hole should be made to suit the size of the bird. The lids can easily be removed for inspection of the nest and for cleaning purposes.

Much more ingenious are nesting baskets which are easy to make for those who have learnt basket-making. Birds are sure to prefer such natural-looking material. It will be necessary to keep these clean and hygienic, as they attract pests, by use of the disinfectant sprays now available which are not dangerous to the birds.

Foreign finches need an enormous amount of nesting material, for they often build large nests. As well as straw and woollen threads (especially hemp rope), they use strips of paper, bits of material, fur, hair, and large and small feathers. A large quantity of this sort of material should be available, as the finches often enlarge their nest while actually incubating. Some birds prefer dark material, others stick to hay and fresh blades of grass, and moss is also well liked. The nest boxes are sometimes packed tight, the nest itself being at the top. Dampness helps the hatching, and it is advisable to avoid the use of very dry material. Some birds take over old nests, especially those of Weavers. These are hung in all sorts of places, are well built and lined with different kinds of soft materials and have an entrance at the side.

Food Utensils

Food and drink must always be available outside as well as in the shelter. If food is supplied only in the shelter, the birds will be disinclined to come into the open; outside seed boxes or automatic seed hoppers can be put on the ground or suspended. Automatic seed boxes (Figs. 9, 10) have the advantage of not needing to be replenished daily; but must function perfectly, and the seed run through properly. Seed boxes of this type must be placed where they can be inspected at a glance. A further advantage is that little seed is wasted. The birds

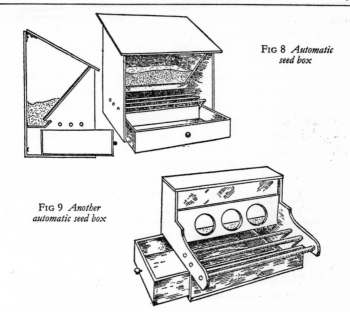

FIG 8 *Automatic seed box*

FIG 9 *Another automatic seed box*

cannot spill it and the husk falls into a tray. A separate automatic box used for each kind of seed, makes it possible to see which seed is most popular.

All boxes must be fixed so that they keep dry and the feeding table put where it is 'mouse-proof'. If suspended, it will be out of the reach of the mice.

If there are insufficient growing plants (and these should include grass and weeds), green stuff must be supplied daily and hung in a rack, rotting leaves and stalks must be removed. These racks can also be used to hold nesting materials but only in the breeding cages.

There are special holders for cuttle fish which most birds like, but this can also be hung. Salt lick is best placed, with the minerals, in a saucer, although not all birds will eat it. Fine grit and lime or ground oyster shell must also be provided and powdered charcoal should be mixed with the grit to prevent gastric trouble.

Good seed mixtures contain all the ingredients needed. Only well-known kinds should be bought, as poor quality or impure ingredients may cause illness. Drinking water must be absolutely pure; this is the best prevention against maladies of all kinds.

Baths

Bathing facilities must be provided in order to keep birds in good condition. Flat stones can be put on the floor of the bird room and a shallow dish of water placed on them close to the wire so that it can easily be filled from outside.

For the cage or inside aviary, it is better to buy glass-enclosed baths which hang on the front of the cage and so avoid water being splashed on to the floor. The bottom of these must be ribbed and not smooth, so that the birds can stand firmly. Flat stones can be placed in the dishes, but they must be cleaned regularly. At all costs deep bowls, in which young birds might drown, must be avoided.

Flower pot saucers make excellent baths, but larger shallow dishes or shallow cemented ponds are more suitable for an aviary. If water is supplied direct from the main it is possible to have a small fountain playing.

Bath water should be changed at least twice daily, and the risk of the birds drinking dirty water avoided.

3. SUITABLE SHRUBS AND OTHER PLANTS FOR AN OUTSIDE FLIGHT

Prunus serotina

Strong-growing shrub—flowers in May and June with bunches of white flowers. The black fruit is appreciated by the birds.

Prunus virginiana

Flowers in May and June with bunches of large white blooms. It can be cut down to a low hedge and is then suitable for nesting.

Philadelphus coronarius Mock Orange Blossom

A strong growing shrub which may reach a height of 15 ft. Flowers in June with delightfully scented blooms.

Rubus fructicosus Blackberry

A strong-growing variety from the Himalaya. Bears large fruit, greatly appreciated by the birds. Will grow in almost any soil, but likes a damp and shady spot. It propagates itself by rootstock and multiplies quickly.

Cotoneaster horizontalis Cotoneaster

Prostrate habit—will spread 4–5 ft.

Flowers May to June with pinkish white flowers. Also very useful against a low wall. Red berries in autumn and winter. The foliage, which stays on all winter, becomes a beautiful dark red and brown colour.

Cotoneaster rotundifolia

Similar to previous variety but upright growing and has larger flowers and berries. Both require a sunny spot. Autumn colouring not so attractive. It usually retains its foliage throughout the winter.

Berberis (Mahonia) aquifolium

An evergreen shrub of spreading habit. Flowers bright yellow in clusters February to May, followed by black berries heavily powdered with violet bloom, and like *Berberis repens*, it has a creeping rootstock. The leaves turn purple during the winter. The dewy blue berries are greatly appreciated by the birds.

Berberis (Mahonia) hortorum

This shrub will reach a height of nearly 5 ft. It flowers in April and May with bunches of yellow blooms and bears in autumn numberless blue berries of which the birds are very fond. The leaves remain on during the winter and colour beautifully.

It will grow on any soil, in either sunshine or shade, and is also very suitable as underplanting.

Viburnum opulus Guelder rose

May grow more than 12 ft high. Blooms from May to June with creamy white flowerets. Later bears red berries which are well liked by the birds.

Vibernum opulus floreplena

Ball-shaped flower umbels, blooming in May and June. The red berries are well liked by the birds.

Sambucus nigra Elderberry

An easy and rapidly growing shrub, which will thrive in any soil, provided there is a sufficiency of humus. It likes sun and moisture. Blooms May–June with numberless white flowers set in umbels. The elderberries are much liked by the birds. Insects attracted to the elderberry make a delicacy for the insect-eating birds.

Carpinus betulus Hornbeam

The Hornbeam makes a close hedge. During the autumn the leaves will turn a beautiful yellow and brown. It flowers in April and May with smallish catkins. It may be trimmed and will grow in any soil.

Ilex aquifolium Holly

If male and female bushes are placed alternately there will be a rich harvest of the bright red holly berries. It demands a sunny spot and not too dry a soil. The variety *pyramidalis* lends itself well for hedges and offers suitable nesting sites. Fruits abundantly.

Juniperus Juniper

An evergreen shrub which grows best on dry sandy soil. Often assumes most decorative shapes. When purchasing from a nursery choose the most freakish growths for the aviary; these are generally unsuitable for gardens and parks, but most attractive to the birds.

Hedera helix Ivy

Very useful for covering fence or wall of an aviary. In places which get little or no sun, the ivy maintains its evergreen colour both winter and summer. The insignificant flowers appear in September and the black berries are eaten by many birds. The special large-leaved variety, *hibernica*, is the most usual.

Ligustrum vulgare Privet

One of the most common and useful of hedge shrubs, which sheds its leaves only in very severe winters. The leaves generally turn a little darker in winter. Privet grows very quickly and can be trimmed into any shape. It is remarkably good for nesting purposes. Cockatiels are very partial to the leaves and will completely destroy a whole hedge, but the small foreign finches find privet a paradise for nesting and roosting accommodation. The black berries are also eaten by the birds.

Any soil is suitable. Privet will tolerate sun or will grow in shade.

Buxus sempervirens Box

The Box is a most useful shrub especially for small nesting Waxbills. The trimmed bushes are the best for nesting but the untrimmed and untrammelled growth is extremely suitable for shelter. This evergreen will do well in sun or shade and on practically any kind of soil.

Crataegus monogyna Hawthorn

This shrub or tree grows quite high and dense and is very suitable for nesting. It blossoms in May and June with scented umbels of pinkish red flowers. The red berries are well liked by several species of birds. It can also be used as a hedge. It will thrive in any soil but likes a sunny spot best.

Deutzia gracilis Deutzia

This shrub will grow from 2 to 3 ft high and blooms in May and June with bunches of white flowers, but is deciduous. It requires a sunny spot and nourishing garden soil. *Deutzia magnifica* will grow more than 9 ft high and flowers in June with double white blossoms in bunches. It requires a sunny spot and nourishing soil, not too dry.

Ceanothus americanus

This grows from 20 in. to 3 ft high. It blooms from June to September, with bunches of white flowers. It loses its leaves in winter and must be pruned in spring. It requires sandy soil and a sunny sheltered spot. *Ceanothus thyrsiflorus* flowers in May and June, and is evergreen.

Symphoricarpus albus Snowberry

This shrub will grow to 5 ft, and has pink blossom in June and July. The large white berries which appear in autumn and stay on until the winter are specially appreciated by the small Quail.

Picea

Various species available; they grow mainly in sandy soil and do very well there. The choice of species will be governed by the space available.

Rhododendron ponticum

Although a very robust grower it can be used as underplanting, but will then flower less prolifically. It needs a peaty mixture and dislikes lime. It retains its dark green leaves in the winter. It is poisonous to Budgerigars and Parrakeets; but is quite safe with other non-chewing birds.

Rosa multiflora Wild rose

There are many species of wild rose which will cover fences and wiring. They also form a thick hedge in which the birds can build their nests. They like a sunny spot and damp soil, and flower in June and July.

Although the shrubs which have been described are useful as well as decorative, they are also valuable because they attract insects. The importance of this has been stated in the paragraphs dealing with the small foreign seed-eaters. During the breeding season all manner of insects from green fly to the larger beetles are devoured greedily.

The behaviour of the birds is often an indication that they have young in the nest. They will be found against the netting trying to discover a way out. If the risk is taken and they are allowed out, they will, in most cases, diligently hunt for insects with which to feed their young. If they are not allowed out, the flight must be well planted with various grasses and weeds. The flight will then resemble the birds' natural surroundings and many insects will be found among the plants.

4. WINTER ACCOMMODATION

Many people think that tropical birds can only be kept in a well-warmed room. Some refuse to believe that our summers, which as a rule do not excel in sunshine and warmth, offer suitable living conditions for these birds. Nothing could be further from the truth.

Experience has shown that our climate offers no special danger for the general run of birds. Once acclimatization has been accomplished, most birds will live their full normal spell of life, and often much longer, in aviaries. In their natural surroundings, which are full of dangers, birds often do not reach the age they attain in captivity, where, even though they become a little less active, they do not have to contend with natural enemies.

If the birds have been kept outside during the summer and the autumn and are still in good condition, many of them will be better off if they remain there during the winter. The shelter must, however, be provided with artificial light, for the long winter evenings and nights are too long for most of these tropical birds to remain without food. The best plan is to have a time-switch so that the light burns until about 8 or 9 p.m. and is switched on again at 6 or 7 a.m.

The ideal method is not to switch this light off suddenly, but to use one or two less powerful lamps and thus obtain a sort of twilight. By switching off the full light suddenly it may happen that the birds stay outside their nesting boxes or away from their sheltered roosting perches, and are thus exposed to the cold night air.

Sometimes birds will breed during the winter. This should be prevented as far as possible, but should they do so it is dangerous to switch off the light without making sure that the old birds are on their nests.

The small foreign finches and other more delicate birds must be brought indoors during the winter and put in a room or other accommodation which can be heated when necessary. The heating should, in case of need, be available instantaneously. The birds must be kept in good condition throughout the winter; if they are not comfortable they soon show it. They sit with all their feathers ruffled and seem to shiver. They improve the moment the temperature is raised. A single bird, if unwell, can be placed in a separate cage in a warm room. Given good nourishing food, to which cod-liver oil should always be added in the winter months, the birds will remain hale and hearty. Birds which start moulting badly during the winter should have special care as they are apt to catch cold much more quickly.

There are various methods of providing warmth, including central heating, but in the case of the latter system it is important to ensure adequate humidity. Coal fires, slow combustion stoves (if no carbon monoxide is formed), oil stoves and the primus type are all suitable, as are also electric fires. Gas heating can be dangerous if the fumes are allowed to escape into the room. The heating apparatus must be kept away from the birds. As a rule, temperatures a few degrees above freezing point are better than the higher temperatures. The latter are really only necessary for sick birds or those recently imported. It is advisable to have some cages on hand so that if the need should suddenly arise the birds can be kept indoors.

A choice must be made of those birds which can be kept outside with complete safety. A shelter in which the birds can spend a great deal of their time can be provided with trusses of straw, reed matting, and bundles of heather; all these will afford extra protection.

If only a shelter and outside aviary are available, new birds should not be acquired during the winter unless they come from similar accommodation. It has been found extremely difficult to acclimatize birds during the winter without the use of warmed rooms or aviaries. Only during the summer can the risk be taken of placing recently imported birds straightaway into an outside aviary, and even then only on warm days. Beginners are advised not to start such experiments, which only too often end in the death of the birds.

The aviary should be so furnished that by the time the nights become cold and wet, the birds have grown used to going into the shelter for the night. A start can be made by placing the food there early during the winter, and when the lights go on in the evening the birds will come in naturally. A certain routine is advisable when shutting the trapdoors between the day and night accommodation. It is much better to close them every night. A little ingenuity will provide a method of closing them from the outside, so that it is not necessary to enter the aviary. The birds will soon become accustomed

Fig 10 *A very good design for combined winter and summer accommodation.* Left: *the entirely enclosed aviary which can be heated.* Right: *the open flight. In between the summer shelter, where nesting facilities and food table should preferably be placed*

to this routine and it will be found that at 'closing time' none remain outside.

Although it is not essential to provide special winter quarters for a great number of birds, those fanciers who wish to house their birds under ideal conditions can build a double-walled bird house. The space between the walls should be filled with glass wool. The windows must be double glazed. By the use of electric heating and a thermostatic control, together with air conditioning, sudden variations in temperature can be avoided. It is, however, an open question whether the resistance of the birds to cold and illness is increased by this method.

5. OBTAINING THE BIRDS

When the cage or aviary is ready, suitable occupants have to be obtained. It is, of course, essential that the paintwork (which must not contain lead) is bone dry, including the paint on the outside of the cage and on the wire netting.

When buying birds, make sure that the source is reliable and the birds absolutely healthy. Purchasing direct from an importer may be cheaper, but it also presents a greater risk. Hundreds of birds will have been imported by ship or air together in one cage, which it is really impossible to keep scrupulously clean. Hence food may be contaminated and infection possibly spread by a sick bird. It is essential to keep the birds in quarantine for about 10 days.

It is a good plan to read all available literature beforehand about their habits, diet, and accommodation. For instance, if any come from Africa or Asia and have been fed on boiled rice, this should be supplied at first and diet changes introduced very gradually.

Birds which have been seen for some time at a bird fancier's or which are obtained from a breeder are less of a risk, but more expensive. The fancier who is just beginning will be well advised to buy locally and not from strangers, from whom he will have little chance of redress.

The best seasons for buying are spring and summer.

Watch out for the following points when selecting birds from an importer:

> birds must not sit puffed up with their eyes closed;
> there should be no soiling on the plumage around the vent;
> there should be no damage to the legs;
> their eyes should be bright and clear.

The condition of the plumage is not of such importance, but birds which have completed the moult are preferable to those still moulting.

The sexes of many species show little difference and it often happens that two birds bought as a pair are really of one sex. Observation of the birds' behaviour after they have settled down will show the difference, and it should be made a condition of purchase that one bird can be exchanged if they do not prove a true pair. It may be wise sometimes to take an extra pair, and change the surplus birds later on.

When the birds have been brought home safely, it is advisable to keep them in separate cages for the first few days. If they are seed-eaters only seed, fresh sand and water should be given, and the birds should have time to get used to their new surroundings. If they do not sit puffed up but remain in good condition, they can be transferred to their permanent home. Should this be an outside aviary, then the season and the weather must be taken into account. From June to September most birds can safely be housed in the open; in the remaining cold months they need to be acclimatized very carefully. If, however, the birds come from an outside aviary, they can be placed in a similar enclosure without undue risk. New arrivals should be placed in a cage in the shelter and left there for a day. Then they should be given freedom to fly about the shelter and investigate, and after another few days the door to the outside aviary can be opened. They should by now be used to the feeding places and not come to any harm.

It is essential to study the lists which are given in Chapter 6 to see which varieties can be kept together safely in an aviary, and not to diverge from them. Any digression may have unfortunate results.

If the birds are to remain indoors, they can go to their permanent quarters after about 10 days' quarantine. After a week a start should be made with a little green stuff, possibly meal-worms, and drops of cod-liver oil on the seed or soft food.

It may be impossible to collect the birds personally so that they have to be forwarded by rail. Provided they are despatched first thing in the morning, they will usually get to their destination in one day. It is, however, better to have them sent by express delivery by train in the late evening. They will then arrive early the following morning and, since they require little in the way of food and drink during the night, they will hardly suffer from the journey.

Travelling cages must be provided with seed or a suitable insecti-vorous food and a little water. A small tin similar to that used for tomatoe purée is the best container for the water. To prevent splash-ing, some moss, bread, cotton wool, or even a piece of sponge can be used to soak up and retain a great deal of water so that some is always available for the birds. The cage should be packed in strong paper with a largish hole in front of the bars so that ample light and air are available, and should be labelled 'Live Birds'.

Immediately on arrival the birds must be transferred to their quarantine cage and given food and drink. They must have sufficient light to see and find their food supply; it is especially necessary to watch this point in winter.

It is important to check immediately that the birds are hale and hearty. If they come from a dealer their nails may well be too long. The little Weavers, in particular, are apt to be troubled by overgrown nails. Snip off the tips of the nails but take great care not to touch the 'quick'. If the claws are held up to the light, a small red line is visible. Only the pale tips beyond this line should be clipped.

6. MIXED COLLECTIONS

It is impossible to state exactly which species of birds should be kept together in an aviary; there are too many species and too many possible combinations.

Moreover, the size of the aviary has an important bearing on the selection of species which may be safely associated with each other. Birds are always less tolerant in a small aviary than in a large flight. Birds which always quarrel in a small aviary will live in perfect peace and harmony in a large space because they are then able to secure their own territory and are able to avoid trespassing on that of other and stronger neighbours with the inevitable consequences of such temerity. Usually the following rules may be applied:

(1) Birds with which it is intended to breed are best kept in breeding pens or in separate aviaries on their own.

(2) Pairs of birds of similar species usually do not tolerate one another unless they are colony breeders, and even then there may be quarrelling unless the aviary is very large. Hens or cocks of related species only will live in peace together; as soon as a bird of the opposite sex appears there will be uproar.

(3) Birds of similar size and habits may be kept together; for instance, a collection of seed-eaters or a number of insect-eaters, always providing they are of different species.

(4) Insect eating and large omniverous birds can be kept together only if of similar size and stamina.

It must always be remembered that the characters of individual birds may not be normal, and hence, when building up an aviary collection, much will depend on observation. The introduction of a new bird into an existing community may lead to great difficulties and trouble. The equilibrium, the natural order of precedence, of the birds, may be instantly disturbed by a single 'intruder'. A 'weaker' bird should be introduced into the aviary first, so that it can explore every nook and cranny and find where it can hide safely. The owner can do much to prevent fights. The feeding-place can be a source of discord and if an alternative spot can be provided this cause of trouble may be removed.

A shortage of nesting and roosting sites can also cause unrest and fighting. Plenty of perches and nest boxes will help to prevent bickering. The nest boxes should not be close together, but well distributed about the aviary.

Below are given lists of species which may, as a rule, be safely kept together. Obviously the number to be kept must depend on the size of the cage or aviary available. The fewer pairs that are together, the greater will be the chance of successful breeding:

A. Cordon Bleu   Common Spice Finch
    Tiger Finch   Three-coloured Mannikin
    Fire Finch   Bengalese
    Red-eared Waxbill   Zebra Finch
    Lavender Finch   Green Avadavat
    Golden-breasted Waxbill   Green Singing Finch
    African Silverbill   Indian White Eye
    Indian Silverbill   Blue-breasted Quail

B. Bronze Mannikin   Bengalese
    Long-tailed Grassfinch   Lavender Finch
    Cherry Finch   Olive Finch
    Red-headed Finch   Grey Singing Finch
    Diamond Sparrow   Diamond Dove
    Zebra Finch

C. Gouldian Finch   Zebra Finch
    Rufous-tailed Grassfinch   Bengalese
    Parson Finch   Blue-breasted Quail
    Long-tailed Grassfinch

D. Budgerigars   Californian Quail
    Bourke's Parrakeet   Weavers
    Cockatiel   Zebra Finch

E. Whydahs   Java Sparrow
    Weavers   Diamond Dove
    Cut-throats   Californian Quail
    Cardinals

F. Indigo Bunting   Golden Sparrow
    Rainbow Bunting   Canaries
    Pileated and Red-crested   Java Sparrow
        Finches   Weavers
    Common Saffron Finch   Pekin Robin

G. Pekin Robin   Whydahs
    Bourke's Parrakeet   Bulbuls
    Cockatiel   Golden-fronted Fruit-suckers
    Shama   Mynahs (not Hill Mynahs)
    Glossy Starling   Virginian Cardinal
    Tanagers   Common Hangnest
    Green Cardinal   Pagoda Mynah

H. Weavers   Cut-throats
    Whydahs   Long-tailed Grassfinch
    Senegal Combassou   Masked Grassfinch

I. Budgerigars   Indian Ring-necked Parrakeet
    Cockatiel   Plum-headed Parrakeet

7. FOODS

The birds described in this book and its companion volume are divided into four groups. This is not an arbitrary division but based on the food and treatment needed. First, and by far the largest group is that containing small seed-eating birds. Secondly come parrots and parrot-like species, which in most cases require a different and rather specialized seed diet. These will be dealt with in Book 2. The third group comprises insect- and fruit-eaters and the nectar feeders. The fourth, the pigeons and doves, the quail, pheasants, and waterfowl, is also dealt with in Book 2.

Group 1

The basis of seed mixture suitable for all small seed-eating birds in Group 1 is best-quality Senegal millet or La Plata millet, and canary seed. The latter must be of good white quality, say Moroccan white.

The proportion in which the seeds should be mixed will vary according to the individual tastes of the species to be kept and for this reason some fanciers prefer to supply each kind of seed separately, in dishes or automatic feeding boxes.

Yellow millet is also used extensively for the feeding of small foreign finches and although this is a much harder seed some of the smallest finches show a preference for it. In addition, small quantities of various other seeds may be given as it is most important to avoid monotonous feeding and rape, niger, linseed, hemp, and teazle are all useful to provide variety.

Seeding weeds and grasses are always acceptable and millet in the spray is a most excellent food, greatly enjoyed by nearly all species.

Excellent seed mixtures, in which various additions have been made to the basic canary and millets, can be purchased and most fanciers will be content to use one of these after having found by experiment which gives the best results.

If, however, the mixing is to be done at home, much experimental work will be necessary. An aviary containing several species of finches should be supplied with three food pots in which canary, white and yellow millet may be given separately, say about 2 oz. per pot. The husks should be blown away carefully, and the contents of the pots weighed daily. After a week the proportion of each seed eaten will be known. It will be clear that the seed can then be mixed in that proportion.

This method, of course, is not entirely reliable. Weather conditions influence the birds' choice of food. The carbohydrates, proteins, water, minerals, fats, calcium, and phosphorus contained in the seeds vary and during the winter more fats will be needed. In a heated winter aviary less canary seed will be eaten than in a frost-proof but cold aviary. It will also be possible to determine whether seeds rich in minerals are preferred during the moult.

The following is an analysis of the percentage of ingredients of various seeds from which it will be seen that the composition of canary seed, white and yellow millet varies very little.

C

Percentage of:	Fats	Carbohydrates	Proteins	Minerals
Canary (white seed)	6	55	14	2
White Millet	4	60	11	3
Yellow Millet	4	63	11	3
Oats	5	56	11	2
Hemp	32	18	19	2
Sunflower	22	21	16	3
Maw	40	12	17	6
Niger	32	15	17	7
Rape	40	10	19	4
Linseed	34	24	21	6
Vetch (Tares)	2	50	23	3
Wheat	2	70	11	2
Barley	2	70	10	2
Maize	7	65	10	2

To compare the food value of these seeds, it is necessary to investigate the effect of fats, carbohydrates, proteins, and minerals on the birds. The percentage may vary slightly with the quality of the seed, but the essential proportion of the constituent parts is not greatly affected.

Fats provide warmth and energy. Carbohydrates also supply energy and heat during the digestive process. Proteins build up the body and replenish wastage and wear and tear. Minerals are indispensable for bone formation and help the operation of the intestines.

When the seeds are given unmixed, it is soon noticeable where the preference lies and this can be followed. If, however, some birds react unfavourably to a certain kind of seed and get out of condition, *e.g.* by growing too fat, then the seed menu must be changed to provide less fattening elements. Cage birds especially should not be given too fattening seeds, as they already have a tendency to obesity as a result of insufficient exercise.

From tests made, birds thrive better on canary seed, mixed or unmixed with millet, than on oats.

Oats stimulate copulation and can be given with advantage before the breeding season. As soon as sitting has commenced the feeding of oats should be discontinued, as the ardent advances of the male might result in neglect of the brood.

A more fatty mixture does no harm during the winter; it guards against cold and in the spring the birds soon lose any excess fat, provided that sufficient exercise is possible. But if the fatty food is continued too long into the spring egg production may cease, for fat birds are bad layers.

Keeping in mind the low percentage of fat in the three basic kinds, it can be readily understood why the addition of maw seed (fat content 40), rape-seed (40), linseed (32), hemp seed (32) may sometimes be necessary. These seeds also have a high mineral and a low carbohydrate percentage.

Although canary fanciers believe that the birds should be forced to eat all the various seeds included in their mixture, and hence give only small quantities so that the birds will eat everything because they are famished, I have never found that the health of the birds was unfavourably influenced if and when they had an opportunity to choose their own menu. I place in my cage (which is 4 ft 2 in. high × 2 ft deep × 5 ft 4 in. long) a number of cold cream jars in a row, each filled with a different kind of seed, and in this way I have discovered which the birds in this cage eat most. Sprays of millet are supplied regularly as extras.

If I am asked to give the exact proportion of seed mixtures, then the relative percentage of these is shown in the following examples of seed preferences of small finches:

	Tiger Finch	Zebra Finch	Bronze Mannikin	Bengalese	Nun	Cuban Finch
Canary Seed	5	3	7	7	24	10
White Millet	4	40	17	50	48	10
Yellow Millet	91	57	76	43	28	80

It will be seen from this that it is not unnatural to house these 6 species of birds together in a room aviary. It would be possible to add the Sharp-tailed Finch, Bicheno's Finch and others which show a definite preference for the yellow millet (65% and 75% respectively).

Starting with the 6 pairs of birds quoted, the following proportion is reached: canary seed 10%; white millet 35%; yellow millet 55%.

If some Bicheno's Finches were to be added to this collection then a theoretical shortage of yellow millet would occur. On the other hand, should a pair of Rice Birds (Java Sparrows), be added, which eat 30% canary seed, 45% white millet, and 25% yellow millet, the result would be quite different.

It would be possible to give numberless examples of small foreign finches which show a special preference for certain seeds and thus prove that the supply of a standard mixture is practically impossible.

The following is a simple way of calculating how much of each is necessary for a particular collection of birds:

(1) Each species of bird should be separated into a not too small aviary for a fortnight and a note made each day of the quantity of seed eaten of the three kinds supplied in separate containers.

Care should be taken to gather up the shelled seeds which have been scattered, and return them to the container.

If, say, 6 species have been tested in this way, it should not be difficult to determine the proportions of each seed eaten. If more than one specimen of any one kind of bird is kept, the result is simply multiplied by the number of such birds.

Now all the weights of the canary seed used must be added, then all the weights of the white millet and finally those of the yellow millet.

In order to calculate the percentages all three figures must be added and this result set over 100. It is then not difficult to see the percentages.

Here is a detailed example:

Collection consists of: 6 Rice Birds;
                       4 Zebra Finches;
                       2 Bicheno's Finches;
                       6 Bengalese.

In a fortnight *a pair* of each kind of birds consumed seeds in the following proportions:

	Rice Birds	Zebra Finches	Bicheno's Finches	Bengalese
Canary Seed	10	3	5	7
White Millet	35	40	1	50
Yellow Millet	55	57	94	43

In order to cover the requirements of the 6 Rice Birds, the results for a pair are multiplied by 3, by 2 for the Zebra Finches, those of the Bichenos by 1, and those for the Bengalese by 3, so that we get:

	Rice Birds (6)	Zebra Finches (4)	Bicheno's Finches (2)	Bengalese (6)
Canary Seed	30	6	5	21
White Millet	105	80	1	150
Yellow Millet	165	114	94	129

Total of canary seed used	62
Total of white millet used	336
Total of yellow millet used	502
Total	900

Calculation of the proportion need only be taken roughly. The requirements will thus be:

$\frac{62}{900}$ canary seed; $\frac{336}{900}$ white millet; yellow millet $\frac{502}{900}$.

$$\frac{62}{900} = \frac{1}{15}; \frac{336}{900} = \frac{1}{3}; \text{ and } \frac{502}{900} = \frac{5}{8}.$$

Take 900 as 100 and we then have in round percentages:

$$\frac{1}{15} \times \frac{100}{1} = 7\%; \frac{1}{3} \times \frac{100}{1} = 33\%; \frac{5}{8} \times \frac{100}{1} = 60\%.$$

For every 14 lb. of seed to be mixed we take 2 lb. of canary seed, $4\frac{1}{4}$ lb. of white millet, and the remainder $7\frac{3}{4}$ lb. of yellow millet.

(2) Place three feeding bowls in the aviary, containing the three kinds of seed and note the quantity used daily, taking care to take the split seed into calculation. Husks should be blown off before weighing. After the weights have been noted for a week or 10 days, add up the total weight of each kind of seed used. The proportion can then be easily calculated.

These calculations are not of much practical value. Only fanciers who specialize in certain species would find it definitely advantageous to discover the very best composition of the seed mixture.

Many fanciers make changes in their collections. Some birds go and others take their places, and it is an advantage to know how the seed mixture should be varied to meet the requirements of the new-comers.

Fanciers with little spare time will find it impossible to pay attention to the requirements of every individual bird in their collection and others may find the foregoing instructions too complicated. For general purposes, the following mixture is suggested as suitable for most of the small seed-eaters: 25% each of canary seed, white millet, yellow millet, and Senegal millet.

Although the birds can be kept alive for many years on this mixture and may remain in excellent condition, it will be found that it is the 'little extra' which will make all the difference, and as more experience is gained the proportions may be varied and other seeds added to provide variety or to suit the special requirements of individual birds.

The quality of the seed is of the utmost importance and seemingly attractive 'special offers' of cheap seed should be carefully investigated before purchase. Such offers often consist of inferior seed which should have been ground in a cattle fodder mixture, but which it has been found more profitable to sell as bird seed. Usually this cheap seed can no longer be germinated and lacks essential qualities. It is the living element in the seed or grain which is of such para-mount importance.

It matters little whether seeds for mixing are bought in packets or by bulk. The main thing is to buy first-class quality, well-cleaned, shiny seeds. It often happens after wet summers that ergot or spurred rye get mixed with the seed; these large violet-black seeds are very poisonous and may lead to paralysis should the birds eat them. They are still more deadly when germinated. Hence, when canary seed is soaked, great care should be taken to see that no violet-black seeds are mixed with it.

Powdered yeast is often added as an extra. It should not be given as a regular ingredient, but only occasionally and in small quantities. An easy way of giving it—the birds will most certainly not take it from a pot—is to add it to the seed which has been made sticky by a few drops of cod-liver oil. It attaches itself to the seed and the yeast is taken in the minute quantities required.

Most seed-eaters also appreciate a little animal food and one of the insectivorous mixtures such as 'Nightingale' food or 'Universal' food, together with a few live insects, should be offered daily. This is particularly important if young are being reared, as many species of granivorous birds feed their young entirely on insects during the early stages.

It is a remarkable fact that nearly all species will partake of the special food I provide for my Zosterops, viz. honey water made from 1 part of clear honey dissolved in 3 parts of water and fresh oranges. Zebra Finches especially are very fond of the oranges.

A special food which should never be lacking in the breeding season is that formed by the germination of various kinds of bird seed. The vitamin content of sprouted seed is very high.

Seeds must be soaked in cold water for 2 or 3 days in summer and 4 to 5 days in winter. The water should be changed daily and when germination has commenced it should be poured off, and the seed rinsed carefully with tepid water and allowed to dry in the open air. When it is offered to the birds they will immediately leave the dry seed in the bowls. There is no better food for young birds.

It is advisable to mix a little clear honey or the raw yolk of an egg with the seed. All this provides a useful change of diet. Stale white bread, soaked and squeezed dry and then crumbled, with a little milk poured over it, will (in addition to their normal food) always remain the staple food for birds when rearing their young. New bread must not be given and in summer care should be taken to see that the milk does not become sour. Carrot juice or ordinary water can be used instead of milk.

The vitamins in the foodstuffs are indispensable to the well-being of the birds. Fresh green stuff, given daily, contains most of the essential vitamins. The two most important, A and D, must be added to the rations during the winter months and throughout the breeding season by dropping a little cod-liver oil in the seed mixture (provided this is not given in an automatic feed box, when the stickiness would prevent the seed flowing freely).

Of the green foods, chickweed, *Stellaria media*, must be named first and foremost. All birds love it; it is rich in Vitamin E. Spinach, tender lettuce leaves and dandelion leaves are always appreciated. But there are dangers to be guarded against. Chickweed obtained from soil which has been sprayed should not be given if it can be avoided; if it is given it should be very well washed. Frozen chickweed must never be given. Lettuce may also have been sprayed (it is, indeed, usually sprayed when cultivated under glass), and must be most carefully washed. A head of lettuce should be given in preference to loose leaves. It will be picked absolutely clean. Any chickweed left over will usually be used by the birds as nesting material, and its moisture content is helpful in softening the egg shell at hatching time.

All kinds of grasses with green seed are delicacies and beneficial to the birds, and should always be supplied when young have to be fed. The plantain, *Plantago lanceolata*, dandelion, *Taraxacum vulgare*, groundsel, *Senecio vulgaris*, shepherd's purse, *Capsella bursa pastoris*, clover, *Trifolium pratense*, and all manner of other herbs and weeds provide seeds which are very much liked. The various thistles, *Carduus* and *Cirsium*, make a greatly appreciated delicacy. There is ample scope for experimenting in feeding.

Grit should be scattered about or placed in a bowl in a corner of the cage, not beneath the perches where it would be fouled. It should be finely graded and should consist of ground oyster shell with which some minerals have been mixed. During the breeding season especially, the birds need pieces of cuttlefish bone. These contain salt and calcium and can be hung or fixed in special clips.

Oyster grit, finely ground egg shell, boiled up or baked in the oven (never from preserved eggs) should always be available during the breeding season for seed-eaters as well as the cuttlefish or a piece of mineralized lime. Most birds are very fond of them and they help to form sound egg shells and aid egg production.

A Norwegian bird fancier has found that dried and finely ground seaweed is beneficial to all his birds and makes their plumage extra glossy. This is not strange since sea water cures are often prescribed for human beings, for sea water contains many minerals which may be temporarily lacking in the human body. Seaweed powder is on the market, and experiments can be carried out with herb mixtures. Every effort must be made to vary the food with 'something extra'. Far too little is known about foreign birds and their food requirements, but it is certain that when wild and in their natural surroundings, they will pick up many entirely different foodstuffs from those that the fancier is able to furnish in the aviary. Every season will provide different food. These varied conditions also make a change in the birds. As winter is the time of rest in nature, so also in the case of birds. If quantities of insects are eaten during the mating season and breeding period, the birds will often confine themselves to seed during the winter; they will be so well fed that they can stand a leaner time quite easily. If they are to be kept in the best possible condition they should not be deprived of this natural cycle. First, a richer menu then a period when less rich food is given, will give the best results.

Cultivation of Canary Seed and Millet

Even a small plot, if sunny, is enough for seed cultivation. This does not mean competing with seed merchants, but birds are passionately fond of half-ripe seeds which are richer in vitamins, especially when rearing their young.

To produce good millet sprays, seeds should be sown about 4 in. apart, leaving 6 in. between the rows. Plants will quickly grow to a height of 3 ft in well-manured soil. Sowing should not be started until night frost is past—at the earliest the beginning of May.

Do not grow too close together. It is only when the plant has plenty of room and can absorb all the sun available that it will grow large and heavy.

The yellowing of the stalks shows that the sprays are ripe and the harvest may be gathered. It is now that the birds may be given the sprays regularly.

Canary seed needs less attention and can be sown more closely. Unlike the millet spray (Senegal millet), the stalks have many branches, and these bear the round seed heads, full of pointed husks. Song birds enjoy these greatly. All other seed-eaters will eat the freshly harvested seed when it has been shaken out and placed in the seed pots.

Group 2

The feeding of the insect- and fruit-eaters and the nectar feeders presents rather more difficulty. Generally speaking they are rapacious feeders and in their natural state consume enormous numbers of many different kinds of insects each day. While it is possible to purchase supplies of certain kinds of live insects, it is not practicable to keep the birds on these alone since such a diet would provide insufficient variety and would be very costly. It is therefore necessary to use, as a basis, a food which is more readily obtainable and which contains all the elements essential to maintain the birds in good health and provide them with a properly balanced diet. Such live insects as are available should be given as a supplement and it will materially assist in making the birds tame if they can be persuaded to take these from the fingers.

Several proprietary brands of insectivorous foods are obtainable, either in bulk or in packets, and these are usually supplied in two or more different grades, modified to suit the special needs of the type of birds to be fed. The best kinds contain a percentage of dried insects such as flies, silkworm pupae, and ants' cocoons, the later being known in the trade as 'ants' eggs'.

Some of these foods may be supplied to the birds without further preparation, others require to be moistened either with water or, better still, with carrot juice or finely grated raw carrot. The carrot is itself an excellent food, has a good vitamin content, and greatly assists in maintaining the natural brilliance of a bird's plumage.

For the sake of convenience the fine-grade foods which should be used for all small and more delicate species will be referred to as 'nightingale' food, and the coarser grade, suitable for the larger species such as the thrushes and starlings, as 'universal' food.

If it is desired to make up an insectivorous mixture at home, the following is a good recipe:

1 pint dried ants' cocoons;
1 pint dried flies and silkworm cocoons (crushed);
$\frac{7}{8}$ pint crushed biscuit or toasted breadcrumbs;
$\frac{7}{16}$ pint dried egg powder;
$\frac{1}{2}$ lb. lard;
1 tablespoonful honey.

First the lard should be grated and rubbed into the crumbs, and then the remaining ingredients added and well mixed in. The mixture should be kept in a tin with a tight-fitting lid and should be stored in a cool, dry place. Sufficient for the day's ration should be moistened with water, milk, or raw grated carrot to give it a crumbly texture, but it should never be reduced to a sloppy or sticky mass. If water or milk is used special care will be needed during hot weather to ensure that it is removed from the food dishes immediately there is any sign of it going sour, when it becomes a source of danger to the health of the birds. When mixed with grated carrot it does not tend to sour so quickly.

Freshly imported birds or newly fledged young may not take readily to these artificial insect foods but they should be encouraged to do so by scattering some live meal-worms or ants' cocoons on top.

Certain species, notably the Hummingbirds, Sunbirds, and Sugarbirds, subsist mainly on pollen and nectar which they extract from flowers, and on minute insects, and for these the insectivorous mixtures are not suitable. Most of the insect- and fruit-eaters are passionately fond of honey, and their needs may be supplied by the following mixture:

1 tablespoonful honey;
1 tablespoonful condensed milk;
1 tablespoonful baby food such as Mellins or Horlicks.

Six to eight tablespoonfuls of hot water should be added and the mixture allowed to cool before being fed to the birds. It should be given in the specially made glass tubes which are available from most birdfood dealers and which have a tube fitted to the base from which the birds can suck the 'nectar'. These tubes should be hung in the cage or aviary within easy reach of a perch, and care must be taken to ensure that the mixture is always fresh. Even in the winter it is advisable to change the supply at least once during the day and in warm weather more frequently.

This food is inclined to be rather fattening and some fanciers prefer to replace the evening feed with a solution of pure honey made in the proportion of 1 spoonful of honey to 3 or 4 spoonfuls of water. This solution has the added advantage that it does not turn sour and will remain sufficiently fresh during the night for the birds to drink it with safety in the early hours of the following morning.

Two or three times a week a little meat extract and a few drops of Vitamins A and D should be added.

One special word of warning must be given—all food dishes and tubes used for feeding insectivorous foods and nectar must be kept scrupulously clean and tubes should be scalded each time before being filled. If the containers are allowed to become tainted with stale food they will be a source of serious danger to the health of the birds.

Another very important point is that all food and drinking water, whether on the ground or hung high up, should always be placed in the shade. If it is exposed to the sun decomposition will set in much more rapidly.

Most fanciers will already have some knowledge of the essential part vitamins play in promoting healthy growth and maintaining good condition. More detailed information as to their use is easily obtainable and there are many preparations available containing various combinations of the most important vitamins.

If it is found that a bird is in need of additional vitamins or that the food being supplied is deficient in any which is essential to its development and health, the deficiency may be made good by adding a few drops of the correct concentrate to the drinking water two or three times a week. Only glass or china vessels should be used.

Live Food

The most difficult part of the diet to provide is live food in the form of live insects. Meal-worms are the least troublesome to obtain but they are expensive and unfortunately the chitin of these larvae is not easily digested by all birds. They are so well liked, however, that unless they are strictly rationed, the birds may well take too many and fall ill. A bird should not have more than 8 to 10 at a time, and the small finches should never have more than 1 or 2 a day. During the breeding season they should be given cut up or if thrown into boiling water can be used whole, as the water will have softened the chitin. If very young worms or those which are still white after casting their skin are selected, they can be given as they are. These insects can be used at all stages of development but the very young larvae or the pupae are the best.

If it is desired to breed meal-worms at home, prepare a box 2 ft by 20 in. wide by 1 ft deep. Drill holes of $1\frac{1}{2}$ in. diameter along the sides about 1 in. from the bottom, and cover these on the inside with fine mesh mosquito gauze. This will admit air into the box when it has been filled up. At the bottom place a layer of chopped straw sufficient to come just above the air holes.

On the straw an old piece of woollen material should be laid, and covered with bran and flour 1 in. deep. Another piece of woollen material must be placed over this, and again meal and bran should be laid. Continue until there are four layers, then cover the whole surface with woollen material. On this must be placed a piece of greased paper with lettuce leaves and some soaked and squeezed bread exactly in the centre to supply moisture. The meal-worms feed on the flour and bran.

If live meal-beetles can be obtained, place as many as possible in the prepared box. The beetles lay eggs invisible to the human eye on the woollen material, and from these eggs come the worms which provide the food for the birds. These worms or larvae become pupae and in time change into beetles.

The box must not be damp nor too cool. The temperature should be kept even so as to speed up the growth process. The lid must fit well and be covered with mosquito netting. Beetles and worms will not crawl out between box and lid if a piece of zinc has been nailed round the top inside edge of the box.

Beetles have one arch enemy which may do untold damage to the whole culture—the acarida found in flour. This mite can multiply enormously in a very short time. There are two ways of getting rid of it. If the box is placed on a grid and heated well during the night, the mites will emerge and settle on a white cloth placed in the box under the lid. To kill the mites it is then only necessary to pick up this cloth and dip it in boiling water. But it is simpler and just as effective to buy some wormwood from a chemist or herbalist. If this is cut up and placed in a saucer inside the box the mites will vanish by the next day.

It is quite possible that the bran or waste flour used for the meal-beetle nursery already contains acarida, which will increase rapidly with heat. It is always advisable when furnishing the box to get rid of the mite in this simple way by the use of wormwood.

Finally, the worms should not be removed every day as this disturbs the brood. A large enough quantity should be taken once a week, and the lettuce leaves and bread changed at the same time.

Another excellent live food are blowfly maggots. These can be bought from an angler's shop as also can *enchytraea* (white worm). Both can be cultivated. A garden is needed in which to breed the blowfly maggots, as the effluvium of putrid meat is very unpleasant. Hang up a piece of meat and it will soon be covered by eggs of the bluebottle fly. If the meat is put in a box covered with a piece of cloth, the maggots will develop rapidly. These can be taken off the meat daily and laid in a bowl of water, which must be frequently changed. The grubs or gentles can then be fed to the birds; the contents of the intestines, consisting of rotting meat, having emptied themselves, the pure white grubs are then most suitable food for the birds. If a large outdoor aviary is kept, a piece of meat or fish can be hung above the wire in such a way that the birds cannot get at it. The meat should be wrapped in a piece of cheese cloth or muslin. Flies will lay their eggs and the grubs will fall down into the aviary where the birds can find them. If a plate is placed just under the bag the birds will quickly see the grubs and pick them up. Young birds do well on these fat grubs.

Enchytraea, thin white worms $1\frac{1}{2}$ in. long, are found in decaying wood and leaves. If kept in a dark box with some leaf mould damped with old leaves, they will multiply quickly. They should be given a little oatmeal as food.

There has been much controversy about the advisability of feeding birds on earthworms. Large birds like them, but some fanciers have refused to use them. It has been alleged that the yellow ring contains poison, and that this is why the birds have sometimes refused to eat these worms. However, it has now been definitely proved that this is not so, and that the sickness or death of some of the birds is not due to this; there is probably another cause which has escaped attention. More and more poisonous weed killers are being used and the soil is then given all kinds of chemical fertilizers. Birds which come into contact with these poisons by eating the sprayed weeds or the sprayed green stuff, like chickweed, will almost certainly die. Is it, therefore, so surprising that they sometimes die after eating earthworms? The digestive organs of these worms must be filled with earth, mixed with countless poisonous substances. Another factor is that earthworms are the hosts of a parasitic roundworm causing 'gapes' to which gallinaceous birds are particularly susceptible.

Earthworms can be used as food but they must undergo special treatment. They should be put into a glass jar, in which has been placed damp blotting paper. The jar should be hung, tied down with a piece of cheese cloth, in a cool, dark spot and after a few days the worms can be used. What has happened is this: the worms, in crawling about, have left the slimy layer on the paper, have eaten the paper, and thus expelled the earth from their digestive organs. In this way the worms, with or without the yellow rings, have been rendered absolutely harmless.

The tubifex and live cyclops used extensively by keepers of aquaria are not scorned by the more delicate insect-eating birds. They must be kept in running water. The tubifex will remain in good condition for quite a time if placed under a dripping tap.

Daphnia are invaluable during the raising of the young. The avadavats and small foreign finches are very fond of them. They can readily be obtained from ponds, as can mosquito larvae. In summer an enormous quantity of insects can be found in the countryside and many are suitable for the birds. Locusts are among the best food. Naturally, not all insects are eaten and it is a pity that the Colorado beetle is taken by so few birds. Flies and mosquitoes killed by 'Flit' or other insecticides must never be given to birds.

Aphis and Daphnia are believed to assist in maintaining the colour of the plumage, especially the red. Scotch kale, carrots, and grass meal also help to stimulate the red colour.

All insect-eating birds are fond of aphis fly, which are found on elderberry and rose trees, mock orange and nasturtium. Both the green and black species are eaten greedily. If branches covered with greenfly are hung in the cage or aviary, the birds will soon be seen carefully picking off all the insects.

Ants' cocoons, misnamed ants' eggs in the trade, are probably the most valuable form of live food obtainable, especially for rearing young during the early stages and all birds, both seed-eaters and insectivorous species, will take them readily, especially when fresh. They can be purchased either fresh or dried but, like meal-worms, they are expensive and if possible the fancier should himself collect them from the nests, preferably on a warmish, sunny day, when the ants have moved the cocoons near to the top of the nest. Nests may frequently be found in old tree stubs and on the sunny side of the stub quantities of cocoons will be concealed behind the bark. After removing the bark they can easily be scraped into a tin. They may also be found underneath flat stones and other damp places. The hills made by the small meadow ants may be shovelled into a large biscuit tin, covered with a close-fitting lid, and so conveyed home to be tipped into the aviary where the birds will quickly sort out the cocoons. The best supply is to be obtained from the large nests constructed by wood ants. These ants are very beneficial to the woods in which they live and they should not be disturbed more than is absolutely necessary, nor should the whole nest be removed. It should be carefully opened and when the required quantity of cocoons have been removed it should be covered up again. The method of collecting the cocoons is as follows: First spread a white sheet on the ground in the sun and round the edge place flower pots upside down with one edge slightly raised with a stone or piece of wood. Then gather a pailful of the cocoons, ants, and nest material and tip it in the centre of the sheet.

The ants will immediately start to collect the exposed cocoons and carry them to the edge of the sheet and place them in the shade under the flower pots, leaving the debris from the nest in the centre of the sheet. When they have completed their task, the pots can be lifted and the cocoons scooped into a tin. The debris should then be returned to the nest. During the whole process it is advisable to wear leather gloves as these ants bite viciously.

If the 'eggs' cannot be collected fresh each day they may be kept for about a week if spread out on newspaper in a cool place. They are, however, only fit for use while they remain a good white colour. Once they become blue or show signs of mildew they are no longer suitable as food for the birds. Should it be desired to lay in a stock to last a little longer they can be sterilized by placing a layer about $1\frac{1}{2}$ in. thick in a saucepan which should then be stood in a pan of boiling water and covered with a lid so that the steam can reach the cocoons. When the water has cooled the cocoons should be spread out on cardboard to dry thoroughly and they will then keep for about a fortnight.

During the winter it is impossible to obtain fresh ants' eggs and the dried variety will have to suffice. It may happen that the birds will refuse to change from the fresh to the dried eggs or from the dried to the fresh ones, and so it is best to give dried eggs at all times, adding some fresh eggs in the summer months.

Another method of collecting small quantities of meadow ants' cocoons is by the use of an exhauster; this is also valuable in the collection of small beetles and insects. It is easily made at home; the illustration speaks for itself (Fig 11). The 'eggs' and the beetles are sucked into the glass container.

Fig 11 *Exhauster*

It is possible to lay in a stock for the winter, and this is cheaper than buying. To do this, gather the cocoons, pick out the leaves, pine-needles, etc. and spread them out in a spot where there is no wind. When they have dried for a day in the open, fill some small preserving jars right up to the top, shaking down the cocoons. Cover with a rubber ring and screw down the lid but do not add water. Sterilize in the ordinary way, but maintain the temperature at 212° F (100° C) for a full hour. Then cool down slowly and carefully fasten the lids.

When these eggs are used during the winter, the whole contents of the jar must be finished quickly. Once the air has got to the cocoons they soon deteriorate. If a refrigerator is available it is advisable to keep them in it.

If dried ants' cocoons are used in winter, they should be soaked in milk for a little while before being given to the birds; they will then swell and can be mixed with the other food.

Ants' cocoons may be dried at home by spreading them out on cardboard or drying frames and placing these in the sun. When they are absolutely dry they can be stored in some cool, dry place; if they are kept in a damp place they will mildew rapidly and are then worthless.

D

Fruit

Only a very few birds live exclusively on fruit, and these are really too expensive for an ordinary bird fancier to keep. Honey food forms part of their diet.

Most of the insect-eaters are also fruit-eaters, and it is therefore appropriate here to enumerate the most suitable kinds of fruit to use.

The ideal fruit, and the most readily obtainable, is the orange; it should be cut across, so that all the sections will be available. The birds can then suck the juice and pick out the pith as well.

The orange is most useful, too, in helping to accustom the birds to insectivorous food. A section should be cut away from the fruity part and some of the insectivorous food put in. The bird will suck the juice and the food will disappear quite readily. Ants' eggs and meal-worms may also be placed on the orange.

Grapes are excellent for most birds. Pears, ripe and sweet, are usually highly appreciated. Bananas cut up and, if desired, mixed with cubes of other fruit, can be served readily in the peels of halved grape-fruit but they should be given sparingly as they tend to fatten the birds.

Some birds like berries, such as the elderberry, which can be hung up in bunches. Tomatoes, cut up and covered with sugar, are also liked. In fact, the real fruit-eaters really scorn very few kinds of fruit. Preserved and candied fruit, currants and raisins are certainly not to be despised. Pieces of fig and date are real treats. Raisins help in taming the birds, and will usually be taken readily from the hand when offered.

Fruit may be sweetened with sugar or honey if necessary and this often makes it more acceptable to the birds. To maintain a bird in healthy condition it is essential that the fruit should be sound. Fruit which has been sprayed has probably been so washed by the rain that there is no longer any danger of poisoning, but to be doubly sure it is better to wash it again.

8. FEEDING AND HAND-REARING YOUNG BIRDS

Feeding

It is obvious that the food given to parent birds while rearing their broods is vitally important to the young in the nest, for they need an enormous amount of building up in a very short time, sometimes only 12 days, and it stands to reason that when the egg content has been consumed and digested only food of the highest calorific value will meet the needs of growth and development of the fledgling.

Weak youngsters are not always the result of degeneration and inbreeding; wrong feeding is responsible for much of the trouble. It is not really difficult to supply the correct diet, though much thought and care should be devoted to it.

Most finches and their kind, which for the sake of simplicity are known as seed-eaters, live for a great part of the year almost exclusively on seeds, but during the breeding season they need a far more varied and nutritious diet. In their natural state they satisfy this need by changing their feeding habits and becoming largely insectivorous. In the early stages their young are also fed mainly on insects, but during the first few days after hatching the parents supply so-called 'crop milk'. The composition of this substance can be influenced by the food supplied to the adults and if seed alone is given, the 'crop milk' will lack the essential protein and vitamin content. This may cause the death of the youngsters after a few days; it may also cause the parents to stop feeding them. Death of an embryo can often be traced to an incomplete food content of the parent birds, resulting in an inadequate supply of the life-giving substance to the egg. In fact incorrect feeding is frequently the cause of breeding failures.

The least the fancier can do is to supply some form of soft food or stale bread soaked in milk and enriched with a few drops of cod-liver oil and vitamins. This is fairly satisfactory and if plenty of undergrowth is planted in the aviary, the birds will themselves find all kinds of small insects and larvae. The rearing food sold in packets for canaries is suitable for many species of foreign birds and to this should be added meal-worms boiled and cut up, *enchytraea*, aphis, ants' cocoons, and banana flies.

Better results may be expected by supplying a special mixture made up as follows: 50 grams cod-liver oil and 50 grams olive oil should be mixed with 1 lb. finely crushed biscuit, 4 oz. bran, 8 oz. skim milk powder and 4 oz. germinated wheat: 2 oz. yeast and 8 oz. fish meal should be added to this if the mixture is intended for insect- or fruit-eating species.

The mixture should be stored in an airtight tin but should not be kept longer than 3–4 weeks. To prepare it for the birds, it must be moistened with water or better still with carrot juice or grated, raw carrot. For insect eaters dried ants' cocoons and boiled, and chopped meal-worms should be added, or if fresh ants' cocoons can be obtained, these are always preferable to the dried form.

This mixture makes a rearing food of really high standard, suitable for the young of practically all species of small birds.

Germinated sprays of millet and other germinated seeds have a higher vitamin value and are softer for the still soft bills of young birds. Ideal, too, are the numberless grasses which are just seeding and can readily be gathered by the wayside. Seed can be sown easily and grown in flower pots. When it starts to grow it can be placed, pot and all, in the aviary and in a short time the birds will have fed wisely and well on it, as will be shown by their improved condition.

Often nestlings will have to be placed with foster-parents, because their own parents refuse to feed them, or abandon them after a few days. These foster-parents should be chosen from species which rear their own young with similar rearing food.

Hand-Rearing

Many imported birds have been taken from the nest and reared by hand. Hence they have become tame and readily settle down to life in captivity.

Fanciers who take the trouble and care to raise the young themselves will possess birds which have no fear of human beings and will readily learn various tricks. Some species can be taught to talk, and they may become so attached to their trainer that they will often completely ignore their own kind. They sometimes lack their normal brilliance of colouring but they are nevertheless quite healthy and will become cherished pets. If it is intended to hand-rear young birds, they should be taken from the nest while quite young. Better still, the whole nest can be removed to a warm and quiet spot and covered with a piece of woollen material (to take the place of the parent bird).

Very young birds must at first be fed every half hour. A fine spatula should be used to open the beak if necessary, and the food should be gently pushed down the back of the throat with a small glass rod. This is difficult at first, because the fledglings will not help, but once they get used to it they will immediately open their beaks wide at the approach of the glass rod and croak hoarsely.

Insect-eaters will grow well if fed with well-washed grubs, fresh ants' eggs, and pieces of meal-worm boiled or fresh. A little stale bread soaked in milk may be given and tepid water must be supplied.

As an alternative the following mixture may be used: crushed rusks or fine breadcrumbs, dried or fresh ants' eggs, grated raw lean meat, a few drops of cod-liver oil; moistened with some milk or orange juice. Of course, insects and small meal-worms can be added.

Nestlings, especially if they still lack feathers, should be placed in a small box filled with moss and feathers and set in a dark, quiet, corner. If placed in the sun the nestlings would immediately dry up and die. The temperature should be maintained at 100° F (36° C). Feeding should take place at first every 2 hours; later every 3 hours. After every feed excreta must be removed. Even when the fledglings have flown these meals should be continued for some time. If allowed to try and feed themselves the fledglings will not get nearly enough to eat, especially in their early stages.

After the first few days, a feed every hour will suffice. As soon as the young begin to leave the nest, a small bowl of similar food and a bowl of water can be put down and one feed skipped. Most birds will quickly begin to feed themselves.

So long as the birds remain in the nest a thorough hygiene must be maintained. 'Dirty nappies' can be removed with tweezers and the remains of food must on no account be allowed to stick to the birds' plumage.

As soon as the birds are able to fend for themselves and will come and beg for titbits from their foster-parent, start can be made with training. The pupils are then naturally confident and with patience and kindness can readily be taught.

9. BREEDING IN CAGES OR AVIARIES

When describing the various species later on, detailed information will be given as to their breeding habits; but it may be helpful at this stage to give a few general directions for breeding.

Generally the beginner starts with an aviary primarily designed to accommodate a mixed collection of brightly coloured or singing birds, in which case males only will normally be kept since they are more peaceful and sing better when no females are present, provided not more than one of a kind is included in the collection. Sooner or later most fanciers will wish to try their hand at breeding and although difficulties will most certainly arise they may expect at least a measure of success. Some kinds of birds are most suitable for a beginner. These include the Bengalese and Zebra Finches, both of which are seed-eaters. If good pairs are bought from a reliable source, breeding may confidently be expected.

The Bengalese will be of incalculable value as foster-parents, when more foreign finches are to be kept. Once the beginner has become accustomed to the treatment of the Bengalese and Zebra Finches and has succeeded in getting them to breed and raise their young, these birds can be given eggs from other species to hatch. Another suitable species is the Silverbill, but this is not so easy to handle as the Bengalese. Nor should the canary be forgotten; if simple rules are observed, this bird is not difficult to breed.

One pair of birds will breed undisturbed in a cage or aviary, but as soon as more pairs of the same species are housed together they will quarrel about nesting material, nesting boxes, and suchlike. The males will fight over the females with disastrous results. An odd female may be persecuted to death and an odd male will disturb a clutch of another bird's eggs.

If several birds are to be kept together, they should be of as many different species as possible and have a varied choice of nesting sites. Then they will have no reason to fight. Listed on pp. 31–2 is a wide selection of birds which can be housed together, but a sharp look-out must always be kept for fighters. Although very different combinations can be found in the aviaries of experienced fanciers, and in some aviaries many pairs of one kind may be kept, it is unwise for the beginner to embark on such experiments.

Most of the birds from which it is best to start breeding belong to species regularly bred in Europe, but they still retain a strong natural instinct to select secluded spots for their nests. The canary is probably the one exception to this rule. Wherever the nest box with the artificial nest in it is placed, there the canary will lay and hatch her eggs. No birds can breed successfully if they are in an all-wire cage set in the centre of a room through which people are continually passing. As has already been emphasized, breeding in a box-type cage is preferable as the birds can always find seclusion there.

It should be remembered that most birds, in their natural state, choose well-concealed nesting sites and the instinct to do so will persist however tame they may have become and no matter how long they have been kept in a cage or aviary.

A first essential is that the birds have a quiet nook where they will feel secure. The open aviary therefore needs planting. Along the back wall, which should preferably be enclosed, nesting boxes should be hung at varying heights and, if possible, partly concealed with bunches of heather or fir branches.

If the shelter is sufficiently light, nest boxes may be hung there as well; many birds prefer that situation. There must be a lean-to or some sort of cover above the nesting boxes so that rain cannot cause damage. As a general rule each pair of birds should have the choice of two nests. This prevents quarrels.

During the breeding season, no change in the arrangement of the aviary can be made. Branches and twigs which cover the nests should be left undisturbed; though they may fade and die, no new ones must be added as they would cause the birds to abandon the nest even if it contained eggs or a brood.

The outside aviary should not be raked over every weekend to show a 'tidy' birds' home to admiring friends. What is needed is not an immaculate garden but a home entirely dedicated to the wants of the birds. It is much better to let the spilled seed germinate and grow and to let weeds flourish. The birds are fond of weeds and all kinds of insects are attracted which, in their turn, are good for the birds.

A little grass and weed seed might even be sown in a corner of the aviary where the rain could reach it; this should be allowed to grow and seed as much as the birds will permit. Experience has shown that in an aviary where chickweed and other weeds are growing shrubs will stand a good chance of remaining undamaged.

A breeding cage should not be too small. There are special types for canaries. When the young are fully grown and independent, they should, of course, be removed to other accommodation.

A general rule is not to breed from birds younger than 8 months. If this rule is not observed the results will prove disappointing and the birds may even die from the strain of laying.

Birds cannot be forced to pair, and a cock and hen selected by the fancier may not always prove to be a suitable choice of mates. If no inclination to mating is observed, a change of male may sometimes have the desired effect. Although two birds may appear to be happily mated, the cock may be infertile, but the hen will still lay and incubate for her normal period. On the other hand the hen might prove to be sterile, in which case no eggs will be laid in spite of the fact that she has constructed a nest and commenced to sit.

Appearances are no guide to such physical defects, and until by trial and error a good pair has been selected, the results may be disappointing. Many species show no obvious differences between the sexes; both sometimes seem to be laying. They will often sit close together, behave as a true pair, and yet eventually prove to be both of the same sex. The only clear indication may be the behaviour of the male towards the female.

So long as the male does not display himself, dance, or hop about with straws or grasses in his beak, it is doubtful whether a pair has been found. Sometimes the song of the male (as in the case of the Bengalese) will be a pointer.

Sexing adult Zebra Finches does not present much difficulty since the females lack the chestnut cheek patches and the chestnut flanks. Only the pure white variety is apt to cause confusion, but in these the bill of the male is dark red and that of the female pale red.

10. COLOUR MUTATIONS AND HYBRIDIZING

It has always been the aim of bird fanciers to obtain new varieties of household pets by cross-breeding, selection, or even in-breeding. There are ample opportunities for experiments.

Mutations often occur unexpectedly among wild birds but seldom survive to become an established variety. Among large flocks of budgerigars in Australia yellow birds have been observed. The wide difference in appearance from the rest of the flock has subjected them to greater risk of destruction, but it has been found that those which survive and breed often produce young which have reverted to normal.

This is not the case with birds bred under controlled conditions. The differentiations, in colour or in shape, can be carefully retained by judicious selection. In this way a wide range of colours have been obtained with budgerigars and canaries. A recent development in canary breeding has been the production of birds approaching red in colour.

In the hereditary factor red was lacking entirely and it was only by crossing with the Hooded Siskin, *Spinus cucullatus*, a species which possessed this red, that the colour factor was introduced into the canary. It is not often that a crossing has led to such a fortuitous result which is also pleasing aesthetically, for as a rule crossing does not produce birds more beautiful than their parents and in most cases the young prove to be infertile.

The expectations and the theory, which are the basis of hybridizing related species, fall outside the scope of this book, and only brief advice can be given. Much patience and luck are essential to success in this line. Obviously there must be close relationship between the species to be crossed, and a guide to this may sometimes be found in the scientific nomenclature.

Birds of the same species are more mutually attracted than birds of related species. In the first instance, therefore, the birds intended for crossing should be segregated and kept out of sight or hearing of others of the same species. Even then it is not at all certain that the selected birds will mate, nor can there be any guarantee that their eggs will be fertile, even if several matings have been observed. It may therefore happen that partners have to be frequently changed, and for this reason it may be an advantage to keep a cock in the centre compartment of a three-division canary breeding cage with a hen on either side. If the birds are to be kept in a well-planted flight, it is preferable that they should have the aviary entirely to themselves and be put together during the winter well before the normal breeding season commences so that they may get used to each other. Successful crossing has been obtained with the following native birds and between native birds and canaries (the first name used always indicates the cock bird):

> Greenfinch × Hawfinch;
> Yellow Hammer × Reed Bunting;
> Bullfinch × Siskin;
> Canary × Chaffinch;
> Goldfinch × Greenfinch;
> Greenfinch × Canary;
> Goldfinch × Canary;
> Siskin × Canary and Canary × Siskin;
> Linnet × Canary and Canary × Linnet.

11. SICKNESS AND TREATMENT

Birds, like other pets, are liable to sickness, but their treatment is much more difficult. It is not easy to diagnose the complaint correctly. Some of the more common and easily recognizable illnesses are described in the following pages. The first golden rule for all sickness is: isolate the bird at once.

A small box cage in which to segregate a sick bird should always be kept available. A still better plan is to make a 'sick bay' which can be warmed by electric lamps placed underneath. All sick birds should be kept warm, and the temperature must be gradually brought up to 85° F (29° C). A thermometer must be placed in the cage to enable the temperature to be accurately controlled. Sick birds suffer less discomfort when they are warm, and it is easier to start the cure.

The cause of the illness can generally be traced to human neglect. Soiled food or drinking water; insufficient sunlight; draughts and bad green stuffs may be at the bottom of all the trouble.

A sick bird can usually be noticed as it will fluff out its feathers, pant for breath, hold its wings away from its body, and tuck its head under its wing. Also it will sleep with both feet on the perch which a healthy bird rarely does.

Colds or Chills

The most frequent complaint is the common cold, usually caused by draught or damp. Shortage of food also increases liability to catching cold. This complaint can easily be remedied if taken in time. The temperature of the cage should be kept at 85° F (29° C) night and day, and sufficient food should be given. The bird will soon begin to recover and the temperature in the 'sick bay' can be gradually reduced to normal. After a few days the bird can be returned to its normal environment, but should this be outside the change must only be made during a spell of fine weather.

Diarrhoea

This is usually caused by bad food. The cure is to segregate the bird in a cage heated to 85° F (29° C). Clean seed mixed with a little finely powdered charcoal should be given, but no green stuffs. The drinking water should be replaced by 3 tablespoonfuls of water to which 6 drops of aloe syrup have been added. Proprietary medicines can also be used successfully. A hard-boiled yolk of egg, rubbed down with a little bismuth and added to the seed, is recommended. In the case of insect-eaters the egg and bismuth must be mixed with the 'universal' food. Rice water can be given to drink. It is imperative that the bird be kept clean so that no faeces stick to the vent feathers.

Even infectious diarrhoea, which may occur with freshly imported birds, can sometimes be cured by this treatment. Another home cure which is sometimes effective, is to give black coffee instead of water. This disease may prove fatal to some birds.

It is remarkable that damp weather often brings on diarrhoea, which indicates that it is not always bad food which is the cause; the dampness brings on a chill in the digestive organs.

Constipation

The whole demeanour of the bird shows that it is in trouble and it sits continually straining without any relief.

Constipation can be brought about by incorrect feeding or by some unknown cause. The addition of a drop of cod-liver oil to the seed and 12 drops of aloe syrup or a little solution of Kruschen salts to the drinking water may bring speedy relief. Another quick and homely cure consists of 2 drops of castor oil given direct into the beak with a fountain pen filler. A little chicory in place of the usual green stuff should be given, but no special heat treatment is necessary.

Chalk Legs (Scaly Legs)

The legs show chalky scales, which are constantly pecked at by the birds, and obviously cause distress. One treatment with tepid water applied with a soft brush and then dabbing with turpentine will usually suffice. The scales drop off speedily once the mite, which has caused them, has been killed by the turpentine.

Spots

It often happens that a bird has a spot from which pus runs. It can usually be removed by a little boracic vaseline. The tiny scab may then be removed with a pair of tweezers, which have first been sterilized. The spot should then be lightly touched with an iodine pencil.

Moulting

This is a natural process, and occurs with all healthy birds. Sometimes moulting ends quickly or it may continue indefinitely. The cause of prolongation of the moult is usually unbalanced feeding and an inadequate supply of necessary minerals. Too little light and air may also be responsible for delayed recovery.

Drops of Vitamins A and D must be mixed with the food during the moulting season. The birds' stamina is somewhat reduced at such times so it is advisable to give them extra warmth.

Plucking of Feathers

The causes of this are many. In the first place the feeding may not be well balanced. It may contain too little Vitamins A and D. Too confined living space and consequent overcrowding is another possible cause, in which case the remedy is to segregate the birds. More often than not parasites are the cause, and for these suitable non-poisonous insecticides can be used.

The trouble becomes much more serious when a bird seems for some reason only known to itself to pluck out its own feathers and also those of its young. If the remedies mentioned above do not bring about a cure, there is little else that can be done except to make sure that the birds are not used for breeding, for once started, plucking may become a persistent habit.

Egg Binding

The cause of this evil, often designated as 'illness', is injudicious feeding. The addition of cod-liver oil to the seed must be continued during the breeding period. Crushed hemp which has become a little old, and egg feed which has gone damp, will give rise to acidity which may be harmful. Salt cuttlefish given without the addition of vita-lime may also cause the hen difficulty in laying. She just sits puffed out, huddled up in a heap on the floor. She can hardly remain upright on a perch and, if human aid is not at hand, the worst may happen.

The remedy is to bring the temperature up to 85° F (29° C). This will generally be enough to cure the trouble. Another suggestion is to run cold water on the bird's stomach and then apply warmth. But this, and also the old method of holding the bird over steam, are rarely effective.

If egg binding continues and the bird is valuable, it is advisable to call in a veterinary surgeon. He will probably give the bird an injection in the thigh with piton, the same remedy as is often used for human beings during difficult confinements, but the dose must not be more than one-twentieth part of a cubic centimeter (c.c.).

Sudden cold during the laying period may also cause egg binding. Alec Brooksbank in his book *Foreign Birds for Garden Aviaries* recommends a preventive which has been hitherto almost unknown, *viz.* add a teaspoonful of gin to a pint of drinking water during the laying period.

Birds suffering from this ailment should not be allowed to bathe. Often the difficulty in laying occurs with only the first egg, and the rest are laid quite normally, but sometimes the trouble recurs with every egg to be laid. In any case, the hen should not be allowed to breed for some time. Young birds sometimes suffer from egg binding, and therefore they should be prevented from breeding until 8 months to a year after they have been cured.

Overgrown Claws

Birds kept in a cage or glass show-case are especially liable to suffer from overgrown claws. The cause may be too small perches, which provide little opportunity to wear down the nails in the normal manner. Weavers are specially prone to this trouble.

The bird should be caught and its nails held against the light so that the little live vein can be seen. The tip of the nail should then be cut off with a sharp pair of scissors, without touching the blood vessel.

Bird Mites and Lice

Various preparations to destroy these pests are available and with all a very fine spray must be used. The birds should not be saturated, nor should the preparation be allowed to enter the eyes, but a very light spraying will cause them no harm. Young and naked birds in the nest should just be covered with a piece of paper on to which the mites will crawl and it can then be removed and burnt. The perches, nest boxes, and cracks or joints in the walls should be carefully and repeatedly sprayed. If this is done at regular intervals no parasites will remain alive.

Other Ailments

All the illnesses mentioned are liable to occur to any bird and seldom prove difficult to cure, but it is more serious if a mortal disease, whether infectious or not, is contracted. Remedies can be suggested but it is essential to have professional treatment, especially in the case of valuable birds, and the veterinary surgeon should immediately be consulted. He will give the necessary instructions for the disinfection of the cages and aviaries. In the case of death, autopsy is desirable so that the cause can be ascertained. It is impossible to be too careful of one's birds and good food and attention to hygiene will keep illness at bay.

MODERN MEDICINES

Aureomycin and Penicillin

New and powerful drugs are now available on a veterinary surgeon's prescription, but they may be found difficult to apply.

Although a penicillin ointment will give an excellent and rapid cure in the case of inflammation, the wound must be cleaned first, so that no pus or scab prevents the ointment taking effect. Boric acid solution or an infusion of camomile flowers can be used for cleansing a wound.

Inflammation of the throat or larynx can also be treated with penicillin. The powder (1 milligram per 10 gram weight of bird) must be dissolved in distilled water and poured into the mouth with a fountain pen filler. For blood infection penicillin injections may be given but aureomycin is better for the purpose. The same proportion, 1 milligram per 10 gram weight, is the correct dose, and a bird suffering from inflammation of the intestines can be cured in 2 or 3 days if given aureomycin 3 times a day. It is best given in the feed of ants' eggs or boiled meal-worms with which the powder has been mixed. A little water should be given afterwards with a fountain pen filler.

Obviously experiments with these remedies are not for the ordinary fancier and the only reason for mentioning them is to give some insight into the development of treatment for bird ailments. It is probable that reliable patent remedies will soon be freely available for common illnesses which have hitherto defied treatment.

12. THE ILLUSTRATED PAGES

A complete index of the species, including illustrations, is on pages 254–62. They are listed under commonly accepted English names, Latin names, and alternative names.

In the captions to the illustrations, only the commonly accepted English names and Latin names are given.

1 Red-collared Whydah
Coliuspasser ardens

2 Yellow-backed Whydah
Coliuspasser macrourus

3 Giant Whydah *Coliuspasser
progne*

4 Jackson's Whydah
Drepanoplectes jacksoni

6 Grenadier Weaver *Euplectes o. orix* (cock and hen)

5 Pintailed Whydah *Vidua macroura*

7 Napoleon Weaver *Euplectes afra afra*

8 Black-bellied Weaver *Euplectes nigriventris*

9 Orange Bishop *Euplectes orix franciscana*

10 Little Masked Weaver *Ploceus luteolus*

11 Madagascar Weaver *Foudia madagascariensis*

12 Taha Weaver *Euplectes afra taha*

13   Speckled Fronted Weaver *Sporopipes frontalis*

14   Scaly-crowned Weaver *Sporopipes squamifrons* (cock and hen)

15 Spotted-backed Weaver *Ploceus cucullatus*

16 Red-headed Quelea *Quelea erythrops*

17 Red-billed Quelea *Quelea quelea*

18 Crimson-rumped Waxbill *Estrilda rhodopyga*

19   Golden-breasted Waxbill *Estrilda subflava*

20   St. Helena Waxbill *Estrilda astrild*

21   Red-eared Waxbill *Estrilda troglodytes*

22 Blue-headed Cordon Bleu *Uraeginthus cyanocephalus* (hen and cock)

23 Cordon Blue *Uraeginthus bengalus*

24 Peter's Twin Spot *Hypargos niveoguttatus* (cock in centre)

25 Orange-cheeked Waxbill *Estrilda melpoda*

26 Yellow-bellied Waxbill *Estrilda melanotis quartinia*

27 Violet-eared Waxbill *Granatina granatinus*

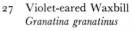

28 Black-cheeked Waxbill
Estrilda erythronotos

29 Sydney Waxbill *Aegintha
temporalis*

30 Lavender Finch *Lagonosticta
caerulescens*

31 Green Avadavat *Amandava
formosa*

32 Strawberry Finch *Amandava amandava punicea*

33 Fire Finch *Lagonosticta senegala*

34 Melba Finch *Pytilia melba*

35 West African Quail Finch
Ortygospiza a. atricollis

36 Red-headed Fire Finch
Amadina erythrocephala

38 Cut-throat *Amadina fasciata*

37 East African Cut-throat
Amadina fasciata alexanderi

39   Black-headed Mannikin *Lonchura malacca atricapilla*

40   Magpie Mannikin *Spermestes fringilloides*

41   White-headed Mannikin *Lonchura maja*

42   Three-coloured Mannikin *Lonchura malacca*

43 Bronze-winged Mannikin *Spermestes cucullata*

44 Common Spice Finch *Lonchura punctulata*

45 African
Silverbill
*Euodice
malabaraica
cantans*

46 Indian
Silverbill
*Euodice
malabarica*

47 Bengalese *Lonchura domestica* (Fawn
variety at front)

48   Bengalese *Lonchura domestica*

49   White Java Sparrow
     Padda oryzivora

50   Alario Finch *Alario alario*

51   Java Sparrow *Padda oryzivora*

52   Cherry Finch *Aidemosyna modesta*

53   Masked Grass Finch *Poephila personata*

54 Star Finch *Bathilda ruficauda*

55 Chestnut-breasted Finch
Lonchura castaneothorax

56 Heck's Grass Finch *Poephila acuticauda hecki*

57 Long-tailed Grass Finch
Poephila acuticauda

58　Parson Finch *Poephila cincta*

59　Red-headed Gouldian Finch
Erythrura gouldiae

60　Orange-headed Gouldian
Finch *Erythrura gouldiae*

61 Black-headed Gouldian Finch *Erythrura gouldiae*

62 Zebra Finch *Taeniopygia guttata castanotis*

63 Zebra Finch *Taeniopygia guttata castanotis* (Pied variety, hen and cock)

64 Zebra Finch *Taeniopygia guttata castanotis*
(White variety; hen and cock Penguin
variety; hen and cock Fawn variety)

65 Painted Finch *Emblema picta*

66 Diamond Sparrow
Steganopleura guttata

67 Pintailed Nonpareil *Erythrura prasina*

68 Bicheno's Finch *Stizoptera bichenovi*

69 Wild Canary *Serinus canaria*

70 Cape Canary *Serinus canicollis*

71　Green Singing Finch, *Serinus mozambicus*

72　Grey Singing Finch *Serinus leucopygia*

73 Yellow Sparrow *Auripasser l. luteus*

74 Saffron Finch *Sycalis flaveola*

75 Black-headed Siskin *Spinus ictericus*

76 Hooded Siskin *Spinus cucullatus*

77 Crested Bunting *Melophus lathami*

78 Indian Rose Finch *Carpodacus erythrinus*

79 Indigo Bunting
Passerina cyanea

80 Lazuli Bunting
Passerina amoena

81   Rainbow Bunting *Passerina leclancheri*
(front view)

82 Rainbow Bunting *Passerina leclancheri*
(back view)

83 Nonpareil Bunting *Passerina ciris*

84 Versicolour Bunting *Passerina versicolor*

85 Olive Finch *Tiaris olivacea*

86   Black-crested Finch *Lophospingus pusillus*

87   Cuban Finch *Tiaris canora*

88 Red-crested Cardinal *Paroaria cucullata*

89 Virginian Cardinal *Richmondena cardinalis*

90   Pope Cardinal *Paroaria dominicana*

91   Yellow-billed Cardinal
       Paroaria capitata

92   Black-headed
       Hawfinch *Eophona*
       personata

93 Green Cardinal *Gubernatrix cristata*

95   Rufous-bellied Niltava
Niltava sundara

94   Northern Blue Grosbeak
Guiraca caerulea

96   Shama *Copsychus malabaricus*
       indicus

97   Orange-headed Ground
Thrush *Geocichla citrina*

98　White-crested Jay Thrush *Garrulax leucolophus*

99　Indian White-eye *Zosterops palpebrosa*

100   Pekin Robin *Leiothrix lutea*

101   Silver-eared Mesia *Leiothrix argentauris*

102   Golden-fronted Fruitsucker *Chloropsis aurifrons*

103 Red-vented Bulbul *Pycnonotus cafer*

104   Red-eared Bulbul *Pycononotus jocosus*

105 White-cheeked Bulbul *Pycnonotus leucogenys*

106 Blue-throated Barbet *Megalaima asiatica*

107 Racket-tailed Drongo
Dicrurus paradiseus

108 Common Mynah
Acridotheres tristis

109   Pagoda Mynah *Sturnus pagodarum*

110   Greater Hill Mynah *Gracula r. religiosa*

111   Lesser Hill Mynah *Gracula religiosa indica*

112   Occipital Blue Pie *Urocissa erythrorhyncha occipitalis*

113 Lanceolated Jay *Garrulus lanceolatus*

114 Violaceous Touracou *Musophaga violacea*

115 Cape Robin Chat *Cossypha caffra*

116 Wattled Starling *Creatophora cinerea carunculata*

117 Long-tailed Glossy Starling *Lamprotornis caudatus*

118   Green Glossy Starling *Lamprotornis chalybaeus*

119 Purple Glossy Starling *Lamprotornis purpureus*

120 Superb Spreo *Spreo superbus*

121 Malachite Sunbird *Nectarinia famosa*

122 Scarlet-chested Sunbird *Chalcomitra gutturalis*

123 White-bellied Sunbird *Cinnyris leucogaster*

124   Mariqua Sunbird *Cinnyris mariquensis*

125   Pucheran's Emerald Hummingbird
      Chlorostilbon aureoventris pucherani (hen)

126　Pucheran's Emerald Hummingbird
Chlorostilbon aureoventris pucherani (cock)

127 Ruby Topaz Hummingbird *Chrysolampis mosquitus*

128 Yellow-winged Sugarbird *Cyanerpes cyaneus*

129   Isthmian Purple Sugarbird *Cyanerpes
       caeruleus isthmicus* (hen and cock)

130   Blue Sugarbird *Dacnis cayana* (hen and
       cock)

131 Purple Sugarbird *Cyanerpes caeruleus*

132 Superb Tanager *Tangara fastuosa*

133 Mrs Wilson's Tanager *Tangara nigrocincta franciscae*

134 Emerald-spotted Tanager
Tangara chrysophrys

135 Bay-headed Tanager
Tangara gyrola

136 Silver-throated Tanager
Tangara icterocephala

137 Black Tanager *Tachyphonus rufus*

138 Silver-blue Tanager
Thraupis virens

139 Scarlet Tanager *Ramphocelus brasilius*

141 Green-billed Toucan
Ramphastos dicolorus

140 Scarlet-rumped Tanager
Ramphocelus passerini

142   Toco Toucan *Ramphastos toco*

143   Spot-billed Toucanet *Selenidera maculirostris*

144   Chestnut-billed Emerald Toucanet
Aulacorhynchus haematopygus

145   Mountain Bluebird *Sialia currucoides*

146 Red-winged Blackbird *Agelaius phoeniceus*

147 Baltimore Hangnest *Icterus galbula*

13. DESCRIPTIONS AND CARE OF THE BIRDS

Nomenclature of the Plumage

The most popular of the aviary birds are described in the following pages, and brief details of their colouring are given.

It is not easy to describe the colouring and markings of a bird's plumage and it is often impossible to convey an accurate impression without the aid of a colour illustration. Where illustrated, the description is sometimes not given. Measurements refer to approximate length.

In following a description it is essential that the reader should understand exactly what area of feathers is meant by such names as rump, neck, nape, shoulders, and so on.

The wings present a further difficulty since they can be inspected either spread or when folded, when certain feathers are concealed. Fig. 12 shows the areas covered by the various types of wing feathers and how they appear when the wing is folded. The wings of different

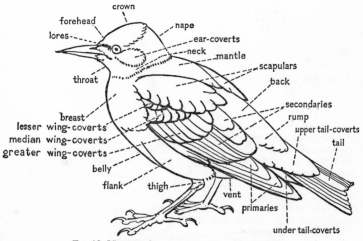

FIG 12 *Names and arrangement of main feather groups*

E

species of birds may differ in shape, but in every case the distribution of feathers is the same.

It is possible, once one is conversant with the plan of the wing, to follow accurately a description of wing markings, including the network of various coverts, and their colouring.

The drawing also indicates the areas of other feather tracts, with their appropriate names. The names given are sufficient to describe almost any bird, and to give more would only cause confusion.

Where names have been translated in the first instance from the German and have given a wrong interpretation, difficulties have arisen. For instance 'Rump' from the German word *Stiesz* really means the part around the vent, whereas it is now used to indicate that lower part of the back which corresponds to the coccyx at the base of the spine.

The scapula (shoulder) and mantle are often confused. If the place of the scapula is fixed into the mind, and in imagination the wing is then folded, it will be found that the illustration is correct.

In the following descriptions this feather nomenclature has been closely followed and only in special cases has a still more detailed indication of area been given.

Paradise Whydah (Widow Bird) *Steganura paradisea*

Origin Central Africa.

The Whydahs rank high among the species most appreciated for grace and beauty. They have a special appeal on account of the fantastic metamorphosis of the cock when he comes into breeding plumage. A dull $5\frac{1}{2}$ in. beige bird is transformed into a gaudy cock with a total length of 20 in. Two of the tail feathers—those in the centre—will be more than 10 in. long. At other times the cock resembles the hen. *Hen* is buff, streaked with dark brown and with dark eyebrow markings.

These birds need a very large cage, or, preferably, a bird room. The long tail is easily damaged in too small a space, and the bird would get no chance to display its graceful flight.

Normally the Whydah is very tolerant; but when nesting is seriously contemplated, the cock becomes aggressive and restive. He will sit as high as possible in the flight and let his long tail hang down. For satisfactory breeding, place 3 or 4 hens with a cock.

In their natural state the Whydahs will lay eggs in the nests of small finches, which hatch them and rear the young. It is remarkable that each Whydah species generally chooses a particular type of finch with which their young roughly correspond in the colouring of the feathers and also in the reflecting papillae, the markings in the roof of the mouth.

The Paradise Whydah usually deposits its eggs in the nest of the Melba Finch (*Pytilia melba*), or *Pytilia afra*. To encourage breeding, keep in the same aviary several pairs of these finches to act as hosts. Breeding successes have also been recorded with the aid of the Fire Finch, *Lagonosticta senegala*. A Bengalese can also be used to hatch the eggs. There are only a few records of this species having been reared successfully.

Sometimes old hens which no longer lay eggs will adopt the nuptial plumage of the male bird and retain this to the end of their lives.

Diet: Various kinds of millet, green food, and germinated seeds. During breeding season, meal-worms, chopped or boiled, ants' eggs, and hard-boiled egg mixed with crumbled rusks. After careful acclimatization this bird becomes hardy and needs special care only while moulting; it can winter in a frost-proof room.

Pintailed Whydah *Vidua macroura* Pl. 5

Origin Central Africa.

4½–5 in. *Cock* in breeding plumage, is 12 in. inc. tail of which the 4 long centre feathers are from 7–10 in. Forehead, crown, and nape glossy bluish-black; cheeks and throat white, the white being continued in a band round neck; upper parts mainly black with rump and upper tail coverts white. Under parts white except for a black-crescent on breast; tail, four central feathers black, remainder and flights blackish-brown. Beak light red; legs slate-coloured. In non-breeding dress cock resembles the hen. *Hen:* Centre of crown sandy, bordered on each side with black;

mantle and scapulars buff heavily striped with blackish brown; rump brown faintly striped; flights and tail dark brown edged with buff; throat whitish; remainder of under parts buff, darker on the breast and flanks, with some darker markings. Beak pinkish brown; legs light brown. Young birds are much like the hen but have horn-coloured beaks.

One of the most frequently imported. Although less colourful than the Paradise Whydah, it is very impressive and graceful. It is rather aggressive and only if one cock and several hens are kept in a large flight is it possible to avoid perpetual unrest, and even then many feeding troughs must be provided.

To encourage these birds to nest, provide a large well-planted flight so that the cock will have an opportunity for his courting, which consists of performing a hovering dance above his ladies. These Whydahs are polygamous —every cock collects 4 to 5 hens or more around him.

The Pintail Whydahs use the St. Helena Waxbill *Estrilda astrild,* and the Red-eared Waxbill, *Estrilda troglodytes* as hosts for their young. With these facts in mind, the fancier can be encouraged to attempt breeding experiments. Even if no results are obtained, it is profitable to keep these birds if only for their graceful appearance.

Queen Whydah (Shaft-tailed Whydah) (Shaft-tailed Widow Bird) *Vidua regia*

Origin South Africa.

4½–5 in. *Cock* in breeding plumage is 12–13 in., the extended shafts of the 4 central tail feathers measuring 7–8 in. Cock in breeding dress: crown and nape glossy blue-black as also are the mantle and scapulars; coverts and flights blackish; cheeks, throat, a narrow collar across the nape, and the whole of under parts a warm tawny-buff; tail brownish with the exception of the 4 central feathers which are extended as bare black shafts with glossy black webbing at the extremities only; beak and feet coral red. In eclipse plumage, cock is similar to hen. *Hen:* Above warm brown, more or less heavily striated with blackish-brown; head and neck buff with a broad band of darkly striated feathers on each side of the crown; under parts whitish with the throat and flanks sandy buff; under wing coverts white; beak and legs brown. Immature birds like hen but paler and less distinctly marked.

One of the more rare species. Rivals Paradise Whydahs in beauty. The 4 elongated tail feathers consist of wire-like shafts, with feathery plumes at the tip. Each cock must have several hens, for in the wild one cock may have as many as 20. The hens can only be distinguished from the Pintail Whydahs by their red legs. The Queen Whydah is a strong bird and has no special requirements; it will soon lose all shyness and is peaceable.

The rather expensive Violet-eared Waxbill, *Granatina granatinus*, is the host of the Queen Whydah. Queen Whydahs were reared successfully by Violet-eared Waxbills in an aviary in South Africa in 1967.

Fischer's Whydah *Vidua fischeri*

Origin East Africa.

Cock: In breeding plumage, 10–12 in. crown pale buff, remainder of head, neck, back, and shoulders black. Rump and upper tail coverts light brown. Under parts cream-coloured. Sides finely barred with black. Wings brown-black. Tail brown-black, the 4 centre long tail plumes light isabel-yellow. Eye brown, bill and legs red. *Hen:* Forehead red-brown, upper parts brownish with dark quills. White throat and light eyebrow stripe. Under parts and sides of the head yellow-brown. Belly white in centre; sides have little dark stripes. Winter plumage of cock similar to that of the hen.

These birds are seldom imported. They are mainly seed-eaters—canary and millet seed. They do not thrive in a cage because of their long tails, which soon become damaged, and are at their best in an aviary with the larger foreign finches. They can safely be associated with others of their own kind.

The young Whydahs resemble outwardly the young of their foster-parents. The young Fischer's Whydahs look exactly like the young of the Purple Grenadier Waxbills, *Granatina ianthinogaster*, when they are chosen as hosts. Sometimes they use the Red-eared Waxbill, for Whydahs do not always restrict their choice to one particular species.

When furnishing an aviary for Whydahs, extra care must be given to reproduce their natural habitat. They are frequently found in reedy surroundings and are accustomed to clambering up and down reeds, which helps to wear down their claws. If reeds cannot be planted, bundles of reeds should be tied up in a corner.

The aviary walls should be lined with birch and willow branches, planted or with their roots in large troughs. Cut branches in water containers can be used, but the containers must be out of the birds' reach. Another way is to cover a frame with fine meshed wire netting, insert twigs of willow or birch, and bury it in sand with a layer of moss on top. This produces a very pleasing effect. It is wise to supply bowls or troughs containing germinating grains or grasses which grow tall as they will provide the birds with their green food and nesting material. Additional bowls should be kept in reserve for changing.

Red-collared Whydah *Coliuspasser ardens* Pl. 1

Origin South Africa.

Cock: In breeding plumage 14 in. Black with a wide red collar in front across the upper breast. Wings black with brown lacing. Long tail black, bill dark horn-coloured, legs horn-coloured. *Hen:* Red-brown above, with fine black striations. White belly and the flanks rusty-brown.

There is a race which lacks the remarkable red band on the chest. Good breeding results have been obtained quite often. It is best to give the cock and hens an aviary to themselves. The nuptial display dance of the cock shows a remarkable resemblance to that of the Crimson-crowned Weaver, *Euplectes hordeacea,* and Neunzig remarks on this and the special ferocity which this Whydah shows towards the Crimson-crowned Weaver. Both the voices of the birds and the nesting habits show a remarkable resemblance.

To breed successfully the hens must come from the same district as the cock, for they must come into breeding condition when the cock dons his nuptial finery.

Various millets, canary seed, green food, germinated seed, egg food, meal-worms, and ants' eggs, may aid in producing a new family successfully. The condition of the parent birds and the arrangement of the aviary also play an important part. One link missing in the chain may be the cause of failure. A good foundation can be laid only when the right birds have been brought together, and, owing to the similarity of Whydah and Weaver hens, this is extremely difficult.

Red-naped Whydah *Coliuspasser ardens laticauda*

Origin North-East Africa.

9 in. *Cock* in breeding plumage entirely black; except for crown, nape, and band along side of head to breast which are carmine red. Tail broad and not very long. In non-breeding plumage, cock is like hen but larger. *Hen* as last species.

This species is sometimes offered for sale, but not frequently. It is hardy and tolerant of birds of equal size. Successful breeding results are unknown, but it has laid eggs in captivity.

The display dance of the cock, with the tail spread, is interesting to watch. The bird comes down to the ground only to perform this dance; otherwise it always remains up among the branches.

Red-shouldered Whydah *Coliuspasser axillaris*

Origin Africa.

6½–7 in. *Cock:* In breeding plumage 8–9½ in. Black and silky. Red shoulder spot (orange on young birds) wings black with brown lacing. Tail and legs black, eye brown, bill grey. *Hen:* Sand-coloured upper parts with black spots, throat and centre of the belly white, orange shoulder spot with smaller black dots. Wings and tail brown-black with light brown margins. Red-brown bill, dark horn-coloured legs.

There are 7 forms of this species; they show only small variations.

Before copulation these birds perform an air ballet, when the cock gives voice to a hissing chattering sound mixed with flute-like notes. They build their domed nest in a low shrub. The cock will chase all birds away from the neighbourhood. The hen first feeds the young on ants' eggs; then meal-worms and seeds, preferably germinated, canary seed and millet, soaked stale white bread, and green food. The nest is kept clean by her. After flying the young do not return to the nest. The hen feeds the youngsters by herself, although the cock will defend them against other birds. After a fortnight the young feed themselves; they resemble the hen, but are a little paler in colouring.

Keep a couple of hens with one cock and arrange the aviary as for other Whydahs and Weavers.

Yellow-backed Whydah *Coliuspasser macrourus* Pl. 2

Origin West Africa.

8 in. *Cock:* Upper part of the back black with yellow mantle. Feathering of the wings brown.

Hen: Upper parts dull brown, feathers with black striations. The feathers on the back have yellow margins. Upper tail coverts brown. Sides of the head and flanks light brown, generally with dark striations. Throat and belly whitish. Wings and tail black with brown margins, and yellow margins to the mantle feathers. Eye brown, legs dark flesh-coloured, bill brown horn-coloured.

Cocks can be recognized when in eclipse plumage by odd yellow feathers in their wings. Supply each cock with 4 to 5 hens if possible; polygamy is presumed but has not been definitely proved. It repeatedly happens that a cock is seen with birds which look like hens but which may be young birds from the previous season or immature cocks.

Diet: Mainly seed, millet, and canary, also paddy rice. Insectivorous food, fruit, and live insects.

Breeding results not yet been reported. Natural planting of aviary and plenty of suitable nesting material should encourage success (see Fischer's Whydah).

Yellow-shouldered Whydah *Coliuspasser macrocercus*

Origin Abyssinia.

Similar to Yellow-backed Whydah but lacks the yellow mantle, which is replaced by black. Tail much longer— the bird's length is often nearly 10 in.

During non-breeding season large congregations of these birds may be seen together with flocks of Red-naped Whydahs *Coliuspasser laticauda*. When breeding time draws near, they separate and some cocks with a number of hens will choose a breeding territory which has very definite boundaries allowing no intruders.

Treatment exactly as other Whydahs. Breeding results have not yet been reported but it should be possible to encourage them to nest if the aviary is arranged according to their requirements.

If the birds are acquired during the eclipse period, a single yellow feather on the shoulder may indicate a cock. But surprises do happen and there have been frequent occasions when rare and unknown species have come into the possession of fanciers. Whydahs, although hardy birds, do not thrive in a wet summer. Cold does not seem to hurt them, but they must be provided with frost-proof accommodation during the winter.

They are ideal for exhibition, but sometimes the sudden change from aviary to cage brings on a moult and they drop their beautiful tail feathers, which may then not be renewed until the following breeding season.

Giant Whydah (Long-tailed Widow Bird) *Coliuspasser progne* Pl. 3

Origin Kenya.

Cock: Similar to hen during non-breeding period but may be distinguished from her by the orange of her small mantle feathers. Cock is larger, 22 in. including long tail feathers of 16 in. *Hen:* Light brown above and under parts light isabel, heavily striated especially on the flanks. Lores, throat, and belly cream-coloured. Wings and tail brown with orange and buff margins. Bill and legs horn-brown. Although it was believed that this species was polygamous, researches by Jackson in Kenya have shown that in the breeding territory of each cock there was never more than one nesting hen.

The claws of all Whydahs and Weavers require attention as they grow very rapidly in captivity. Those of the Giant Whydahs particularly need care and should be inspected and clipped regularly.

Giant Whydahs are liable to suffer from 'scaly legs' caused by a parasite, which can be killed by a solution of ammonia carbonate or methylated spirits. In the wild the birds rub their legs along the razor-sharp canes and the parasites cannot get a hold. If rings are fixed on the legs, these have the same effect through their constant rubbing, and act as a preventive.

A pair may be kept in a very large aviary, with other smaller birds. Giant Whydahs are among the easiest and hardiest of birds to keep.

Diet: Ordinary seed such as millet and canary, hemp and sunflower, and green food.

Breeding results may only be expected in a really large and well-planted aviary, with plenty of cover. The hen will hatch the eggs which are laid in a nest on the ground and will rear the young by herself.

Jackson's Whydah *Drepanoplectes jacksoni* Pl. 4

Origin: Highlands of Kenya.

Cock: Deep black, brown wings with yellow and brown margins. Bill grey, legs black, tail long and arched like the tail of a cockerel. Lengthened crown feathers which form a collar. *Hen:* Light brown with dark striations. Out of breeding season, the cock is like the hen, but considerably larger, and with more massive head. 13 in. inc. large tail.

Imported only at irregular intervals and rather expensive. The care necessary is similar to that for the Giant Whydah. A large aviary is, of course, essential. Giant and Jackson's Whydahs may be kept together.

Although opinions as to the polygamy of Whydahs differ, experiments with Jackson's Whydahs have fairly definitely proved that the species is monogamous. There are always a number of birds around a cock in nuptial finery, but it may be assumed that these are really immature cocks, which take 2 years to become fully adult.

The display and dance of Jackson's Whydah is most interesting. With every feather erect and stretched neck the cock will jump straight upwards from the ground with wings fluttering while he moves his legs as though cycling. The stiffly held tail is thrown forward over the back until it touches the crown of the head. Displaying cocks will jump 3 ft or more into the air. A circle on the ground, 2 ft in diameter, is trodden flat, while a clump of grass in the centre will remain untouched. The cock will run round and round this clump, interrupting his circling at frequent intervals to perform the display.

The species has been bred successfully. A nest made of grass was suspended like a hammock from the branches. The 3 eggs laid were hatched in 12 days. The young were reared exclusively on seeds, canary seed, and millet; although live insects and insectivorous food were available, these were not fed to them.

These birds readily grow tame. Shrubs with green leaves will soon be completely destroyed and it is better to plant pines or conifers.

Very hardy birds, but should be accommodated in a frost-proof room during winter.

Long-tailed Combassou (Steel-blue Whydah) *Hypochera hypocherina*

Origin East Africa.

4½ in. *Cock:* Black with a green metallic sheen. Wings glossy black-brown. The 4 centre tail plumes are black and about 8 in. long, the remaining feathers being short, black-brown with white end margins. Eye brown, bill flesh-coloured, legs brown. *Hen:* Upper parts brown, narrow light brown and a wide black-brown band along the head. Eye stripe buff as well as the sides of the head. Throat, centre of abdomen, and under tail coverts white. Tail black-brown. Bill horn-coloured brown.

This bird cannot be mistaken for Senegal Combassou because its bill is reddish, not white, its legs are brown not red, and the Senegal Combassou is much smaller. According to Neunzig these Combassous develop their long tails in the aviary during breeding season. The only species with which this Whydah might be confused is the Steel-blue Finch, *Hypochera amauropteryx,* which comes from the western and southern parts of Central Africa. The wings and tail of these birds are brown-black, difficult to distinguish from those of the wholly black bird. The legs, however, are lacquered and its tail plumes are not elongated. Its bill is also red.

Brood parasitic on the Black-cheeked Waxbill, *Estrilda erythronotos,* and the young resemble each other. They are reared on insects. The song of this species consists of a clear flute-like note with cheeping sounds. It is hardy and can winter in frost-proof accommodation. Care and feeding do not call for any special consideration; the normal seed menu for foreign finches is sufficient.

Senegal Combassou *Hypochera chalybeata chalybeata*

Origin West Africa. Senegal.

4½ in. Like the Whydah, the Combassou has an eclipse plumage. In breeding plumage the cock's beautiful steel-blue colour, compared with the drab colouring of the hen, makes him particularly attractive. But after, the colouring of the cock resembles that of the hen. During breeding time, the cock is restless and will hover over the other birds, sometimes creating quite a panic with his chattering song.

This species has been known to breed in captivity, but success is rare. If breeding is attempted, the flight should be small and well planted. Both nesting materials and diet should be as varied as possible. Old Weavers' nests, artificial nests at various heights must be provided, and a quantity of material supplied to offer choice and a variety of nesting sites. It might also be wise to supply 2 or 3 hens for the cock. The Combassous, like the Whydahs, are polygamous and parasitic, and use Fire Finches, *Lagonosticta senegala,* for the hatching and rearing of their young. St. Helena Waxbills, Blue-breasted Waxbills and Melba Finches are also believed to be used as hosts.

The Combassous, however, do not seem to have forgotten how to hatch a brood, for Neunzig cites several instances of this species having incubated and reared their own young.

Grenadier Weaver *Euplectes orix orix* Pl. 6

Origin South Africa.

5¾ in. *Cock* deep black and velvet orange, except the upper half of the mantle, wings, and tail which are brown. *Hen* is brownish. Will breed much more readily than other species, so it is regrettable that hens are not always obtainable. They like to use green bark and fresh grasses for their nest, which is egg-shaped with a funnel-like entrance passage at the side, and is larger and finer than that of other Weavers. It is usually suspended between 2 to 4 strong branches of low trees. The bird in nuptial finery is quieter than other *Euplectes*, but males of the same species are fiercely chased. Though slightly less colourful, this hardy bird is to be preferred for breeding purposes.

During nesting period, Grenadier Weavers like to eat ripening grain and will also search for small beetles and other insects. The young are fed mainly on animal food during the first few days, so that ants' eggs and small meal worms must be supplied or they would not survive.

Their natural home is in boggy places where they suspend their nests between the reeds, and it is advisable to plant some reeds in the flight.

Black-bellied Weaver (Zanzibar Red Bishop) *Euplectes nigriventris.* Pl. 8

Origin Eastern Kenya, Manda, Zanzibar, and Kwale Islands.

4 in. *Cock:* smaller than the Orange Bishop, *E. orix franciscana,* and has the crown of the head deep orange-red, and the whole of the under parts velvety black with the exception of the thighs, which are buff, and the under tail coverts, which are orange. It does not develop the pronounced ruff on the nape which the larger species has during the breeding season. *Hen* is difficult to distinguish from the Orange Bishop hen. Normally she is a little smaller and the under wing coverts and inner edges to the flights are paler buff. In eclipse the cock resembles the hen.

Less frequently imported than the Orange Bishop, this species makes an interesting addition to a collection of weaver. It requires the same care and feeding. It is a common coastal bird in eastern Africa, where it is usually seen in small parties. It is polygamous, and many nests may be constructed in a comparatively small area, but each cock has its own limited breeding territory. The nests are usually built in tall grass, bushes or in clumps of reeds, in swampy ground, and each hen lays 2–3 pale blue eggs which are sometimes spotted with dusky brown.

Orange Bishop *Euplectes orix franciscana* Pl. 9

Origin North-West and East Africa.

5 in. Obtainable nearly all year, but the choice of a pair is difficult due to the close resemblance of the cock and hen. It is only when the males begin to don their nuptial plumage that there can be any certainty of obtaining a true pair. The cock grows a thick orange ruff on the back of his head, while his head and

abdomen become jet black. During spring both sexes are light greyish brown in colour, and lighter grey underneath. With correct feeding, cod-liver oil during moulting, and 'universal' food throughout the year, the cock will regain his original deep orange colour. The bird must not be kept away from the light.

Although a pair can be kept in a good-sized flight together with small finches, the cock while courting becomes very aggressive towards every bird which approaches the nest, especially those of their own species. They are not so fierce with larger birds. Although they will busily build nests, nothing much will come of attempts to breed in a communal flight. It may be advisable to supply one cock with several hens if serious breeding is contemplated, as these birds are certainly polygamous. Their main point of interest is the annual return of their gaudy plumage and the building of round nests, which they will construct here and there and abandon almost as soon as they are completed. They use fresh stems of grass for building. In a roomy flight, where a corner has been planted with maize, there is every chance of good breeding results. In between the stems and right at the top of the maize the birds will be able to suspend their nest; this most nearly approaches their natural breeding ground.

Hardy birds, well worth keeping, if only for their gaudy colouring, their continual movement, and sprightliness.

Crimson-crowned Weaver *Euplectes hordeacea*

Origin Africa.

5¾ in. *Cock:* Sides of the head and upper part of the throat black, back red-brown, the remainder of the upper parts and neck scarlet. The rest of the under parts black. Under tail coverts brown. Wings and tail black sometimes with lighter margins, bill black, eye brown, legs flesh-coloured. *Hen:* Upper parts light brown with brown striations, light yellow eyebrow strips. Under parts white to buff. Flanks and crop with dark striations on a light brown ground colour. Wings and tail brown-black with lighter margins.

The hens may easily be confused with those of other species, but the birds usually come in a consignment from a particular district so likely to be of one species.

Breeding successes have been reported in the United Kingdom. The nests are built with grasses, often against wire netting where branches and twigs have penetrated from bushes growing outside the aviary. So deep are the nests that the eggs cannot be seen. The hen incubates for 10 to 12 days.

Crimson-crowned Weavers may be kept with other Weaver species and need exactly the same care. They must be protected against frost in winter, but can be kept outside during the day.

Napoleon Weaver *Euplectes afra afra*
Pl. 7

Origin West Africa.

5 in. Closely resembles the Orange Bishop, when the two species are in eclipse plumage but the Napoleon Weaver cock is bright buttercup-yellow. It seems easier to breed but success depends on the space and food provided. All Weavers need a varied insect menu, in addition to seed, to ensure their own physical fitness and also adequate feeding for their young.

Those fanciers who provide this may, with patience and in spite of frequent disappointments, rear a nest of Weavers, although the brood may consist of only 2 or 3.

The nests are fixed between branches of birch, suspended at various heights. A little patch of growing maize is an advantage. The *cock* is vivid yellow and black in colour; he will sit on top of the stems and display his finery, blowing out his yellow collar and dancing up and down like a Black Cock, making a hoarse hissing noise all the time. He will chase away every other bird, especially those of his own species which though tolerated in the wild, are the most furiously persecuted in captivity. The *hen* is much more modest and unpretentious in colour, and closely resembles the hen of the Orange Bishop. She will rummage in and around many nests from which she will finally choose one in which to lay and incubate.

The cock generally builds the nest by himself and takes an active part in rearing the young. If the birds have been accustomed to take meal-worms daily from the hand, which they learn very speedily to do, the cock as well as the hen will take these to feed the chicks. Stale bread soaked in water must be given at this stage as well as the seed mixture.

There is a danger that the cock will not retain his full vivid colours in captivity, mainly because of the lack of essential foodstuffs.

These birds are much better in a roomy aviary than a cage. Once acclimatized, they can winter in an unheated room, even in an outside flight, if ample protection is provided from north and east and a covered shelter is available.

Taha Weaver *Euplectes afra taha* Pl. 12

Origin South Africa.

4 in. *Cock:* Head, neck, and all of the under parts black. Crown and back yellow. Wings and tail brown-black with light brown margins. Bill black, eyes brown, legs brown horn-coloured. Winter plumage resembles that of the hen. *Hen:* Upper parts brown with dark striations, under parts white with a brown tinge. Yellow-brown eyebrow stripe, light horn-coloured bill.

It is best to buy Weavers during the winter, when they are in full plumage and it is easier to differentiate between the sexes.

Care and feeding as for Napoleon Weaver. *Diet:* Seeds, canary seed, and millet, to which stale white bread soaked in water and some insects can be added during breeding. Winter in an unheated room or in a frost-proof shelter.

Cape Weaver (Yellow-shouldered Weaver) *Euplectes capensis*

Origin Cape Colony.

Nearly 7 in. *Cock:* Silky black, rump golden yellow, wings black with a yellow shoulder spot, flights, with brown margins. Upper mandible black, lower mandible horn-coloured. Legs light brown, eyes brown. *Hen:* Light brown upper parts with black striations, rump olive-yellow, under parts dirty white with brown markings. Wings black-brown with whitish margins. Bill brown horn-coloured.

This species is not imported regularly; the few consignments that come in consist mainly of cocks. Breeding results have been reported, but they are exceptional as few hens are imported. There are 6 sub-species. These birds are closely related to the Whydahs

This can be proved by a successful crossing with the Red-shouldered Why-dah, *Coliuspasser axillaris*.

Diet: Seeds, millet, canary seed, and rough rice, green food, and sometimes insects. Ants' eggs are essential in rearing the young.

Madagascar Weaver *Foudia madagascariensis* Pl. 11

Origin Madagascar, Mauritius, and Seychelles.

5 in. *Cock:* In breeding plumage almost entirely crimson, the feathers of back, mantle, and scapulars being marked with black and flights and tail brownish. Through the eyes is a black line, and beak is steel black. Legs brown. *Hen:* Rather similar to a hen sparrow. In eclipse plumage the cock is like the hen.

At one time this beautiful Weaver was frequently imported, but has become rare on the market. It is inclined to be very quarrelsome in an aviary and will bully and torment birds far larger than itself, especially in the breeding season.

It builds a typical Weaver nest, suspended between branches of low trees or among reeds, and the eggs of a pale blue number from 4–6.

In a wild state it feeds on grass seeds and insects and also invades the growing crops, especially rice, and in captivity does well on the diet described for other Weavers. Once acclimatized it is hardy and can winter in an outside aviary provided it has access to a draught-proof shelter.

Little has been recorded of this species breeding in captivity but no doubt the young are reared very largely on insects, particularly in the early stages, with green seeds added to their diet at a later stage of their development.

Little Masked Weaver *Ploceus luteolus* Pl. 10

Origin North-West and North-East Africa.

Nearly 5 in. *Cock:* Head black to the light yellow superciliary eye stripe, remainder of upper parts yellow to greenish-yellow. Sides of neck and under parts yellow, wings brownish, the feathers laced with yellow-green. Tail brown with yellow-green sheen. Eyes red-brown, bill black, legs flesh-coloured. *Hen:* Upper parts light olive-green with yellowish upper tail coverts and dark striations along back. Cheeks and under parts light yellow, lores white, and bill grey. Outside the breeding period, cocks resemble hens in every detail.

One of the most free-breeding of all the species. The song of these Weavers is very soft and not disturbing, but they are aggressive while breeding and it is advisable to keep them separate or in a large flight. They build or weave small but sturdy pouch-like nests, which they line with soft feathers. The eggs, 4 in number, are incubated chiefly by the hen and hatch in 12 days. Cock and hen both feed the youngsters. During rearing time especially they must have meal-worms in addition to ants' eggs, and occasionally egg food. Other insects are readily eaten. A few weeks after flying the young birds change to a diet entirely of seed.

Normal diet: Various millets, oats, hemp, canary seed, much and varied green food, insectivorous food, sometimes fruit.

These birds may winter outside if an adequate and frost-proof shelter is attached to the aviary.

Spotted-backed Weaver (Village Weaver) (V-marked Weaver) *Ploceus cucullatus* Pl. 15

Origin West Africa.

6½–7 in. *Cock:* Head and throat black terminating in a point on upper breast; broad collar of dark chestnut. Mantle and back golden yellow, mantle bordered with broad black band forming a V-shaped mark on shoulders; wing coverts and inner secondaries black edged with yellow; outer secondaries and flights dark brown with narrow edging of yellow-olive. Rump yellow. Upper tail coverts olive, tail light brown with olive-yellow edging. Breast golden-yellow merging into chestnut where it joins the black of throat. Remainder of under parts bright yellow with chestnut tone on flanks. Eyes red, bill black, legs dark flesh-coloured. *Hen:* Crown, nape, and sides of neck olive with yellow stripe above eyes. Mantle and back olive-brown; the feathers edged with grey; rump olive. Wings brownish-black edged with yellow and primaries with broad yellow on the inner web; tail brown with olive wash. Chin, throat, and breast yellow, belly white, under tail coverts yellow. Eye very dark, warm brown. Bill, upper mandible brown, lower mandible pale horn. Immature cocks are very similar to adult hens but when they have acquired adult plumage they are said to retain the full colouring and not to have eclipse plumage.

This bird is sometimes known as the Village Weaver because of its apparent fondness for human company and may be found in large and noisy colonies at most native villages in West Africa.

These are powerful birds and better kept with larger birds, and then only outside the nesting season unless they prove to be peaceable. It is better to have a number of hens. They can be induced to breed. Sometimes the cock builds a small nest near the main one and spends the night in it. The hen incubates for about 15 days. Insect food and germinated wheat is necessary for rearing the young. Several broods in one season have been reported.

Treatment as for other large Weavers. They are hardy once acclimatized and able to winter outside provided they have access to a good shelter.

Half-masked Weaver (Vitelline Weaver) *Ploceus velatus vitellinus*

Origin West and North-East Africa.

5 in. *Cock:* In breeding plumage—lores, ear coverts, and cheeks jet black; forehead chestnut fading into golden on crown and bright yellow on nape. Mantle and back olive, wings yellow (feathers have blackish centres), tail brownish, chin and throat black shading into chestnut on upper breast, rest of under parts bright yellow. Eyes yellow, bill black, and legs flesh colour. *Hen* and cock out of colour are similar, a brownish olive streaked with blackish brown. The cock then has a more vivid colouring of the back and is brighter underneath.

This much smaller species is more peaceable than other Weavers. They are more suited to an aviary than a cage and will breed only in a large space. They build a pouch-shaped nest, with a short entrance tunnel from below, woven from grasses and fine rushes and suspended from the branches of low trees. It is solidly and beautifully made.

During mating time, the cock dances around the hen with fluttering wings and spread tail, making hissing noises. The 2–4 pale greenish-blue eggs, with brown markings, are hatched in 12 days. As with all Weavers, the young must be fed with many insects, meal-worms, grubs, and ants' eggs, also 'Universal' food. Of all the Weavers, this species is the easiest to induce to breed, and sometimes there is more than one brood a year.

Normal diet: Seeds, millet, canary seed, paddy rice, green food, some-times insects.

These Weavers are entertaining. In a flight planted with rye and oats, they will climb up and down the stalks as soon as the grain begins to ripen. They are hardy, and can winter out of doors.

Scaly-crowned Weaver *Sporopipes squamifrons* Pl. 14

Origin South-East Africa.

4 in. Black and white scale-like mark-ings on head. Lores black, back grey, sides of head grey-brown, white cheek stripe; black stripe on both sides of throat. Under parts whiter. Wings black laced with white, eyes red, bill pink, legs light horn-coloured.

On first arrival these Weavers never look very flourishing, but after a period of careful tending they grow into lively and active birds. They will roost in a nesting box at night and often inhabit it during a greater part of the day. They will evict other birds, including Zebra Finches, from the nests, but they always return to their own nests eventually and squabbles then cease.

Cock and *Hen* cannot be disting-uished, except by the song of the cock, which is not loud but quite pleasant. During breeding time the birds are apt to fight and can only be kept with such birds as other Weavers, Whydahs, Cut-throats, possibly also Budgerigars.

Although mainly seed-eaters, Scaly-crowned Weavers do not dislike insects while breeding and ants' eggs are

essential in rearing the young. They will build their own nests in nest boxes, and will also take possession of an old Weaver's nest and enlarge it, lining it with feathers. Hatching will take 12 days, both birds taking turns at incuba-tion during the day but occupying the nest together at night.

They can winter in an unheated room and may remain in an outside aviary during the day.

Speckled-fronted Weaver *Sporopipes frontalis* Pl. 13

Origin East and West Africa.

Nearly 5 in. Black beard stripe, black and white scale-like marking on the head. Neck red-brown, back brown-grey, tail with white margins. Under parts white, breast and sides showing a little isabel colouring. Eyes brown, legs and bill pink horn-coloured.

It is difficult to select a pair, the *Cock* being indistinguishable from the *Hen* except by his song.

Unlike the Scaly-crowned Weavers, these birds are docile and will live har-moniously with all other birds except when breeding. They will roost in a nest box which they fill entirely with moss, grass blades, and feathers, and will also retire there during the day. They eat all kinds of seeds and avidly pick up aphis and ants' eggs. They are trusting and rarely fly away when ap-proached. They are much less active than Scaly-crowned Weavers, and if kept by themselves in a cage would be rather dull, so company is needed. They like the sun, and as they are seldom in good condition on arrival they should be given a sunny spot in an acclimatizing cage.

Good results have often been obtained from breeding. Hatching takes 12 days and the rearing food should consist mainly of ants' eggs. They should be kept in a warm room in winter.

Red-billed Quelea *Quelea quelea* Pl. 17

Origin Africa.

4¾ in. One of the species most frequently imported, pairs usually available. *Cock:* Has a wine-red bill and may be recognized by this even in his simple winter plumage. *Hen:* Has a pale yellow bill. The French name for the bird *travailleur* (worker) designates it as active and industrious. Immediately upon being put into an aviary, the cock, often assisted by the hen, will begin to build a nest. They start by making a hoop which they extend each side to form a ball-shape with an entrance at one side. They use for preference fresh strong blades of grass, so a plentiful supply of these must be available. The birds are always busy and often destroy one nest in order to start another, sometimes next to the old one. If no material is available, the Weavers will worry other birds and pull out their tail feathers which they weave between the wire netting. Several pairs can be kept together, as they are colony nesters and more liable to breed successfully under these conditions. No serious fighting will occur, provided there is ample room.

Diet must include an abundant supply of insect food and half-ripe grain. Hardy birds; can winter in an unheated outside flight provided they have completely shed their nuptial finery before the really cold weather sets in. Moulting birds naturally need more care.

They may be kept together with Budgerigars, Cut-throats, and Zebra Finches. If only a single pair is kept it can be safely housed with smaller finches, if accommodation is adequate.

Recommended for beginners, but

little is known of their breeding habits in captivity.

Red-headed Quelea *Quelea erythrops* Pl. 16 and 17

Origin West and East Africa.

4½ in. *Cock:* Head and throat carmine, throat darker. Upper parts striated brown, under parts buff, belly white in the centre as are sometimes the under tail coverts. Wings light and dark brown with yellow margins. Tail very dark brown with light brown margins. Bill black, legs flesh-coloured. *Hen:* Has no red on the head or throat; she has a brown-white throat, light brown on the upper parts with white eyebrow stripes, bill horn-coloured brown.

Care and treatment similar to the Red-billed Weaver which they closely resemble, but the cock works less diligently at nest building.

Successful breeding has frequently been reported. Insect food during breeding time is essential. Special attention should be paid to their nails which are apt to overgrow. If some bamboo is planted in a corner of the aviary, the birds will keep their nails short on it.

Hardy birds, can remain in the aviary summer and winter, if adequate shelter is available.

Baya Weaver *Ploceus philippinus*

Origin India.

6 in. *Cock* in breeding plumage. Crown of head and breast golden yellow. Mainly brown above and whitish on under parts. In eclipse like the hen, which is similar in colour to the House Sparrow.

A single cock or hen can be kept with other birds and will build beautiful nests almost continuously. A pair must be kept separate from other birds if breeding is desired, unless in a very large aviary. They will defend their nest ferociously against all intruders. During mating time the cock will flutter near and above the hen, constantly uttering its hoarse chattering song. There is no better nest-builder than this species.

Treatment as for following species.

Bengal Weaver *Ploceus bengalensis*

Origin Burma.

Nearly 5 in. *Cock:* Crown and nape yellow, remainder of the upper parts dark brown, plumage of mantle heavily striated. Black-brown lines on both sides of throat and chin. Under parts are red-brown, darker on the flanks. Eyes brown, bill black, legs flesh-coloured. *Hen:* Upper parts brown with a red-brown lacing. Under parts lighter with brown striations. Bill light brown.

During winter the cock has a yellow spot on both sides of the neck and a yellow stripe above the eye. The species is difficult to distinguish from the Baya Weaver which however has a yellow breast. It is difficult to get a pair; the hens of the various species of Weavers are very similar in appearance and in eclipse plumage the cocks and hens are much alike.

These weavers are best in a large aviary or bird room where they can weave their remarkable nests sometimes consisting of two compartments. Keep a number of pairs together as they are colony breeders.

There will be fights over the hens at first, but the birds will settle down and active building will begin. The material used consists of soft blades of grass as well as strips of paper, hemp teasings, raffia, etc.

Easy to keep and quite hardy, but their *diet* must be varied and besides seed must include insectivorous food

in which some meal-worms are mixed every day. Sweet fruit and green food should also be supplied. The hens will probably start laying and hatch during the summer months, but few details of breeding are available probably because so few fanciers have bred these birds. One disadvantage is that every variety has to be kept separately for breeding.

Cocks are usually kept by themselves; they are very suitable to form an aviary collection with other species of Weaver and the brilliant and varied colouring of their breeding plumage makes a fascinating spectacle. Even during winter, when they are in eclipse plumage, they can remain outside if an adequate shelter is available.

Cordon Bleu *Uraeginthus bengalus* Pl. 23

Origin Central Africa.

4¾ in. inc. tail 2 in. *Cock:* Is readily recognizable by the broad crescent-shaped spot of red in his cheeks. *Hen:* Is much duller in colour and lacks the red cheek spot.

Although these birds have a reputation for being delicate, this is probably so only immediately after their arrival; once settled down, they have been known to live to quite an old age; some have lived in a flight for 14 years.

They nest very readily. The cock brings the various building materials and the hen weaves the artistic nest, which she lines with soft grasses and feathers. The nest is usually domed with an entrance at the side, but in an aviary these birds will occupy a hollow log or nest box and entirely fill it. The nest box must be fixed somewhere high up, so that the birds are out of the line of general flight in the aviary, for they are apt to leave the nest when frightened or disturbed. The hatching of 4–6, sometimes even 7, eggs is shared by cock and hen and incubation takes a fortnight. The fledglings leave the nest after some weeks; their colouring then is still duller than that of the hen. Several pairs can be kept together as they are not very aggressive, even during the breeding time. The cock executes an amusing little dance during the courting period, tripping around the hen with a straw in his bill. His song is sweet and pleasant. The birds breed more easily in an indoor aviary than they do outside; they cannot stand sudden big changes in temperature, or wet weather.

Keep in a moderately warmed room in winter where the winter sun can penetrate. Although their main *diet* consists of the well-known seeds, in their natural surroundings there is an ample supply of small spiders and beetles during the time the young have to be fed. Hence, in captivity, plenty of small ants' eggs and meal-worms must be added to the menu. Egg food is a satisfactory substitute for other natural foods.

Hybrids have resulted from crossing with the St. Helena Waxbill, the Blue-breasted Waxbill, and even with the Bengalese.

Blue-headed or Blue-capped Cordon Bleu *Uraeginthus cyanocephalus* Pl. 22

Origin Kenya, Somaliland, and Tanzania.

5 in. *Cock:* Whole of head, throat, breast, flanks, rump, and upper tail coverts soft, clear blue; mantle, back and wings earth brown; centre of abdomen and under tail coverts buff-brown; tail dark blue. Iris red; beak dusky-red; legs and feet pinkish-brown. *Hen:* Forehead, face, breast, thighs, rump, and upper tail coverts soft blue, not so bright as cock; crown, nape, mantle, back, and wings pale earth

F

brown; centre of abdomen and under-tail coverts pale buff-brown; tail dark blue. Iris, beak, legs, and feet as cock. Sometimes the blue of the forehead is replaced by earth-brown.

These birds frequent the dry desert country, where they are seen in pairs or small parties. Their behaviour and habits are said to be similar to those of the Cordon Bleu, but they are shyer. Their domed nest of dry grass is usually placed in a low thorn bush, often in association with hornets, and 4–6 white eggs are laid. Their food consists mainly of grass seeds and insects, especially termites, and it is very probable that the young are fed entirely on insects in the early stages.

It was not until comparatively recently that they were imported in numbers, and at once became firm favourites with bird keepers. They are a little hardier than the Cordon Bleu, but the same food and treatment suits them well. In the winter months they require some protection and are then better kept indoors, either in cages or indoor flights. They should not, however, be encouraged to breed by too much artificial heat, as it is almost impossible to find suitable rearing food, such as greenfly and fresh ants' cocoons, at that time of year. If they show any inclination to start nest building it would be better to separate the sexes until the following spring.

Blue-breasted Waxbill *Uraeginthus angolensis*

Origin South Africa, Angola.

4¾ in. Almost entirely like the Cordon Bleu, but the blue is more extensive and the red spot on the cheek of the cock is absent. *Cock:* More intensely coloured than the *Hen.* They come from a more temperate zone, and are hardier than the Cordon Bleus. They breed more readily. Insects are a necessity when rearing the young.

Golden-breasted Waxbill *Estrilda subflava* Pl. 19

Origin West Africa.

3½ to 3¾ in. *Hen:* Is slightly smaller than the *Cock*; throat and breast olive grey, dark yellow underneath, sides grey with fine yellow wavy lines; lacks red eyebrow stripe of cock.

The song, a monotonous chirping, may be heard from early morning till late at night. The mating display is most charming to watch. Eggs are laid nearly the whole year round in the rather untidy nest, built from all kinds of different materials, high up, either in a nest box or in a bunch of heather. The nests are lined warmly with hair, wool teasings, and feathers. Unfortunately the eggs of this species are very often infertile. If fertile, the 3–5 white eggs are hatched in 11 days, being incubated alternately by cock and hen. When the young appear, fresh ants' eggs and egg yolk should be given.

They can be induced to breed in an inside or outside aviary. Although they are not very tolerant during the breeding season, they do not disturb the nests of kindred and other small birds. The young are yellow-grey when they leave the nest, with yellow-red tail feathers and black bills.

They may be kept outside in summer, but should be brought indoors during winter in a sunny room, which need not be heated.

Cape Orange-breasted Waxbill *Estrilda subflava clarkei*

Origin South Africa.

Nearly 4 in. *Cock:* Upper parts dark grey-brown. Abdomen bright yellow without an orange tinge. Black lores, eyebrow stripe orange-red, bill red, rump red. Sides striped with yellow and black. *Hen:* More yellow in tone and without red eyebrow stripe.

Usually obtainable although slightly more expensive than the Golden-breasted form. They are better breeders and nearly always rear their young well.

Although they thrive and show up well in an aviary, the other inhabitants should not be too large or too lively or the Orange-breasted Waxbill will become intimidated and remain hidden in a corner. With Tiger Finches, Cordon Bleus, and other kinds of small finches, they will live in complete harmony. During breeding time they will defend their nest (usually made in a nest box with fine grasses, fibres, hairs, and so on) ferociously. The 4–6 eggs are incubated by both parents alternately and hatch in 12 days. The young may remain in the nest for more than 3 weeks and even after flying will return to the nest at night, for some time longer. These fledglings are exactly similar to young Tiger Finches with whom there is a close relationship. Crossings with the Tiger Finch have repeatedly been successful. It is important that the parents become thoroughly accustomed to the rearing food beforehand. This should consist of hard-boiled egg, germinated seeds, finely chopped mealworms, and ants' eggs. However, young birds have been reared on germinated millet alone, to which cod-liver oil has been added. Canary rearing food will also be eaten. Once they have started to breed, these Waxbills may raise as many as 4 families in one season. Crossings have been reported with Cordon Bleus, Fire Finches, St. Helena Waxbills, and Red-eared Waxbills.

The birds' song is monotonous and soft, and resembles the clinking of glasses.

The acclimatization of the newly imported birds calls for extra care. They must be kept warm and given plenty of fresh drinking water to which a little disinfectant should be added every three days. Green food must be supplied sparingly. The birds will soon recover their good condition in a sunny enclosure; they are then ready for the outside aviary, but should not be moved outside before June. They need not come inside again before November. Their accommodation need not be heated, but it must be frost-proof. The West African form has been known to live for 8–10 years in a cage. A winter sojourn in a cage indoors is suitable, but transfer to an outside aviary should be undertaken with great care as the birds will be less resistant to cold as a result of having been kept in warm surroundings.

A cage is not recommended for permanent residence as melanism (blackening of the feathers) is apt to occur. This will disappear in a short time after the birds have been moved to the open-air aviary. It is essential they be given insects, gentles, aphis, and so on. An aviary with grass and weeds growing in it is ideal.

St. Helena Waxbill *Estrilda astrild* Pl. 20

Origin Central Africa.

4–4½ in. inc. tail 2¼ in. *Cock:* Can be recognized by the stronger red colour on the breast which is present at all seasons. In good health the plumage of these birds is always tight and glossy. Their song is insignificant, consisting only of a gurgling sound with some flute-like call notes. During mating season the cock sings continuously.

These Waxbills will nest readily and usually rear the young well, provided they are accustomed to the use of rearing food, consisting of fresh ants' eggs, egg food, and finely chopped-up mealworms. The temperature should not be allowed to fall too low, as they cannot stand cold and damp. They are active, but the cocks are very pugnacious during the breeding season and fighting sometimes leads to the nest being deserted. One pair can be kept in an indoor aviary with other small birds.

The nest is usually built high up and is domed: 3–5 rather pointed white eggs are laid and the cock and hen share in incubation.

When the birds are actively engaged in building a nest they are fascinating to watch. The young hatch after 11 days, and leave the nest in a fortnight. They are somewhat duller in colour, lacking the red lores, and their beaks are black. They must be wintered in a warm room. Successful hybrids have been obtained with the Black-rumped Waxbill, the Orange-cheeked Waxbill, and the African Silverbill.

Red-eared Waxbill (Pink-cheeked Waxbill) (Common Waxbill) *Estrilda troglodytes* Pl. 21

Origin Central Africa.

3½–4 in., tail 1½ in. *Cock* and *Hen* difficult to differentiate. During the breeding season the colour of the cock becomes more intense pink over the whole of the abdomen. The loud 'chirrupy' flute-like notes which the cock produces during his courting dance makes him easily recognizable. He dances round the hen with a blade of grass in his bill. Both then sometimes produce a soft gurgling song and soft call notes.

Unfortunately they are very easily frightened; the greatest attention must be paid to providing them with a quiet and undisturbed nook.

They like to use a nest box in which they will construct a beautiful nest with a narrow hidden entrance passage. As it is normally lined with hair and wool, suitable material must be supplied. The nest boxes should be fixed at varying heights, always allowing a choice.

Usually 3–5 eggs, white and pointed, are laid. The birds rear the young on ants' eggs, egg food, and soaked seeds. Hatching, which is carried out by both parents, takes 11–12 days and a fortnight later the young leave the nest. The fledglings are then a pale grey colour; their bills are black with white gapes. After a few weeks they begin to assume adult plumage. Although they will do well in an outside flight during summer, they must be kept in a frost-proof room during winter, and will be better for extra warmth and protection during the moult.

They are lively and tolerant birds, and should be satisfactory to keep in a mixed collection where they will usually live for many years. During moulting season, a few drops of cod-liver oil will prove most beneficial. They breed in the spring and again in the late summer. The latter months are preferable, because fresh ants' eggs, which are indispensable, are then readily obtainable.

Good results have been obtained by crossing with Orange-cheeked Waxbill, Golden-breasted Waxbill, and Crimson-rumped Waxbill.

Crimson-rumped Waxbill (Sundevall's Waxbill) *Estrilda rhodopyga* Pl. 18

Origin East Africa.

4½ in. Difficult to distinguish *Cock* from *Hen,* but the red over the eyes and on the rump is a little deeper and the white on the throat a little wider in the case of the cock.

Although imported very rarely, this species will breed more readily than the closely related Red-eared Waxbill, but sometimes take a year or two to settle down before they attempt to nest.

A pair in my own collection built their nest on the floor in an indoor aviary. The completed nest was very large and feathers, hemp teasings, woollen threads, straw, and grass were used in its construction. The first clutch consisted of 4 eggs which were abandoned. The second nest was made in a nest box with a narrow entrance at the side. The eggs laid in the nest were hatched and the young appeared, but a sudden change in the weather caused the parents to abandon these as well. The third nest was even larger than the other two and again 4 eggs were laid. These hatched and the young were reared on cut-up meal-worms, grubs, and ants' eggs, and soaked seeds.

The birds are hardy, but bring them indoors during winter.

Orange-cheeked Waxbill *Estrilda melpoda* Pl. 25

Origin West Africa.

4 in. *Hen:* Coloured like *Cock,* but less vivid and a trifle smaller. Cock and hen have a soft 'chirrupy' song but the cock's is much louder and he dances and displays amusingly during his courting. He fans his tail widely while he bobs up and down. These birds are peaceable but usually remain shy.

They prefer to build in a nest box. The nest is domed and the sitting bird will draw blades of grass over the entrance hole to hide itself while brooding. Sometimes the pair will sit together on the 3 to 4 almost round white eggs.

They leave the nest whenever other birds approach too closely, so must have a quiet spot. Given suitable conditions they should hatch their eggs in 11 days, the chicks are generally satisfactorily reared and leave the nest after a fortnight.

Orange-cheeked Waxbills are always imported in great numbers and are not very expensive. Once they have settled down, they usually live long.

Although their breeding is not always easy, many satisfactory results have been recorded.

Dufresne's Waxbill (Swee) *Estrilda melanotis*

Origin Eastern South Africa.

Cock: 4 in. Cheeks, throat, and lores black, head grey, back olive, rump scarlet. Abdomen yellowish white. Tail black, bill—upper mandible black, lower red. Legs black.

Hen: Less colourful, and lacks black on cheek and throat.

Only rarely imported but has been successfully bred in England. The birds are charming and peaceable but best suited for an indoor aviary. Largely seed-eaters, only eating insects when rearing their young. They prefer to build in a low tree or isolated bush and as a rule several nests are made in succession. Eggs are usually laid but the rearing of the young seems to present difficulties. Period of incubation is 14 days, and the young will leave the nest after 3 weeks, returning there to sleep at night.

Yellow-bellied Waxbill *Estrilda melanotis quartinia* Pl.26

Origin Abyssinia to Uganda.

$3\frac{3}{4}$ in. *Cock:* Head and breast grey, back olive green, belly yellow, rump and upper tail coverts red, upper man-

dible black, lower mandible red, legs black. *Hen:* Is paler in colouring.

Seldom imported, but price moderate. They are delicate at first and need careful handling until they have become acclimatized; they require extra warmth and should always be given spray millet during the first few weeks after arrival.

Very suitable for an indoor aviary and show a readiness to breed. Pairs will roost together in a nest box, and will also build in such a box, the nest being constructed of fine grasses and lined with small soft feathers. The 3–4 eggs are hatched in 12 days. After a further 3 weeks the young will fly but return to the nest for the first few nights. A fortnight later they become independent. So far as is known the young will be successfully reared only if fresh ants' eggs are always available.

These birds require plenty of sunshine. They can live in the outside aviary during the summer and must only be associated with the smaller types of finches. Keep in a moderately warm room in winter.

Black-cheeked Waxbill *Estrilda erythronotos* Pl. 28

Origin South-West Africa to Southern Rhodesia.

About $4\frac{1}{2}$ in. *Cock* and *Hen* alike. Crown and nape grey with dark pencilling. Back vinaceous, rump and upper coverts carmine red, tail black. Wings greyish to white with clearly marked black barring. Primaries brown with pale cross bars. Cheeks and chin black, the remainder grey to light grey. Middle of the abdomen black as well as under tail coverts, and legs. The remainder of the abdomen grey with a carmine sheen, narrowly barred. Bill black, eyes red. Under tail coverts of the cock black, those of the hen more grey-brown.

Song is insignificant but melodious and low. The hen's call consists of two short flute-like notes; the male's call of three notes, of which the last is prolonged and high pitched.

The condition of the birds on arrival determines whether their acclimatization is easy or difficult. Birds which look ragged need the utmost care; if they have high temperatures, they must be given fresh water several times a day, with some disinfectant added, and fed on fresh ants' eggs, meal-worms, and millet. But even these efforts may fail to save them. Modern preparations, like the sulpha drugs, will give good results, but these are usually beyond the reach of the ordinary fancier. Infra-red rays are beneficial and a sunny position for the cage is essential. Even when acclimatized, they are not hardy or easy to keep.

The birds are active and like to find seclusion among dense foliage. They also enjoy basking in the sun and will rummage about on the floor of the flight in search of insects, which they cannot do without.

Diet: Fine egg food, germinated seed, stale white soaked bread, to which a few drops of cod-liver oil have been added, plenty of green food, insects.

They will breed in a large flight or cage and build in a nest box, the nest sometimes having a side entrance protected with a porch. They appreciate dense cover and the nest box should be hidden from view by thick foliage. Incubation takes 12 days. Ants' eggs, green fly, and many small insects are essential to rear the young, as neither meal-worms, egg food, nor the germinated seed will be taken the first few days after hatching and many broods

have been lost through lack of suitable food. Bengalese have sometimes been successfully used as foster-parents; they are undoubtedly an aid to the rearing of 'difficult' birds.

Black-cheeked Waxbills are partial to bathing. They can stand cold nights, as they are used to great differences between night and day temperatures in Africa, but they must spend the winter in a warm and sunny room. They should only be kept by the more experienced fancier.

This species is used as a host by the parasitic Long-tailed Combassou, *Hypochera hypocherina.*

Violet-eared Waxbill *Granatina granatinus* Pl. 27

Origin West and South Africa.

5¼–6¼ in. (tail 2½ in.). *Cock:* Dark rich brown above, forehead and rump feathers deep violet blue, under parts chestnut, tail black, violet cheeks, red bill. *Hen:* Is much lighter on head, back and under parts, while cheeks are also very pale violet.

Of rare importation, this Waxbill requires the greatest care and should only be acquired by an experienced fancier. The song of the cock is a little like that of the lark. The hen also sings but much more softly. Although they can be kept with other birds, only one pair of Violet-eared Waxbills should be in the aviary, as the cocks are very pugnacious towards their own kindred.

Breeding is said to be difficult, but successes have often been achieved. Much care needs to be given to providing as varied a menu as possible and a quiet and secluded place for nesting.

Diet: Although all Waxbills need some insects in addition to their seed diet, the Violet-eared Waxbill can only be kept in prime condition with a daily quota of insects, ants' eggs, grubs, and meal-worms. It cannot be emphasized too strongly that in most cases too little thought is given to the fact that during breeding season and when rearing the young, the seed-eating bird will take the most diverse food, such as charcoal, cuttlefish, finely ground egg shells, a lot of green food, such as chickweed, sometimes grass and weed seeds, usually meal-worms, fresh ants' eggs, cheese mites, and gentles. A diet varying slightly from that of the adult so-called seed-eaters is necessary for the successful rearing of the youngsters. The birds require a great deal of watching and care at that time. As a rule, if a brood fails it is the fault of the fancier; the birds themselves are only too anxious to rear their young, and owners must see to it that everything they need is available.

Lavender Finch (Grey Waxbill) *Lagonosticta caerulescens* Pl. 30

Origin West Africa.

Cock: 4¾ in. Larger than the *Hen*, more vivid, the grey being clear of any brown or smokey tone and the crimson of rump more brilliant. During the mating season recognizable by his flute-like call notes.

Lavender Finches are peaceable and good for the community aviary; they will play like tits and, full of curiosity, climb up and down the branches. They soon become tame. When they go to roost, sitting in a row with their heads inclined towards one another, they sing a soft murmuring song which finishes on a long drawn-out note.

They have a tiresome habit, which they share with the Zebra Finch, of plucking one another's feathers, so they often look ragged, although they are really quite healthy. It is, therefore, advisable to keep one pair only in the flight and not a number of pairs together. They soon recover, but when a consignment arrives from Africa these little birds often look a sorry sight and it is hard to pick a pair.

They will nest readily in the outside flight or the room aviary. They build themselves a round nest in a box bush, but also use nest boxes when these have been made cosy and dark by partially closing up the entrance, leaving only a 1½-in. hole. They need a lot of nesting material. The 4–5 round white eggs hatch in 11–12 days, and the young will leave the nest after a fortnight.

Breeding results have been achieved regularly in the bird room. Hybrids from crossing with the Fire Finch have been reported. Soaked seed, fresh ants' eggs, and egg food essential for the rearing of the young. This species can be allowed at liberty during the summer once the nest has been made.

The birds should spend the winter months indoors in an unheated room.

There is a sub-species which has a black beak.

Black-tailed Lavender Finch *Estrilda perreini*

Origin Central Africa.

4¼ to 4¾ in., slightly larger than the Lavender Finch. *Cock* and *Hen* show no outward differences. These birds resemble the Lavender Finch, *Lagonosticta caerulescens*, but they are on the whole a darker grey and their bills black instead of red. The upper tail coverts are red in both species but in *Estrilda perreini* the under tail coverts, tail, and legs are black. The eyes are red. These birds are very seldom imported.

Little is known about their care and

treatment. It is most difficult to select a true pair and if a fancier is lucky enough to find this species in a consignment it will be necessary to purchase several and carefully watch their behaviour in order to distinguish between cocks and hens. In addition to the seed diet of the small foreign finches, meal-worms can be recommended, preferably cut up, and other small insects.

According to Delacour the species has been bred in captivity, but the young birds were difficult to rear. This clearly points to their being insect-feeding, especially when rearing young.

Fire Finch *Lagonosticta senegala* Pl. 33

Origin West Africa.

Nearly 4 in. *Hen:* Is dull brown and only has red on the rump and upper tail coverts and a narrow ring round the eyes. Eyelids yellow, bill of both sexes red, and both have small white dots on sides of breast.

Fire Finches are among those most frequently imported, no doubt because of their gorgeous colouring and charming disposition. When they arrive they often look in poor condition and must be acclimatized most carefully, for a sudden drop in temperature and damp weather may cause casualties.

Once settled, they will breed readily. They prefer nest boxes provided to building in the open, although they have been known to nest in a box bush. For nesting material they will take hemp teasings, small blades of grass, and hairs. They are among the most good tempered of aviary birds and several pairs can be kept together. 3–4 roundish white eggs are hatched in 11 days and the young can usually be reared safely if appropriate rearing food

is supplied. They have to be accustomed to ants' eggs, small meal-worms, and yolk of egg. They like freshly dried ants' eggs, if these are soaked in warm water.

Young birds are grey-brown and show only a little red on the tail feathers. Beginners will enjoy keeping these birds. Of all small foreign finches the Fire Finches are the most suitable to set free in the garden during the summer months. Care must be taken always to place the seed pots inside the aviary so that the birds have to go in regularly to eat while at liberty. They will often build in the near vicinity of their aviary.

Vinaceous Waxbill (Vinaceous Fire Finch) *Lagonosticta larvata vinacea*

Origin Senegambia.

$4\frac{1}{2}$ in. *Cock:* Crown and back of head dark grey. Above bill a dark stripe which broadens over eyes and cheeks. Throat is black as is the lower part of the abdomen. Back, breast, and abdomen are a deep wine red, and there are a few small white spots on the sides of the breast. Tail feathers dark red, wings brown, bill grey. *Hen:* Is grey-brown above with a red sheen, the abdomen is soft pink running into beige, head light grey.

Although only rarely available, it is certainly worth while to obtain a pair, for they are peaceable in the flight and nest readily. They will build a round nest from all kinds of material and share in incubation. The 3–5 eggs will hatch in 11 days. When a consignment arrives it is very difficult to pick out a pair, especially as the family is so extensive and the hens of many species are very similar. Treatment as for the Fire Finch.

These Waxbills have a flute-like call

and the cock sometimes makes clucking noises. They must be kept in a moderately warm room during the winter.

Bar-breasted Fire Finch *Lagonosticta rufopicta*

Origin West and Central Africa.

4 in. *Cock:* Forehead, sides of head, and lores pinkish red. Crown and neck grey-brown; back brown; upper tail coverts red. Wings grey-brown to brown, chin, throat, and breast pinkish red with fine white dots on the breast. Remainder of under parts yellow brown. Bill red. Legs brown. *Hen:* The pinkish red is paler.

Imported now and again, often in a mixed consignment when the hens especially may be mistaken for other species. When a pair has been obtained the birds must be most carefully acclimatized, when they become strong, but they must pass the winter indoors. In this way they will remain healthy for many years.

As breeding birds they are very much like the Common Fire Finches. They will associate with them and with all other aviary inhabitants quite peaceably. They much prefer to build their nest in a thick shrub and will line it with feathers. The hatching will take 12 days and the young should be reared on ants' eggs, germinated millet, and finely cut-up meal-worms.

The most obvious difference between the Bar-breasted Fire Finch and the Common Fire Finch is the small white spots all over the breast of the former; on the Common Fire Finch these spots occur only along the sides. Taking into account the 9 more or less differentiated races of the Fire Finch, some slight idea can be obtained of the difficulties which arise when attempting to identify hens, which due to their paler colouring and less definite markings vary little from each other.

Sydney Waxbill (Red-browed Finch) *Aegintha temporalis* Pl. 29

Origin Australia.

4 in. Upper tail coverts and rump wine red, forehead olive grey, back olive, red eyebrow stripes. Lores and bill red, breast and belly whitish.

It is difficult to tell *Cock* and *Hen* apart, except by the behaviour of the cock during the mating time. Successful breeding results have therefore not occurred very frequently. The young cocks can be picked out quite quickly from the young hens because they begin to sing at an early age. The older cocks often do not utter a note.

These birds will build a nest of fine grasses in a nest box or in a dense shrub. They also like to occupy a coconut shell. The 4–5 eggs are incubated by both hen and cock and hatch in 13 days, but the young remain in the nest for 3 weeks after.

One of their idiosyncrasies is that they will also feed the young birds of other species. Young Zebra Finches seem to know this, for they immediately attach themselves to the Sydney Waxbills and allow themselves to be fed by them. The young Sydney Waxbills start to feed themselves at an early stage.

The best rearing food for these birds consists of germinated millet and soaked stale white bread, mixed now and again with some egg food. During rearing time they will also eat meal-worms which at other times they leave alone. Green food is indispensable.

Sydney Waxbills are tolerant of other birds. They can stand the British climate, but should spend the winter nights in the shelter and be allowed outside only during the day. Hybrids have been recorded with the African Silver-bill and St. Helena Waxbill.

Tiger Finch (Avadavat) *Amandava amandava*

Origin India and Indonesia.

3¾ in. *Hen :* Is dark brown and yellow-beige on abdomen, black lore stripe, upper tail coverts red, and black tail. She also has white spots on the wings and a red bill.

Only when adult and during the courting season do the *cocks* sport beautiful plumage. At other times they resemble the hens and can only be distinguished by their quaint song. The hens also sing although more softly, when no cocks are present. During courting, the cock is very active, prancing around the hen and displaying his spread tail. The birds will nest readily but nearly always only in shrubs or box bushes where they will build a hanging pouch-shaped nest, sometimes provided with two entrances.

The hen lays 4–6 eggs, which she incubates by herself. The rearing of the young is not always successful, probably because their surroundings are not quiet enough. One peculiarity of this species is that the birds will take large black chicken feathers into their nests and arrange them to be able to see through if danger threatens.

Incubation lasts from 11–12 days. The young are light brown and have black bills and dull white spots on the wings. Tiger Finches are among the most frequently kept birds because of their four good qualities: gorgeous colour, pleasant song, easy breeding, and strong constitution. They are certainly among the first species to be acquired and cannot fail to delight any fancier.

Green Avadavat *Amandava formosa* Pl. 31

Origin India.

4 in. These are not nearly so hardy as Tiger Finches and beginners are not advised to start with them. The green of the upper parts and yellow breast of *Cock* are much more intense than of the *Hen*.

Although they may be kept outside in summer they must be brought indoors during the winter. Once they have become acclimatized they may live to a considerable age. As well as seed they need plenty of insects. They are more difficult to breed than the Tiger Finches, and the rearing of the young is dependent on a constant supply of ants' eggs and meal-worms, or grubs.

Strawberry Finch (Chinese Avadavat) *Amandava amandava punicea* Pl. 32

Origin Indonesia and Thailand.

3½ in. *Cock:* generally smaller than the Tiger Finch, also darker above, brighter red along under parts, with small white dots instead of black. *Hen* also smaller and darker in colour.

The closely related Yellow-bellied Tiger Finches *Amandava amandava flavidiventris* which come from southern China and the islands of Lombok and Timor are also sometimes available. The lores of the cock are red, abdomen orange-yellow, and small white spots also appear on breast, not only on sides. Upper parts lighter and under parts more yellow.

Care and breeding of both species exactly similar as for the ordinary Tiger Finch, but they do not seem to like breeding in a cage; they need ample space which can only be provided in an aviary. Among the strongest of the smaller finches and may even winter out of doors during the coldest months.

They need a lot of sunshine. The brilliant colouring of the cock is dependent on this and an ample supply of insect food. If no live insects are supplied, the beautiful red colour will disappear after a few years and black will take its place (melanism). The young are reared mainly on insects. Ants' eggs, chopped up meal-worms (raw or boiled), and aphis must be supplied during the nesting period. Egg food and germinated seed may be given with advantage. Quantities of green food, especially chickweed, are essential.

They have the sweetest voices of any of the small finches. Crossings have been obtained with hens of Cordon Bleu, Golden-breasted Waxbill, and Zebra Finches, and with cocks of Golden-breasted Waxbills.

Peter's Twin Spot *Hypargos niveoguttatus* Pl. 24

Origin East Africa.

Nearly 5 in. *Cock:* Head brown-grey, back red-brown, upper tail coverts, neck, sides of head, and chin carmine red. Under parts black with white spot markings on the flanks. Wings red-brown to black-brown. Tail black with carmine red; centre plumes with black tips. Bill black-grey, legs horn-coloured. *Hen:* Less red on the head, paler in tint, and less spot markings.

Imported only on rare occasions and is always rather expensive.

The birds must be acclimatized with care, especially if they arrive in poor condition. They like the sun and must be kept warm at first; later on they become quite hardy and can stand cool nights well but must have frost-proof accommodation in winter.

Diet: Millet in the spray, and other types of millet, both dry and in germinated form, cut-up meal-worms,

either raw or boiled, ants' eggs, preferably fresh, and canary seed. Only a little green food needed at first, but grass seed germinating or in the ear can be given. Stale white bread soaked in milk and egg food with a few drops of cod-liver oil (especially in winter). Fruit, such as oranges, is popular. These birds show up quite well in an indoor cage, but even better outside in a summer aviary where they cause no trouble to other birds. They will hunt for insects in the sun, and spend much time on the grass under shrubs. They like to make their nest, for which they need grasses, coconut fibres, and feathers, a little above the ground in a dense shrub, such as box or dwarf conifer, but they also use nest boxes. They construct a narrow covered slip-in passage with grasses. The nuptial display of the cock is performed on the ground; he will carry a feather or a blade of grass in his beak, and dance round the hen with spread wings and upstretched neck. The hen responds by swiftly moving her tail from side to side. During nesting period, when incubation is shared, kindred species are chased away from the neighbourhood of the nest.

After 13 days the young hatch and will fly in another 3 weeks. Meal-worms should now be given and, if possible, ants' eggs. Egg food, soaked bread, and germinating seeds are essential for a long time after the young have left the nest. Bengalese have sometimes reared the young but, probably because the wrong kind of rearing food is supplied, the birds do not grow and eventually die.

Their song consists of a soft rustling 'chirruping' with a few deep flute-like notes and is pleasant to hear. The markings and colouring make these birds among the most attractive of African Finches. Crossing with Cordon Bleu has been successful.

Aurora Finch (Crimson-winged Waxbill) (Crimson-winged Pytilia) *Pytilia phoenicoptera*

Origin Central Africa.

Nearly 5 in. *Cock:* Head and back grey, back and rump washed with red. Upper tail coverts carmine red, as are the centre tail plumes. The remainder is black-brown. There is much red and brown on the wings. Under parts are grey, and the breast narrowly barred with white. Eyes red, legs flesh-coloured, bill black. *Hen:* Browner in colour with more wavy markings on breast and belly. Legs red-brown.

These can be thoroughly recommended; by their steadiness and confidence in a cage or room aviary they rapidly win everyone's heart and soon settle down to breed. One essential condition for their health is a sunny room; they prefer to sit in the sun in the open and on the ground.

Diet: As ground birds they consume a quantity of insects, spiders, ants' eggs, etc. Next to a preference for millet and millet sprays, they like germinated grass seeds. During breeding time ants' eggs are essential; either fresh or dried and soaked in hot water, mixed with egg food. If care is taken to maintain a constant supply of maggots, grubs, finely cut-up meal-worms, and occasionally a twig with aphis, it is certain that the young will be safely reared. Disappointments have often occurred through lack of correct rearing food.

They like to build in a box bush but will also use a nest box. Their nest is constructed untidily from grasses and hair, fibres and feathers; the inside entirely lined with small feathers. The 4 eggs are hatched in 12 days, both birds taking turns at incubation. After leaving the nest the youngsters are still fed for a considerable time by the parents. The fledglings attain their adult colouring only after several months.

The song of the cock is soft and short, but melodious, and usually heard towards the evening. It is amusing to watch a pair during nuptial preparations. The cock will hop with elevated tail round and round his hen, bowing and scraping and uttering his quiet little love song.

These Waxbills need extra care during acclimatization, especially rest and sunshine, but in time become reasonably hardy. They must winter indoors in a moderately heated room.

Abyssinian Aurora Finch *Pytilia phoenicoptera lineata*

Origin Abyssinia.

Is a slightly larger race, distinguished by its red bill, but its requirements are similar. When a consignment comes from Abyssinia it often includes birds of this sub-species.

Melba Finch (Crimson-faced Waxbill) *Pytilia melba* Pl. 34

Origin South Africa.

Nearly 5 in. *Cock:* Forehead scarlet, also throat and cheeks; grey lores, head and neck grey, back and wings olive green. Red tail, yellow band to lower edge of breast. Belly white with black barring, sometimes broken up into spots. Bill red, eyes red-brown, legs yellow-brown. *Hen:* Does not have the red on her head, which is entirely grey, and she is also much paler in colour than the cock.

There are many sub-species in Central and South Africa which differ greatly in colour and markings. This race only is imported with any regularity and then in small numbers.

It is delicate on arrival. Only experienced fanciers should attempt to keep these birds, as their acclimatization requires great care. They must be kept warm during the first few weeks and placed in a sunny spot. A disinfectant should be placed in the drinking water every few days; a little lime water can be added. No green food at first.

Diet: Millet and canary seed, millet in the spray, various grass seeds, 'nightingale' food on which some ants' eggs and *Enchytraea* may be sprinkled.

Although these Waxbills will agree with birds of other species, they become ferocious and even dangerous during the breeding period. More than one pair cannot be kept together. Their song is sweet and lovely. The birds spend much time on the ground in the sun, and grow fairly tame; they are always lively and inquisitive. Although they require warm accommodation during winter, they can be moved to a favourably situated, sunny aviary during the summer. Only in this way can satisfactory breeding results be obtained; there is no record of breeding from birds kept in a cage. If the summer is wet and chilly, it is advisable to heat the birds' shelter by a lamp which should be kept burning all night.

This species will build a domed nest in a dense shrub; usually preferring to build in the open although they sometimes make use of a nest box. The hen alone will form the inside of the nest and likes to line it with small white feathers. Both parents share incubation of the 3–4 eggs which hatch in 13 days. The young remain in the nest for a fortnight or more before flying and are then fully fledged. They are then fed for another fortnight by their parents. Best results are obtained when the hatching and rearing are done by the parent birds themselves; attempts to use the Bengalese have usually been a failure. Although the youngsters will shed their nest feathers after 4 weeks, it is only at 7 months that they assume full adult plumage.

The successful rearing of the young depends on the correct food being available; this should chiefly consist of live insects, such as ants' eggs, aphis, *Enchytraea*, and cut-up meal-worms, with egg food, green food, and bread and milk.

South African Quail Finch *Ortygospiza atricollis muelleri*

Origin South Africa.

3½ in. Can be distinguished from the West African species which follows by the white orbital ring round eyes, white lores, and much larger chin spot.

The sexes can readily be distinguished as the *Hen* lacks black on cheeks and throat is grey. During breeding season, the pairs segregate themselves from their kind, and the cock will defend his breeding-ground against all comers.

This species is different from all the other finches, as it is almost entirely terrestrial, scrabbling in the sand, and taking dust baths. If the aviary is turfed the birds are concealed in the grass.

Although no reports are to hand of successful breeding results, these birds often build a dome-shaped nest with an entrance at the side, in a corner, on the floor. If they are kept in a cage, it is advisable to fit a false roof of mutton cloth or muslin, as when the birds are frightened they fly upwards and are apt to damage their heads.

West African Quail Finch *Ortygospiza atricollis atricollis* Pl. 35

Origin Central and West Africa.

3½ in. *Cock:* Head and throat black with a small white chin spot. Upper parts grey-brown, lower parts brown, with black and white barring on breast and along sides. Eyes brown, upper mandible black, lower pinkish red, legs flesh-coloured. *Hen:* Head does not show any black and whole colouring is paler.

Acclimatization needs care; it is reported that it is far more difficult to keep the hen alive than the cock; these birds need warmth, bathing water and some damp moss in a corner of the cage. They will develop into excellent aviary birds, but cannot endure a wet summer and need ample cover, with a good growth of grass on the aviary floor. This can be maintained by regular spraying of the turf.

They should not be kept as cage birds, for they are not satisfied with ust a layer of sand, but need small growing plants and the many tiny insects always found in the soil.

Diet: Although mainly seed-eaters and like various grass seeds, small millet, and green food, they also enjoy ants' eggs, aphis, and other small insect life. For breeding they should be accommodated in an aviary containing large clumps of grass. On or in such a clump or on moss they will build a round nest of grass blades, coconut fibre, etc., and furnish it with a narrow slip-in passage. The cock and hen incubate the 2–3 eggs alternately and they hatch in 14 days. The young are reared on seed and small insects.

The birds usually roost in the aviary on a clump of moss or the bark of a tree, a little above ground. They are quick on the ground; like true ground birds, their movements are very rapid. When they sense danger they flatten themselves on the ground, with wide open mouths.

They will live in harmony with all other birds in the aviary, including their own kind. During the breeding season mild skirmishes may occur between the cocks. More than 10 races which show very little outward difference are known from various parts of Africa.

Attention must be paid to their legs, as inflammation of the toes occurs frequently. A thick layer of good clean sand and fresh bathing water will prevent this. These birds need a warm room during the winter. For fanciers with experience they are most attractive.

Cut-throat (Ribbon Finch) *Amadina fasciata* Pl. 38

Origin Africa.

5 in. It is easy to distinguish the *Cock* and *Hen* of this very common species as the hen lacks the red band on the throat. The cock's song is barely audible, but he may often be seen trying to sing with his throat feathers puffed out. Given ample nesting opportunity, these birds are not difficult to breed in an outside aviary. But if they are kept by themselves in a cage the chance of success is much greater.

They will breed in nest boxes and build with any material available; the hen lays 4–6 eggs and the parents will take it in turns to incubate. After 12 days the young appear and must be fed with meal-worms, ants' eggs, germinated seeds, and soaked bread.

A common failing is to inspect the nest while the cock or hen is sitting or protecting the young. This may be the cause of failure of many attempts at breeding which would have succeeded if the nests had been undisturbed.

The birds need all kinds of minerals, especially lime. During winter, cod-liver oil is good; during spring, green food and mixed grit should be given. The dreaded egg binding which frequently occurs with this species can be effectively combatted by this diet.

These birds are hardy and will live for years; they may be kept in an outside flight.

East-African or Abyssinian Cut-throat *Amadina fasciata alexanderi* Pl. 37

Origin East Africa.

5 in. *Cock* differs greatly in colour and markings from the ordinary well-known species, which is beige-brown with brown markings. The very dark barring and the extra wide red collar are particularly noticeable. The scaly marking is more extensive and the basic colour a deeper beige brown. *Hen* is similar to the hen of the Cut-throat but rather more boldly marked. There is no difference in the care of this sub-species.

Red-headed Finch *Amadina erythrocephala* Pl. 36

Origin South Africa.

5¼ in. It is easy to distinguish the sexes; the *Cock* has gorgeous colouring while the *Hen* wears a very sober beige suit, without any red on the head.

Importation from South Africa is limited. Although some are bred each year, they are few and far between. It is practically impossible to breed in an aviary together with other birds. By themselves, Red-headed Finches will readily build in a nest box or they may occupy some old nest and furbish it up a little to suit their own taste.

While breeding they must be left in peace, and no attempt made to investigate the nest. They are very susceptible to disturbances. Once the young have been hatched, successful rearing is merely a question of the correct rearing food, which should be that described for the Cut-throat. Nests with 3–4 young are normal.

It is worth while concentrating on these birds. Demand always exceeds supply, and expense and trouble are amply repaid. If you are unlucky enough to possess only a cock or a hen, crossing with a Cut-throat is a possibility.

Bib Finch (African Parson Finch) *Spermestes nana*

Origin Madagascar.

3¾ in. *Cock* and *Hen* alike. Forehead, lores, and upper tail coverts light olive-brown. Tail black, under parts light brown with a pink tinge with some scaly markings. Under tail coverts grey with yellow-brown margins. Upper mandible black, lower mandible horn-coloured, legs flesh-coloured.

Few fanciers keep this species, mainly because it is so difficult to obtain a true pair. It is necessary to purchase several and then wait until the cocks perform their nuptial dance and sing their pleasant song. During the breeding season they will chase other birds from their nest and persecute them, so they should be kept apart in a small aviary or large cage. Their nest is built in any suitable receptacle, or in a low shrub; it is simply constructed from fibres and grasses, entirely lined with feathers and plant fibres.

One of the most free breeding species; broods of 6 young three or four times in close succession are no exception. This species may be crossed with others, such as Bengalese, Indian

Silverbill, and African Silverbill. Incubation takes 12 days, and the young remain in the nest for 3 weeks. Another 10 days will then see them entirely independent and they will not disturb their parents when new families are being reared.

Diet: Various types of millet, canary seed, and much green food. Ants' eggs, especially during rearing time. Then hard-boiled egg, with soaked stale white bread should also be given, as well as germinated seed.

The birds incubate alternately in the day, and together in the night. They can winter in the shelter of the outside aviary, but a frost-proof room is better.

Bronze-winged Mannikin (Bronze Mannikin) *Spermestes cucullata* Pl. 43

Origin Africa.

3½–3¾ in. Bronze-winged Mannikins do not breed easily, but are very popular for their sharply defined marking in contrasting colours of glossy black, grey-brown, and snow white, with a vivid spot of greenish bronze on shoulders. They are bustling and lively. The song of the cock is barely audible, but this is the only certain way in which to distinguish him.

If breeding is to be attempted, the birds must be given a cage or small aviary to themselves, and in it should be placed some nest boxes and a variety of nesting material, wool and kapok fluff, hemp teasings, moss, and grass blades. They will construct a simple nest in a nest box and will hatch 4–6 eggs in 12 days, the cock and hen sitting alternately.

This species lends itself to hybridizing with the Bengalese, providing the intended pair are kept in a cage by themselves. If kept with other species, both these birds will be very ready to

fight when hunting for suitable nesting sites and will even chase larger birds. As a rule their own nest will suffer in consequence, and other nests too.

In addition to 'foreign finch' seed, Bronze-winged Mannikins will use for raising their youngsters finely cut-up meal-worms, ants' eggs, and soaked stale bread. They also need green food.

Rufous-backed Mannikin *Spermestes bicolor nigriceps*

Origin East Africa.

3½ in. *Cock* and *Hen* alike. Black head and breast, back and wings brown, belly white. A white-barred marking on the wings and the rump and upper tail coverts have white transverse stripes. Tail black, eyes brown, legs black, bill grey.

The very slight difference between the outward appearance of the sexes usually necessitates the purchase of quite a number if it is desired to obtain a true pair, which can only be selected by close observation of their behaviour.

This species entirely disappeared from the market for many years and only recently again became available. It has therefore been necessary to refer back to records of the 1930's for information on their care and breeding. It was said then that this was the most peaceful species of all the Mannikins.

A seed mixture, such as given to foreign finches, is necessary, while meal-worms and soaked stale bread form the basis of the rearing food. Only a little green food should be given. These birds will soon build a nest of grasses and coconut fibre in a nest box, and the hen will lay 3–4 eggs, which are incubated by both parents alternately. After 13 days the young will appear and remain in the nest for another fortnight. They are then fed for another 3 weeks by the parent birds and roost with them in their nest. After the moult and loss of nest feathers, they must be separated from the parent birds or they will be chased away.

Magpie Mannikin *Spermestes (Amauresthes) fringilloides* Pl. 40

Origin South and West Africa.

4½–4¾ in. These birds are much easier to breed than the Bronze-winged Mannikins. They are quieter and the cock is recognizable only by his song (which is almost inaudible) and his behaviour during mating season.

Kept in a flight with larger birds, they will give little trouble, but for breeding they need a cage to themselves. They will build a simple nest in the nest box provided; it will be constructed of diverse materials, and will usually have a slip-in passage. These birds will incubate their 4–6 eggs, sitting alternately for 12 days, and the young are normally reared without difficulty. It takes from 3 months to a year for the young to change their greybrown colour to the full colour of the adult.

Diet: Treatment and rearing food as for the Bronze-winged Mannikin.

African Silverbill *Euodice malabarica cantans* Pl. 45

Origin West and Central Africa.

4–4½ in. *Cock* and *Hen* alike. Light brown above, very pale buff below. Wings dark brown, rump and tail blackish. Bill silver grey. These are among species most frequently available to the trade. They are one of the easiest to breed and will also hatch the eggs and rear the young of other species of the same size. This will be appreciated by fanciers who have left on their hands the eggs of birds which are too restless

to hatch and rear their own young, such as the Red-eared Waxbill and the Cordon Bleu.

If a pair is desired, the best plan is to purchase a number of these birds. Only the soft song of the cock makes him recognizable and as he generally begins to sing as soon as he has settled down, it should not be too long before the fancier is able to distinguish between the sexes.

Although the plumage is not so colourful as usual with foreign species, the behaviour of these birds is so charming that it is a real pleasure to keep them. They will breed best in a cage; they are easily frightened while breeding, and need a quiet and secluded corner.

They will build in a nest box from different kinds of fine materials, constructing a narrow slip-in entrance. The nest they will line with soft material and feathers. The 4 eggs will be hatched in 12 days and the young will leave the nest 3 weeks later. It is not exceptional for as many as 20 youngsters to be reared by one pair in a season.

This species can be crossed, among others, with the Common Spice Finch.

Diet: Normal foreign finch seed and during breeding some cut-up mealworms, ants' eggs, soaked bread and hard-boiled egg. Green food must also be supplied.

Indian Silverbill *Euodice malabarica* Pl. 46

Origin India.

4½–4¾ in. Sexes alike, but *Hen* smaller in head. Chocolate brown above with white rump.

Though not very hardy, this species is regularly available and is a good breeder. The *Cock* is only distinguishable by his song, and if a true pair can-

G

not be obtained, crossing with an African Silverbill might be attempted; it has often had good results.

Although the birds will use a nest box, they prefer to take over a Weaver's nest which they will close up entirely and provide with a narrow entrance passage. Their clutches are much larger than those of the African Silverbill, and sometimes number as many as 8–10 eggs. They will live in harmony with others of their own species and sometimes 2 pairs will nest and raise their young together. Diet and treatment during breeding similar to that for African Silverbill.

Common Spice Finch (Nutmeg Finch) (Spotted Munia) *Lonchura punctulata* Pl. 44

Origin India.

4½ in. One of the best-known species and always available. In a community cage or large cage and also outside these birds are charming and lively; the cock sings a peculiar humming and buzzing melody. They are extremely easy to keep; they eat chiefly seed and can stand winter climate if protected.

Breeding, however, is far less easy than with the African Silverbill or Bengalese. It is difficult to obtain a true pair as the birds are so much alike and only their behaviour during breeding time can be a real guide. If the pair begin to nest, complete quietness must be ensured for at the least noise the birds will leave the nest and, though they may return later, small chance of success remains. In a cage by themselves, they sometimes settle down to breed, and must not be disturbed. It is safer to use Bengalese to hatch and rear young. Hybrids with the Bengalese and the African Silverbill have been known.

To cross these species it is best to choose a Bengalese hen and pair it to a Spice Finch cock.

These birds will build a nest in a high shrubbery or use a nest box; in a cage only a nest box will be used.

White-rumped Mannikin (Sharp-tailed Munia) *Lonchura striata acuticauda*

Origin Asia.

4½ in. Mostly dull brown faintly striated, rump and breast buff-white. Tail blackish with centre feathers extended to narrow point. This species is almost certainly an ancestor of the Bengalese.

The *Cock* can be distinguished from the *Hen* by his song. When displaying he assumes an upright posture, and rocks backwards and forwards, spreading his tail.

Very suitable for a community flight or cage, where they can nest without disturbance. Unfortunately they are seldom imported. A pair of birds, kept by themselves, can rear a large number of young every year. Treatment as for Bronze-winged Mannikin.

Bengalese Pl. 47, 48. Domesticated.

Around 5 in. Originally produced in Japan over 200 years ago from stock imported from China—a domesticated form of the Sharp-tailed Munia, *Lonchura striata auticauda*. Frequent reference has already been made to the outstanding qualities of this bird as a foster-parent. The Bengalese is better bred in a small cage than in a flight with other birds. It is so tame and gentle that it would offer little resistance to any bird attempting to usurp its nest, but would simply go to another nest box. The 6–8 young are usually raised without difficulty in a cage. Egg food with soaked bread, meal-worms, and a quantity of green food are rearing necessities, in addition to the normal seed diet.

In a cage, not too large, the charming family life of this species can be followed. The cock will blow himself out until he looks like a ball of feathers and will then sing his rattling song.

Cock and *Hen* look exactly alike; only the song differentiates the cock. Pure white Bengalese have been reared as well as fawn and brown pied birds. The pure white is the least hardy.

One of the latest and most charming varieties to be produced is the single- and double-crested white Bengalese. A totally black variety is offered very occasionally. The birds will commence to breed at the early age of 8 months.

Every fancier of foreign finches should possess several pairs for use as foster-parents if necessary. The Bengalese will adopt young fledglings just out of the egg, but it is better to place eggs which have been under a hen for a few days with those of a Bengalese pair in a similar advanced stage of development, though this must not be taken too literally. Birds reared in this way are inclined to seek the company of the Bengalese later on, so it is wise to remove the young, once they have become independent, and place them with their own kindred. This may be necessary to ensure successful breeding from the young birds at a later stage.

For beginners, these birds are very suitable. Once they have been reared successfully the experience gained may be of considerable help in breeding more difficult species.

The Bengalese will build its nest from various materials, usually in a nest box, preferably entirely enclosed with only a small entrance hole at the front so that the birds are hidden completely while incubating. This will take up to 14 days and the young will fly in a further 3 weeks. It is advisable to add a few drops of cod-liver oil to the rearing food and to offer the fledglings soaked seed until they are old enough to go on to a normal seed diet.

Mineral mixture with cuttlefish and lime is essential, for the caged birds have no other means of obtaining these essential elements.

The Bengalese needs a daily bath, and being always kept in a cage, the claws tend to become overgrown, even if extra thick branches have been provided. These long nails must be cut occasionally, or the birds in flying from the nest may become entangled with the nest materials and drag some of their young out of the nest.

Black-beaked Bronze Mannikin
Lonchura leucogastroides

Origin Indonesia.

About 4 in. *Cock* and *Hen* alike. Upper parts chocolate brown with fine wavy markings. Head and breast black, belly white. Tail and rump brown-black.

Diet: Subsists solely on seed and will be quite happy with various millets, together with canary seed and green food. The young are reared almost exclusively on seed, although they like bread and milk. As they are closely related to the other Mannikins and therefore also to the Bengalese, they are in great demand. The resulting young of various crosses with different species have proved fertile.

They thrive in breeding cages and are suitable birds to use as foster-parents for other species, provided that species can be reared on seed alone.

White-headed Mannikin (White-headed Nun) (Maja Finch) *Lonchura maja* Pl. 41

Origin Indonesia.

4¾ in. Sexes alike but head and beak of *Hen* smaller. This species is friendly and tolerant. Not easily induced to breed.

Kept as a pair or crossed with a Bengalese in a cage, breeding may result. Cut-up meal-worms and soaked bread are suitable as rearing food, in addition to the seed diet. Incubation takes 12 days. The young will leave the nest after another 25 days, and have to be fed for a long time afterwards before they become independent.

Except for the difficulty of inducing them to breed, White-headed Mannikins are very suitable for the fancier to start with. They will even winter in an outside aviary and, if well looked after, may live for more than 10 years.

Three-coloured Mannikin (Tri-coloured Nun) *Lonchura malacca* Pl. 42

Origin India.

4¼ in. Sexes alike. One of the more frequently imported species. Its wants are simple. It is quite hardy, so may be kept outside in winter. But, as yet, it cannot be classed as a free breeding bird. Now and again a report has been given of a successful brood, but this is exceptional. It is not known whether this is because of incorrect feeding, or insufficient attention to making the nesting facilities as much like the birds' natural surroundings as possible.

These birds live in reedy surroundings, in long grass and near rice fields and build their nests there, hung between the sturdy stems. If bamboo or ordinary cane or rushes are planted in the flight in addition to the ordinary shrubs, it is possible that the birds will nest more readily. Sometimes they will take over an old nest and rebuild it.

Stale soaked bread and germinated seed must be made available in addition to the ordinary seed once the birds have young. Their song is inaudible.

Black-headed Mannikin (Black-headed Munia) (Black-headed Nun) *Lonchura malacca atricapilla* Pl. 39.

Origin India and Burma.

4½ in. *Cock:* Entire head, nape, and throat glossy black, remainder of plumage dark chestnut with a splash of black on belly. Beak silver-grey, legs dark grey. *Hen:* Similar and difficult to distinguish from cock, but usually has a less robust beak and is a little smaller in head.

Of all species of Mannikin, this is the one most often met with by the fancier. Breeding is exceptional and takes place only when the flight has been specially planted to meet their needs. Hybrids have been produced with Bengalese, Common Spice Finch, and White-headed Mannikin.

Diet: Seeds, also hard-boiled egg, soaked bread, much green stuff, finely chopped meal-worms; ants' eggs and germinated seeds during the rearing period.

If breeding is not desired and the birds are kept only as pets, they will be found friendly, quiet, and never disturbing in a mixed collection. They like perching high up in the flight. Their song is barely audible.

Java Sparrow (Rice Bird) *Padda oryzivora* Pl. 51

Origin Indonesia.

5½ in. *Cock:* Main colour is dove-grey. Head and tail black, white cheek patch. Lower breast bluish tinge, belly and under tail-coverts white. Beak rose pink edged with white, feet flesh coloured.

Cock and *Hen* practically indistinguishable except for the song of the cock, which is pleasant and not too loud. The beak of the cock is a trifle more robust.

One of the best-known cage birds, but often kept separately as it is reputed to be a disturbing element among other small birds. This might be expected, as it has a large, powerful beak.

It is preferable to keep a pair with other birds of the same size. Pairs by themselves will be slow to nest and breed; indeed it may take a couple of years even before they will start a family.

Diet: Usually consisting mainly of millet, canary seed, some hemp, and some oats, must be varied, and the birds need quantities of green stuff and insects.

If breeding results are to be expected, insectivorous mixture, grated apple or pear, and some berries must be supplied, and during breeding time, mealworms, ants' eggs, and bread and milk should be given. Another important factor is the hardening off of the birds; if they have become sufficiently tough they may even winter in an outside flight. When completely acclimatized the chance of breeding is much greater. But these birds cannot be described as domesticated, and the secret of the Japanese fanciers, who have even succeeded in producing a white variety, has not yet been discovered.

If white and pied Java Sparrows, which breed more easily, are also kept in the aviary, the imported birds may be induced to breed. There must be adequate space between the nests—usually hollow logs or nesting boxes—as each pair will defend its territory against invaders: 3 ft apart should be sufficient. It is better to choose large, peaceable birds as co-inhabitants of the aviary; they will not be inquisitive and poke about and inspect all the nest boxes, disturbing the sitting hens. Should breeding take place in winter, the birds must be kept in a warm room, if possible connected with a small outside aviary, so that they can enjoy a little fresh air every day.

The hours of darkness can be shortened by providing artificial light for these birds until about 9 p.m. and again about 7 a.m. It is too long for foreign birds to be allowed to remain in darkness from 5 p.m. to 8 a.m., if they are attempting to rear a family.

White Java Sparrow Pl. 49

Origin A domestic variety of *Padda oryzivora* produced in Japan. 5½ in.

The Japanese have from time immemorial shown a talent for the domestication of birds. In addition to the well-known Bengalese they have cultivated a white variety of the Java Sparrow. Before the war the Japanese exported large quantities of these birds but today only a few seem to be left in Europe.

The White Java Sparrow is much more tranquil than the normal variety, and breeds readily; the raising of its young seems to offer no difficulty. The young are not always completely white; often they will be partially coloured.

When in good health, the plumage of this bird is wax-like. Only when ill or in discomfort will it sit fluffed out. This rarely happens as the bird is very hardy. This species can be recommended to a fancier who is just beginning.

Pectorella Finch (Pectoral or Pectoralis Finch) *Lonchura pectoralis*

Origin Australia.

4½ in. These and other Australian species are difficult to obtain apart from the comparatively few which are bred in captivity.

Cock: Cheeks and throat black, fawn line over eyes. Upper parts grey-brown. Chest white, barred black. Breast pinkish-brown with white spots on back and flanks. *Hen:* is easily distinguished by the feathers of the ear coverts and throat which are brownish, and by the black-and-white barred appearance of the fore-neck.

The song of the cock consists of a series of 'chip-chip-chip' notes only.

Out of breeding season the sexes live apart in separate flocks. While courting the cock bows and scrapes, hopping round the hen on the ground. Both birds will then perch quietly bill to bill, after which they will diligently search the ground together picking up twigs and grasses. The cock will drop his wings and flirt his tail up and down.

In their wild state these birds nest in a large grass clump, and in captivity they will hunt for a secluded corner in the flight, using an open nest box. They then proceed to fill this with grass blades and reeds and make a shallow depression which they will line and partially cover with fine grasses and fibres. Their 4–6 eggs are incubated by both parents alternately, but the hen does most of the work. The young hatch after 13 days and will leave the nest in another 3 weeks. A fortnight later they will be independent. Their plumage assumes adult colouring only slowly, and it is not until they are a year old that they resemble their parents. Crossing with the African Silverbill is possible.

Diet: Similar to that given to the Cherry Finch (p. 166); this applies also to the rearing of the young.

Chestnut-breasted Finch *Lonchura castaneothorax* Pl. 55

Origin Australia.

Nearly 4½ in. Sexes alike. Not at all hardy on arrival and must be acclimatized very gradually and carefully.

Its requirements are similar to those of the Common Spice Finch (p. 162), and it needs the same care. Its nest is built in a low shrub or in a nest box. A long entrance passage made of grass blades hides the interior from inquisitive eyes. This bird has often been bred in captivity. Hybrids with the Yellow-rumped Finch, with the African Silverbill, and the Bengalese have been recorded.

Yellow-rumped Finch (Straw-rumped Finch) *Lonchura flaviprymna*

Origin Australia.

Nearly 4½ in. Although this species in its natural state shows some resemblance to the Chestnut-breasted Finch —and discoloration of the yellow plumage may make this resemblance greater—it has whitish cheeks and plain buff under parts. Sexes alike.

Treatment as for other Mannikins; it builds its nest similarly. It has frequently been bred in captivity. It has a great liking for grass and weed seeds.

Cherry Finch (Plum-head Finch) (Modest Finch) *Aidemosyna modesta* Pl. 52

Origin Australia.

4¼–4¾ in. *Cock* is easily distinguished from the *Hen* by the carmine red spot on the forehead and the black spot on the chin.

As with most Australian Finches, the acclimatization of these birds is a problem, especially in the early stages. The fancier would do well to buy a pair which he knows to have been in a cage or aviary for some time, or which have been bred in captivity.

Cherry Finches will build a round domed nest in a cage or flight. They will also build in a nest box and, after laying 4–6 eggs, will commence to incubate, the cock and the hen taking it in turns to sit for the 12-day period.

They share in rearing the young. As well as the regular seed diet, egg food and grass seed make a good rearing mixture, provided green food is also given liberally. But breeding and rearing these birds is not always easy; they are very susceptible to any disturbance and will quickly abandon their eggs. If not chilled, however, these eggs can be hatched by a pair of African Silverbills or by Bengalese. The former are preferable, as they are closely related to the Cherry Finch, and it is quite possible to rear hybrids of the two species. Lack of minerals may have something to do with unsuccessful rearing. A mixture of grit and cuttlefish, specially packed for foreign birds, is a help. The young do not leave the nest until 3 weeks after hatching, and they become independent a fortnight later.

As with all Australian Finches, once the Cherry Finches become used to an outside flight and are carefully acclimatized, they can winter in an unheated bird room. They are in a class by themselves, and offer more variety than the small African species.

Long-tailed Grass Finch *Poephila acuticauda* Pl. 54 and 57

Origin North Western Australia.

Nearly 7 in., inc. 2½-in. tail. Readily reared, a pair of these birds are best kept in a cage or small aviary by themselves. During breeding season they become very aggressive, and have been known even to kill small finches. The *Hen* is difficult to distinguish from the *Cock* but, on the whole, she is smaller and has a smaller black bib.

Long-tailed Grass Finches are ideal for the cage. If kept by themselves, they will breed and rear their young. They are not very susceptible to disturbances, but the young, once they have become independent, must be left in the cage to which they are accustomed. It is better to move the old birds. Frequently when the young birds have been moved to new surroundings they have refused to take their food and have died after some days. Their cage should be provided with a roosting nest, which the birds will use when not breeding. They take a fortnight to hatch their eggs.

Rearing food should consist of hard-boiled egg mixed with rusk crumbs, finely chopped meal-worms, and plenty of green food. A lime and mineral mixture must be given throughout the year; this is essential for all Australian Finches. Half-ripe seeds of grass and grain make an excellent rearing food for the young.

As a rule, the birds can winter in an unheated room; when kept in cages a frost-proof room is recommended. A bird room usually has so many nooks and crannies that wintering presents no difficulties, and the greater freedom of movement is also better for the birds. But cocks and hens should be kept apart or they will start breeding. It is pleasant to have young birds in the winter, but they must then be kept in a warm room.

They can be reared in a large flight, together with Zebra Finches, Diamond Sparrows, and other larger birds, provided that ample nesting facilities are available; if not, fights may well be frequent.

Although their export from Australia is now prohibited, birds have been reared in Britain in such quantities that they can always be obtained, even if their price is still rather high. If young birds are bought, breeding should not be attempted until they are more than a year old.

A fancier who is just beginning would be well advised to start off with the small African Finches, before embarking on this much more expensive species.

Heck's Grass Finch *Poephila acuticauda hecki* Pl. 56

Origin Northern Territory, Australia.

7 in. including long tail. Distinguished from the Long-tailed Grass Finch by its sealing-wax red beak. Sexes alike, but the hen is generally less bold in appearance and may have a slightly smaller bib. Probably it is safer to sex these birds by their behaviour. If there are a number of both sexes together a cock will usually select a hen and sit close to her, distending his throat in a wheezing, almost silent song, and bob up and down on the perch.

In confinement they require the same treatment as described for the Long-tailed Grass Finch, and will breed just as readily. Unfortunately, however, they do not restrict their breeding activities to the spring or summer months, but will continue to lay clutch after clutch throughout the year if allowed to do so. Apart from the risk to the hen of laying cramp and exhaustion, rearing the young during the winter months entails a deal of extra work to maintain an adequate supply of green food and live insects, and it is far better to be content with two or, at the most, three broods in a season, and to

separate the cocks and hens during the winter. This does not entail caging every bird separately, as it is quite safe to keep all the birds of one sex together in a large cage or indoor aviary. It is preferable, however, that the cages should be as far apart as possible, to prevent the cocks from seeing or hearing the hens, otherwise they will remain restless and may become quarrelsome.

Parson Finch (Black-throated Finch) *Poephila cincta* Pl. 58

Origin Australia.

4½ in. Resembles the Long-tailed Grass Finch in every respect except that it has a short tail, black bill, red legs.

A less common bird, but among the best of breeders. *Cock* and *Hen* are difficult to tell apart, and only when a great number are together can a difference in marking and in depth of colouring be observed. Their sex can be determined with certainty only during the breeding season; even then what seems to be a duller-looking hen may turn out to be a young cock.

If a pair have been obtained, it is fairly certain that they will nest. They like a nest box, in which they will fashion a round domed nest built of blades of grass, teasings, and small roots, lined with feathers and hairs.

The 4–8 eggs are incubated by both birds sitting alternately, and both parents share in rearing their young. Here, again, the Bengalese can be used if necessary, but if the parents are willing to feed their young everything will go well. Three clutches may be laid each season. As this species is apt to disturb others, it is better to keep a pair apart.

They need the same food and treatment as the Long-tailed Grass Finch. They may, if necessary, be wintered in an unheated room, but moderate heat is better.

Masked Grass Finch *Poephila personata* Pl. 53

Origin Australia.

5 in. *Hen* and *Cock* are difficult to tell apart; the hen is a little less pronounced in colouring. The behaviour of the cock during the courting period is conclusive. Much care is required to acclimatize these birds, but once they become accustomed to their new environment, climate, and food, they grow hardy, and will breed readily in a small aviary.

Treatment is similar to that for the Diamond Sparrow (p. 173). They usually rear their young quite well, but it is advisable to use the Bengalese, at any rate for the first clutch of eggs. Charcoal seems to be essential to these finches, for pieces of charcoal as big as eggs are always found in their nests when they are wild.

It is perfectly easy and natural to breed from birds bred and reared in this country; within a week after their purchase they will begin to build their nest. Imported birds need longer and are best kept with other birds. It is only during the breeding time that they will chase other birds away, and may cause trouble. Crossings with the Long-tailed Grass Finch are possible, and will result in a red-billed variety of the Masked Finch.

This species is inclined to disturb the peace of an aviary by its frequent alarm calls.

Gouldian Finch *Erythrura gouldiae* Pl. 59, 60, and 61

Origin Australia.

About 5 in. The gaudiest-coloured of finches. *Hen* much paler on head and under parts. Three forms are obtainable, the Black-headed, Red-headed, and Orange-headed Gouldian; all are expensive and, moreover, imported birds are difficult to acclimatize. They should be placed in a warm room (70° F or 21° C) and must be kept in quarantine for some weeks until they become accustomed to a diet of seed, green food, lime, and minerals. Even then a bird which looks quite healthy may suddenly die in the cage.

These birds are very sensitive to draughts, but once acclimatized they will become hardy and live for a long time. They may even be kept in an unheated room in winter.

Fortunately quite a few Gouldians are bred now and the young are reared without difficulty. It is, however, advantageous to leave both hatching and rearing to the Bengalese, so as to reduce risks to a minimum and allow the Gouldians themselves to start on a new nest. The young Gouldians, once they become independent, must be removed from the Bengalese and placed with other Gouldians, with whom they will team up after a short time.

In nest boxes and hollow logs, they will build nests, selecting materials of a dark colour—grasses, roots, moss, and feathers. The young are hatched in 16 days. They have inside their bills typical phosphorescent spots, which enable the parents to find in the dark nest the exact place in which to deposit the food.

Before the breeding season, the cocks and hens take little interest in each other. They will chase one another away from the highest roosting perches but as soon as breeding begins the cock will start to sing his peculiar song, often sitting next to the hen and beginning to dance, at the same time bowing deeply.

The hen will remain passive, although sometimes their bills will touch. This courting is most interesting to watch.

The cock will soon begin to collect and carry blades of grass and other nesting material, after the birds have carefully inspected and chosen a nesting box. Often 6 eggs are laid and hatched and this performance may be repeated four times a year. If the eggs are placed under a Bengalese, a large number of young can be raised, though sometimes disappointments occur.

Rearing food should consist of egg mixture, a meal-worm or two, soaked seed, grass seed, with some grated apple, and much green food, especially chickweed. If the parent birds, before the young are hatched, will not eat egg food it is advisable to let the Bengalese take over the rearing. The young birds need a year or more to attain their full colouring; the actual time depending largely on whether the spring is sunny or not.

The Yellow or Orange-headed is rarer and much more expensive than the normal coloured birds, but treatment should be the same.

These birds need, first and foremost, light and air in order to thrive. They are suitable for the more experienced fanciers, and even they cannot always boast of success. The many unknown factors, however, lend special interest.

Bicheno's Finch (Banded Finch) (Double-bar Finch) (Owl Finch) *Stizoptera bichenovi* Pl. 68

Origin Australia.

4 in. These birds, though fairly rare, are not difficult to breed. Only their white rump feathers distinguish them from Black-ringed Finches. It is difficult to tell *Cock* or *Hen* apart. The hen has narrower black bands, and is smaller

and duller in colour. Both cock and hen are easily frightened, and a sudden shock may cause their death.

They are very lively, something like tits. They need an aviary in which to move about freely, and there they will build a neat little nest in the open, in an abandoned nest, or in a nest box. The nest will be lined with soft materials, wool and feathers, and in it 4–6 eggs will be laid.

As a rearing food, hard-boiled egg and powdered rusks, with a few drops of cod-liver oil and a little honey mixed together, can be given and, if possible, fresh ants' eggs and finely cut-up meal-worms. Much green food and soaked seeds are also needed. The eggs of these finches may also be hatched by the Bengalese, which will raise the young admirably.

A remarkable phenomenon occurs when this bird and the Black-ringed Finch are crossed. All the young will look like Bicheno's Finches, and will have their characteristic white rumps, which are the more striking since black usually supersedes white. When these youngsters are paired among themselves the result will be 25% black and 75% white rumps. Hybrids have been produced by crossing with the Zebra Finch.

Although they can winter in a frost-proof enclosure, they will do much better if kept in a temperature of about 65° F (18° C).

Black-ringed Finch *Stizoptera bichenovi annulosa*

Origin Australia.

4 in. This bird, like Bicheno's Finch from which it can only be distinguished by its black rump feathers, is now rare. It is bred occasionally and by exchange or purchase it is some-

times possible to obtain an unrelated pair.

It needs exactly the same treatment as that for Bicheno's Finch. It is possible to breed from Black-ringed Finches, but considerable care is necessary.

Zebra Finch *Taeniopygia guttata castanotis* Pl. 62, 63, and 64

Origin Australia.

4¼ in. This is the best known Australian finch and is as common and perky as a sparrow. It is readily available almost everywhere. It is quite domesticated and can be obtained in many colours. Entirely white Zebra Finches are most charming, as are also the silver winged, the fawn coloured, the isabel, the pied, and even those whose colouring is pastel blue.

See Appendix A for colour breeding.

This species has been crossed with the Diamond Sparrow, the African Silverbill, and other species.

Star Finch (Ruficauda Rufous-tailed Finch) *Bathilda ruficauda* Pl. 54

Origin Australia.

4½ in. *Hen:* Is recognizable by the less intense red of the chin, forehead, and cheeks. Care should be taken not to mistake for a hen a young bird which has not assumed adult colour.

These Finches are favoured by fanciers. Not only are they peaceable, beautifully coloured, and lively, but they breed freely if they can be kept in a separate enclosure where they are unlikely to be disturbed. A pair may be housed alone in a cage and will produce and rear 2 or 3 broods in a season.

The young—usually 4 of them—are hatched in 13 days, and after another 25 days will leave the nest. A nest box is often used and in it a dome-shaped nest with a narrow entrance is made from rope teasings and grass blades. But if some broom twigs are hung in the outside flight and hay mixed with them, the birds will soon build their nest in the broom and prefer this to a nest box.

Attempts to breed from birds less than a year old usually end in failure, and even when fertile eggs have been laid, rearing of the young seldom succeeds. The eggs are best placed under the African Silverbill or the Bengalese, and a number of young will then be reared.

If the Finch, when 2 years will rear its own young, the results will be better still and 3 families a year will not be exceptional. Cold weather during the laying period may cause egg binding trouble.

On the whole, results with these birds are more satisfactory when pairs are kept separately. They should be kept together in a larger community flight only when not breeding and during winter. They will then have sufficient space in which to take adequate exercise. As soon as the young birds have become independent they should be placed in a large flight where they can learn to use their wings. They will develop well, and in a year will be ready to mate. Naturally, new blood must be provided from time to time; this can be done by buying or by exchange with other breeders.

Crimson Finch (Blood Finch) *Neochmia phaëton*

Origin Australia.

Nearly 5 in. *Cock:* Mostly red, with a brown suffusion, the brightest colour being on the head. Upper parts show a brown suffusion as do also the wings. Under parts black on the abdomen. Fine white spots on the sides of the breast. Bill red, legs grey. *Hen:* Brown-grey on top, band on the forehead, throat and sides of the head red. Belly brown-grey, breast greyer with fine white spots. Wings and tail paler than the cocks.

These birds are scarce and fairly expensive. Although difficult to acclimatize, once over this they will certainly not be found delicate, and can withstand moderately cold weather. Millet, niger seed, and especially millet in the spray, should be given at first. Ripening grass seeds should be hung up in the cage. Crimson Finches are not very suitable to be kept with other birds in an aviary as they are rather aggressive. The cock should even be separated from his own hen when they are not breeding, for he can be aggressive even to her.

These birds belong to the insect-eating foreign finches and will not long survive on a diet of seed only. Kept as a pair in a cage, they will give any amount of pleasure, and will probably begin to breed. Grass blades, hemp, and coconut fibres will serve as nesting material and an open nest box will probably be their choice. Some fine feathers should be supplied with which to line the nest. The 4–5 eggs are hatched in 12 days, the cock and hen each taking turns at incubation. After a further 3 weeks, the youngsters will leave the nest. In addition to germinated seeds, small meal-worms and, if possible, ants' eggs must be given. Once these Crimson Finches have started breeding, they will keep on, and sometimes rear as many as 5 families one after the other.

Painted Finch *Emblema picta* Pl. 65

Origin Australia.

4¼ in. This species is rare and expensive and must be acclimatized carefully, so is more suitable for the experienced fancier. *Cock* and *Hen* can be readily told apart, the scarlet on the head of the hen being very restricted; they are beautiful birds. Once they have settled down they soon lose their timidity, never quarrel with others, and are ready to breed. It is better to keep them on their own, so that they are not disturbed. The young hatch in a fortnight and will leave the nest after 25 days. They must be reared on seed, soaked bread or rusk, hard-boiled egg, fresh ants' eggs and a meal-worm or two. Green food should always be given.

Fire-tailed Finch *Steganopleura bella*

Origin Australia.

4½ in. *Cock* and *Hen* alike. Upper parts brown with narrow black bars; sides of the head, shoulders, and wings lighter brown, also striped in black. Black lores. Rump and upper tail coverts carmine red, under tail coverts and vent black. Under parts grey-brown with faint bars. Eyes brown with a blue orbital ring—bill red, legs flesh-coloured.

Very seldom available. Fanciers have not yet succeeded in keeping them alive for long; not even when they have been fed almost exclusively on insects. Successful breeding in captivity has not yet been recorded. Though these birds originate in Australia, they are also found in Tasmania. Hence changed climate conditions cannot be the reason for the difficulty experienced in acclimatizing them.

Only really experienced fanciers should attempt to keep these beautiful and readily tamed birds, for they need very special care and attention.

Red-eared Firetail *Steganopleura oculatus*

Origin South-West Australia.

4½ in. *Cock* and *Hen* alike. Their name is apt. There is a red spot behind the eye, which is itself enclosed by a blue ring. Back olive coloured; rump, fiery red; breast brown-black with white spots. Rest of plumage covered with fine wavy cross barring (as in the Fire-tailed Finch). Flanks show large white spots on a blackish background. The bird is closely related to the Diamond Sparrow *Steganopleura guttata*. No information so far available as to this species ever having been imported.

These birds live in eucalyptus woods and in boggy places. They are never found in flocks but always in pairs. They are nearly always on the ground grubbing for insects and small snails. Their voice is a complaining 'wee-wee' and by this call it is easy to lure them closer to the observer. They build a very frail nest, practically without lining, of long wiry grasses, usually in a forked branch and more than 10 ft above ground.

Diamond Sparrow *Steganopleura guttata* Pl. 66

Origin Australia.

4½ in. This can be numbered among the more easily bred species, especially as the only stock now obtainable is aviary bred.

If a pair in full colour can be obtained, and can be placed in a bird room or aviary, breeding results will be almost certain. It is, however, difficult to get a true pair; the *Cock* and the *Hen* are exactly alike and only the song of the cock can distinguish them.

Diamond Sparrows are unsuitable for a cage; they need space and room in which to exercise, or they tend to become fat and unfit for breeding. They build a nest in the open or make use of a nest box. They make a substantial domed nest from thick grass blades and fibres which they will line with some soft material, preferably feathers.

The 4–6 eggs will be incubated alternately by hen and cock, and the young are usually reared satisfactorily. Hard-boiled egg mixed with rusk, much green food, fresh ants' eggs, and finely cut-up and preferably boiled meal-worms should be given, as well as soaked bread and seed diet. Minerals are needed, so a good grit mixture should be supplied.

If, in the first year that they breed, these birds refuse to feed their young, place the newly hatched youngsters in the charge of 2 or 3 Bengalese pairs, so that each pair has not more than 2 or 3 young to rear. The young Diamond Sparrows need much more food than many other small birds and a pair of Bengalese will find it difficult to cope with a complete brood of such gluttons. At 4 months, the young exactly resemble the adults and need not be separated, if the flight is large enough, for the birds are peaceable and may even be kept with other kinds of finches during the breeding season. In a small flight the young birds are sometimes chased persistently, and if this happens they must be caught and provided with separate accommodation.

Diamond Sparrows are inclined to breed all the year round, but it is better to allow breeding only in spring, summer, and beginning of autumn. For the winter the pair should be separated and kept apart. With a normal transition from autumn to winter they do not need heated accommodation. If, however, they have been kept in a warm room during the winter, the transition to a room without heat must be gradual; sudden changes in temperature may be fatal.

This species is regrettably still very expensive. Another handicap is the difficulty of determining the sex. Fanciers have sometimes been deceived into thinking that breeding must be difficult, whereas they have actually been keeping as pairs two cocks or two hens!

Three-coloured Parrot Finch *Erythrura trichroa*

Origin New Guinea.

5½ in. A rare bird in the trade. Once it has become acclimatized it is hardy and can be left in the outside flight. It is lively and will be constantly on the move between branches and floor.

Sexes alike. Forehead and cheeks blue, rump and tail scarlet, remainder green.

Diet: Seed, 'universal' food, various insects, quantities of green food, and germinated seeds.

Once these birds start nesting, for which they use a nest box, they will breed well, and are quite capable of rearing their young. Several pairs may be kept in a large aviary. Hybrids with the Red-headed Parrot Finch have occurred frequently, and the off-spring are fertile.

A fancier who is lucky enough to own one or more pairs should make every effort to breed from this rather rare species. Birds bred in this country are not only hardy, but keep their colour well in captivity.

Equally rare, but one of the most rewarding species, is the Red-headed Parrot Finch, *Erythrura psittacea*, which breeds fairly quickly in captivity. Several pairs can be kept together.

Pintailed Nonpareil (Pintailed Parrot Finch) *Erythrura prasina* Pl. 67

Origin India and Indonesia.

5½ in. inc. long tail. This Parrot Finch is less rare but difficult to acclimatize. Fanciers who wish to secure a pair would do well to buy more than one to avoid disappointment. The colouring of the adult cock is gorgeous; one may easily mistake immature cocks for hens. Much care and trouble are needed to rear them successfully, and they are usually found only in the hands of experienced fanciers.

Once settled down, they mix with other finches and eat normal seed diet. They successfully rear their young, requiring for this germinated seeds as well as meal-worms and ants' eggs. When first imported they will eat unpolished rice almost exclusively; later they will take to canary seed.

These birds need plenty of space. Cooped up in a cage they will sit motionless and soon become fat and ill. They are best kept with Long-tailed Finches and Zebra Finches, whose example in feeding they will follow.

During the mating season the cock will dance around the hen flirting his tail up and down, and making most strange noises. The nest is sometimes built in a nest box or may be constructed in a bush or other similar cover. The eggs are incubated by the parents alternately, and the young appear in 13 days.

They may be kept together with other pairs in a large flight, although this may lead to chasing, but never to serious damage. Hybrids with kindred species, including the African Silverbill, have been obtained.

Wild Canary *Serinus canaria* Pl. 69

Origin Canary Islands and Madeira.

5⅛ in. These ancestors of domesticated canaries in their various colours are imported only very rarely.

It is 400 years since the wild canary was first brought to the continent of Europe; it has now conquered the whole world. Its colour variations are unending, and new ones are continually being added.

The song of the wild canary is like that of the domestic bird, but many variations have been developed. *Cock* distinguished from *Hen* by song.

Unless a fancier wants the absolute prototype to produce yet more hybrids, there is little point in importing wild canaries. They do not settle down readily and the best plan is to pair cocks to domestic hens. In size the wild bird is smaller than the domestic. Breeding should be done systematically; the best plan is to concentrate on one or two specified varieties. Pedigrees must be recorded carefully; only the best birds should be retained for breeding stock, and the pairs should be selected. Sound advice from experienced fanciers is valuable.

Hybrids of canaries with the Green Singing Finch, the Grey Singing Finch, the Black-headed and Hooded Siskins, common Saffron Finch, British Siskin, the Pileated Finch, and the Red-crested Finch have all been successfully bred. More difficult and rare are crossings with the Linnet, Goldfinch, Greenfinch, Chaffinch, Twite or Mountain Linnet, Yellow Hammer, and Brambling. With care and patience many other experimental crosses will no doubt prove successful.

Green Singing Finch *Serinus mozambicus* Pl. 71

Origin Central Africa.

5⅛ in. This graceful little bird, lively and with beautiful colouring, can be kept with small finches in a cage or aviary. The song of the cock is delightful to hear; it is often kept alone and sings incessantly. The *Hen* can be recognized by the necklace of dark spots on the throat, the *Cock*'s throat being clear yellow. Their flight is silent and butterfly-like.

Unlike many finches they do not huddle together during the day, although they will readily share a communal roosting perch high up in the aviary at night.

Kept by themselves in a cage, a pair will make a nest in an open-fronted nest box. As material they like fine woollen threads and hemp teasings. They sometimes build an open nest in the flight, high up in a tree or shrub. The hen alone will construct the nest and incubate the eggs, while the cock sings diligently near the nesting site, and later close to the sitting hen. The eggs hatch in 13 days, and after another 3 weeks the young will leave the nest. For weeks afterwards they will still be fed by the cock. When they become independent they must be separated from the parents who will probably have already started on a new brood and no longer tolerate them in the same cage. Immediately after the breeding season the pairs break up and remain apart until next season.

The Green Singing Finch is closely related to the Canary and hybrids are easily obtained when a cock is mated with a small canary hen. The young should be fed with canary rearing food or with bread soaked in egg yolk.

Frequently after their arrival, they suffer from inflamed eyelids. They appear to become very shortsighted and often cannot find their feed boxes, especially if these are placed only in the shelter. If the birds are allowed to remain outside at night, they may take a long time to find their way into the shelter and lack of food will quickly cause their death, so food must also be supplied in the open flight where it can readily be seen.

Their breeding season in Africa is from September to January, so they breed more readily in a cage or indoor aviary where an even and reasonably warm temperature can be maintained.

Diet: Mainly seed-eaters, but during the breeding season they also eat many insects, finely chopped meal-worms, egg food, and ants' eggs. They are partial to sprouted grain and grass seed, which they like to extract from the ear, also plenty of green food. They can be wintered outside.

Grey Singing Finch *Serinus leucopygius* Pl. 72

Origin Senegal Gambia to Sudan.

5⅓ in. The dull grey of this little Finch is fully compensated for by its extraordinary singing qualities. As the sexes are alike it is advisable to segregate these birds so that they may be studied individually to determine which are cocks and which hens. A cock kept by himself will sing practically the whole year through, stopping only while moulting. Although at first sight insignificant, they will soon win the fancier's heart by their liveliness, dainty butterfly-like flight, and song. They can be quickly tamed, are always cheerful, and can withstand most vicissitudes

of climate, including really cold weather. They are mainly seed-eaters, but during the breeding season like to be provided with an extra diet similar to that given to the Green Singing Finch. They agree with most birds, except their own kind and their own young, which are soon chased away when independent.

A pair will usually settle down to nesting fairly quickly high up in the flight. In a nest box they will build a home which is a work of art and this they defend fiercely against all comers. The hen does the work, and the cock sings and feeds her by regurgitation. He also feeds her during the fortnight incubation period. After leaving the nest the young are still fed for a considerable time by the cock. They are well able to winter in an outside flight.

Hybridizing with various species has proved successful—with the Canary, Green Singing Finch, and Yellow-rumped Serin. Grey Singing Finches make few demands and can easily be kept in a cage where they will soon begin to breed.

When first imported these birds often suffer from inflammation of the eyes owing to contamination from dirty perches in transit. The feathers around the eye will be found to be sticky. Punctilious cleanliness and fresh bathing water will soon remedy matters.

Hens sometimes suffer from egg binding but a few drops of cod-liver oil on the seed will soon cure the trouble, and it is always advisable to supply plenty of vitaminized lime.

Yellow-rumped Serin *Serinus angolensis*

Origin Tropical Africa.

5⅔ in. The main difference between this bird and the Grey Singing Finch is the pattern of the colouring. The Yellow-rumped Serin has a distinct necklace, like the hen of the Green Singing Finch. This and its larger size make recognition easy, for the gorgeous deep lemon yellow on the rump is usually concealed by the folded wings. It is all the more surprising to see it flash into view when the bird flies and this gives an added charm to the species.

One of the most attractive of the foreign singing finches. Yet its simple grey feathering discourages many fanciers from buying it, also the difficulty in distinguishing the sex, which can only be determined by hearing the cock sing.

Saint Helena Seed-eater *Serinus flaviventris*

Origin Cape Colony.

5½ in. *Cock:* Upper parts olive green, head and back striated with black. Forehead band and eyebrow stripe yellow, ear coverts yellow green. Under parts and part of the cheeks yellow, with olive green moustacheal stripe. Wings black with yellow margins. Eyes brown. Upper mandible dark, lower mandible light horn-coloured, legs black. *Hen:* Upper parts grey-brown, striated with black, rump greenish-yellow, forehead and eyebrow stripe dull white, cheeks and under parts white, breast and sides brownish, black markings on the flanks. Wings with yellow and white margins.

These birds are not imported regularly, but sometimes appear in mixed consignments. Their song is rather like that of the lark. Hybrids between the St. Helena Seed-eater and a Canary have produced very good song birds. The cocks, often offered singly, are exceptionally melodious songsters.

These finches have been bred frequently in an aviary. They make cup-shaped nests like that of the Canary in a dense shrubbery, near the ground, or they may choose a nest box in which to build, using woollen threads, fine twigs, grass blades, fibres, and hairs: 4–5 eggs form the clutch and incubation lasts 13 days. During rearing period, canary rearing food or egg food with rusks should be given, as well as germinated seed and a quantity of green food. The birds will eat greedily and sometimes like finely cut-up meal-worms. Ants' eggs are always acceptable.

Diet: Ordinary canary seed mixture, to which some hemp has been added.

The birds can stay in the outside aviary throughout the year if provided with an adequately protected shelter.

Cape Canary *Serinus canicollis* Pl. 70

Origin Cape Colony.

5½ in. *Cock:* Forehead and crown yellow, neck olive grey to grey, back and rump olive yellow, striped except on rump with dusky grey. Ear coverts grey, lores black, cheeks brownish yellow, breast yellow, merging into white on the belly; under tail coverts yellow. Wings black with yellow, tail brown-yellow, bill grey horn-coloured, eyes brown, legs horn-coloured. *Hen:* Chin to chest greyish and usually more distinctly striped on upper parts. Young birds heavily streaked brown and black above, buff and black below.

These birds are often delicate on arrival but soon become strong and are very suitable for an aviary containing a mixed collection of small seed-eaters. They are active and cheerful and the cock has a delightful song.

Diet: Normal canary mixture, weed seeds, green food, and occasionally live insects. They appreciate insectivorous food or a little soaked canary rearing

H

food especially when breeding or rearing the young, when egg food mixed with rusk crumbs may be given.

Hybrids with the ordinary canary have been produced, but no details are available.

During cold weather, keep in a fair-sized cage or indoor aviary where heat can be provided.

Alario Finch *Alerio alerio* Pl. 50

Origin South Africa.

4½ in. *Cock:* Head and neck black, wide black bands along the flanks. Upper parts red-brown, under parts white. Wing coverts red-brown and the remainder of the wings black. Tail red-brown, eyes brown, legs black, bill horn-coloured, under mandible lighter. *Hen:* Grey-brown, dark striations on the red-brown upper parts. Stripes above and below the eyes white. Back slightly lighter. Under parts dull buff-white. Tail red-brown with centre of each feather dark, almost black.

Not regularly available, though the prices asked are moderate. When imported, usually offered as pairs.

The cock has a soft, pleasant song and sings all the year round. These birds may be kept with others especially Weavers. If in a cage, special care should be taken not to let them get too fat.

Diet: White and brown millet, millet in the spray, and canary seed. They do not care for green food.

A cock kept with a canary hen will generally accept her as mate, and hybrids have been reared. I have no details available of breeding Alario Finches in captivity, but it would be advisable to give the birds a small, quiet aviary, where they can remain undisturbed, and when feeding young a liberal supply of insects would be essential. A thick shrub should be provided in which they could build, and also a nest box. Delacour reports the breeding of these birds but gives no details.

The Alario Finch, kept together with other good song birds, will imitate their notes quite well, but in doing so may forget his own.

Golden Sparrow (Arabian Golden Sparrow) *Auripasser luteus euchlorus*

Origin Southern Arabia.

5 in. *Cock:* In breeding plumage has yellow mantle, uniform with the head and rump. The flight feathers are blackish, edged with white; central tail feathers black edged with white, outer feathers white with black at the tips and on inner webs. Whole of body feathers bright golden yellow. Bill black. Out of the breeding season upper side becomes more brownish grey and bill is horn-coloured. *Hen:* Yellowish grey above with pale yellow breast fading to white on belly. It is a good size and better kept in a flight with other larger birds. It is seldom imported.

It is bold and restless, and in a well-planted flight may spend much of its time hidden in the thick undergrowth. It does not breed freely, and builds a slovenly looking nest in a nest box, where the hen alone will incubate. The young are reared mainly on insects, small caterpillars, small beetles, and meal-worms. Green food, seeds, especially germinated seeds, are also part of their diet.

These birds are hardy and well able to winter in an outside flight.

Yellow Sparrow (Sudan Golden Sparrow) *Auripasser l. luteus* Pl. 73

Origin East Africa.

5 in. *Cock:* Whole head and under parts canary yellow; mantle and edges

of inner secondaries chestnut; wings dark brown to blackish, with chestnut edging; a white bar across secondaries; rump yellowish. Bill black in breeding season, horn-coloured for remainder of year. *Hen:* Head, mantle, and rump buffish-brown with a few black or dark brown streaks on the mantle; flights and tail dusky brown with lighter edges; the white bar on secondaries less conspicuous; below buff washed with yellow. Bill horn-coloured.

Immature birds similar to adult hen but whiter below. Treatment as for Golden Sparrow. Their nest is larger and domed with an entrance at the side. All kinds of material are used and it is lined with soft down and feathers. Hybrids of both species with the House Sparrow have been bred.

The Yellow Sparrow is hardy and can winter in an outside flight.

Mexican Rose Finch *Carpodacus mexicanus*

Origin Mexico.

4¾ in. *Cock:* Front of head, neck, and rump carmine red, remainder of upper parts brown with dark markings, under parts white, striated brown. A reddy-pink gloss on breast. Bill and legs dark horn-coloured. *Hen:* Like cock but lacking the carmine red.

Useful as cage birds, they are more in their element in the aviary. Unfortunately they do not regain their carmine red colouring after moulting in captivity, but turn a yellowish brown. In behaviour they resemble the linnet. They commence nesting in June, building in the open or in a nest box, and the nest is constructed of plant fibres, lined with hairs. The hen alone incubates and the eggs, usually 4 in number, hatch in 13 days. She feeds the young by herself for the first few days, giving them ants' eggs at first, and then canary rearing food. The parents must be left in peace during breeding season or they will abandon their nest. They sing pleasantly, and enjoy bathing frequently.

Diet: Canary seed mixtures, insectivorous food, various berries, live insects.

Frequent breeding successes reported, as well as crossings with canaries and linnets. These finches may winter out of doors if a good night shelter is available.

Indian Rose Finch *Carpodacus erythrinus* Pl. 78

Origin Northern Europe and Siberia, wintering in India and Burma.

6 in. *Cock:* Prevailing colour crimson, most brilliant on head, hinder parts of the rump, throat, and breast; upper back, mantle, and wing coverts with dusky centres; remaining wing feathers and tail dark brown with rosy margins; abdomen bright rose fading to buff-white on the under tail coverts; beak and feet horn-brown. *Hen:* Generally brown, darker on the crown, nape, wings, tail, and throat; back and rump slightly olivaceous.

In common with other species of Rose Finches, the beautiful rose colour of the cock usually fades in captivity and is seldom fully recovered after the moult, when it becomes dull brown.

Diet: Chiefly a seed-eater but also fond of flower buds of fruit trees and hawthorns, of young leaves and other green food, also berries. In spring it eats insects and no doubt the young are partly fed on live food. Feed on a similar diet to other finches of its size and when nesting supply with various insects and with bread and milk or a canary rearing food.

The nest is placed fairly low down, in climbing plants or small bushes, and is composed of dry grasses lined with hair and fine rootlets. The eggs, 4–6 in number, are pale blue, spotted with black and light red.

Once acclimatized, it is hardy and may be wintered in an outdoor aviary.

Purple Finch *Carpodacus purpureus*

Origin United States of America.

5½ in. *Cock:* Crown and rump carmine red, remainder of the upper parts including head, neck, flanks, and upper breast red-brown. Lores paler. Belly and under tail coverts white. Bill horn-coloured, legs flesh-coloured. *Hen:* Upper parts olive brown with light markings, olive and green stripe on the ear coverts and along the throat. Under parts white with olive green striations on the breast and flanks. Wings and tail grey-brown with olive brown margins.

Imported frequently, they are offered at moderate prices, though only cocks are available as a rule. Their song is soft, but slightly complaining, and monotonous. The head and throat feathers are usually raised when the birds are singing. Treatment exactly as the Rose Finches; their behaviour is similar.

They are peaceable with other birds in a large space and can remain in the same aviary during the winter. As so few hens are imported, it might be of interest to attempt a crossing with a Canary hen.

Saffron Finch *Sycalis flaveola* Pl. 74

Origin Brazil, Venezuela.

5¾ in. *Cock:* Forehead and crown bright orange, sides of head yellow. Upper parts greenish yellow with indistinct dusky streaks. Under parts clear yellow. *Hen:* Duller than cock, orange on crown less pronounced. Upper parts more brownish grey and with grey throat. *Young:* Grey-brown above with olive wash and blackish streaks. Under parts grey-white with undertail coverts and thighs yellow. Towards the end of their first year they develop a yellow band across the throat and chest.

These commonly imported birds are one of the most attractive species for flight or large cage. In the former they will soon start breeding and are not aggressive towards other birds: 2 or 3 broods per season are not exceptional. The Saffron Finch can easily be crossed with a Canary hen and the colour of the hybrids is beautiful. It is rather larger than a Canary and very active. Cocks are often kept singly as song birds, because they have a clear, sweet voice.

For breeding, a nest box must be provided in which the pair will build an untidy nest from any materials available. Incubation lasts a fortnight and the young require ants' eggs, rusk crumbs mixed with egg yolk, soaked or germinated seeds, and a variety of green food, in addition to normal seed diet. It is a year before the young birds begin to assume adult plumage and cocks take 3 years to attain their full colouring.

Pelzelni's Saffron Finch *Sycalis flaveola pelzelni*

Origin Argentine, South Brazil.

5½ in. *Cock:* Upper parts olive-green streaked with black. Lower back and rump greyish. Forehead deep orange-yellow. Remainder entirely yellow; sides, paler with dark markings. Wings dark brown with yellow margins. Eyes brown, bill horn-coloured, legs brown-yellow. *Hen:* Smaller, upper parts brown-yellow, throat white, abdomen grey-white with a yellow glow and brown markings on flanks.

Only occasionally imported. Care and feeding the same as for Saffron Finch.

Diet: Canary seed and all kinds of millet, insects, much green food. They sometimes take insectivorous food, and are fond of ripening grass seeds, which it is advisable to supply during breeding time. For nesting they use nest boxes and abandoned nests of other birds. The nest will be lined with wool and hair. Incubation takes 14 days.

Saffron Finches are hardy, tolerant of other birds, and will breed in a large cage and in the aviary. Crossings have taken place with canaries and kindred varieties.

Song Sparrow (Rufous-collared Sparrow) *Zonotrichia capensis*

Origin Central and South America.

5½ in. *Cock* and *Hen* practically alike. Crown grey with black dividing lines. Grey eyebrow stripe, black ear coverts with white markings. Chestnut-brown neck; back and shoulders brown, streaked with black, remainder of upper part brown, under parts white-grey. Wings brown with grey markings, tail brown, bill brown, legs dark flesh-coloured. Hen is a little larger than cock.

These birds are on sale regularly at low prices, and are suitable for cage or aviary because of their very peaceable nature. Their song is pleasant and can be heard often at night.

Diet: Insectivorous food and a seed mixture, in which oats, hemp, and canary seed is included, a quantity of green food and berries.

Neither breeding results nor crossings have yet been recorded.

Black-headed Siskin *Spinus ictericus*
Pl. 75

Origin South America.

Nearly 5 in. *Cock:* Black head, neck, and throat. Rump, upper tail coverts, and whole of the under part yellow, wings and tail black with green-yellow and white margins, remainder of upper parts striated greenish yellow. Bill black, legs brown. *Hen:* Head and upper parts olive grey, under parts grey, belly white. Tail black-brown.

Usually only cocks are imported but sometimes a pair may be obtained. Few fanciers choose them, their high price and rather dull colouring being against them, but they are sometimes purchased specially for crossing with the Canary, English Siskin, or Goldfinch. They need to be carefully acclimatized to new surroundings.

Diet: Is most important and they require extra warmth and fresh bath water always. Canary seed and millet, green seeds, maw, rape, niger, and linseed should be given, also some weed seeds, aphis, and other insects.

Their song is reminiscent of the Goldfinch. Their nest is cup-shaped and lined with wool and feathers. Their 4–5 eggs take 13 days to hatch. The birds are very active and like to clamber about high up in the aviary where they will hang from branches and from wire netting. It is advisable to cover the top with glass or plastic to protect them from cats and other predators. A branch can be suspended underneath this covering so that the birds cannot damage their tails on the wire when giving an exhibition of their trapeze acts.

A large cage in which natural branches have been fixed in water, and keep fresh for a considerable time is also suitable as breeding accommodation, but care should be taken to ensure that the top of the water container is covered or the birds may get in and be drowned.

Keep in a warm room during winter.

Yarrell's Siskin *Spinus yarrelli*

Origin Brazil.

4 in. *Cock:* Crown and neck black, back olive green, and the remainder of the body feathers yellow. Wings black and yellow. Tail black, legs and bill flesh-coloured. *Hen:* No black on head, upper parts have more olive yellow, tail and wings brown.

Infrequently imported; they often arrive in a very weak state and need much care and plenty of insect food to become acclimatized. Treatment and diet similar to that of the Black-headed Siskin. Both species enjoy quantities of aphis.

Breeding results have not yet been reported, but with careful treatment should be possible. Only small hen canaries would be of any use if it is intended to attempt hybrid breeding.

Yarrell's Siskin should be kept in a sunny well-planted aviary during the summer, when it should breed successfully; it needs a warm room in winter.

Mexican Siskin *Spinus mexicanus*

Origin South America.

4½ in. *Cock:* Head, cheeks, an dupper parts black, white markings on wings; remainder clear yellow. *Hen* less colourful. In a communal flight these are peaceable and tolerant. A pair usually become much attached to each other, and are worth keeping for their happy and affectionate disposition.

They breed fairly readily. The cock pursues the hen rather persistently, but will interrupt the chase with a pleasant song, something like the Goldfinch's, although more powerful. Cock and hen will join in building their cup-shaped nest high up in the branches of a dense shrubbery. It is constructed of hemp teasings, blades of grass, and mosses, and lined with fibres. The outside is reinforced with bits of bark and roots. During breeding season they are very pugnacious, and more suitable for a large cage, in which they can live alone, and will breed successfully.

Diet: Mainly seed, particularly weed seeds. Rusks mixed with hard-boiled egg and fresh ants' eggs serve as rearing food for the young.

If possible they should winter in a well sheltered outside aviary.

Hooded Siskin *Spinus cucullatus* Pl. 76

Origin South America.

4–4½ in. Imported chiefly for crossing with the Canary to obtain the greatly sought after 'red factor'. To effect this crossing the Hooded Siskin cock should be introduced to a Canary hen of medium size. At first the birds must be kept apart in a cage with a wire partition. When they begin to show an interest in each other the partition can be removed and the pair allowed together. Young cocks resulting from this cross will be a beautiful red-brown and the hens will closely resemble the Siskin hen.

These lively birds will clamber up and down in the shrubbery and both *Cock* and *Hen* will sing constantly. Ideal occupants of a communal flight. *Hen:* Mainly grey on upper parts with wash of vermilion on back and bright vermilion on rump. Under parts orange-red with some white.

The birds are always together during the breeding season; the cock will follow the hen about and feed her. The hen alone incubates the eggs in the cup-shaped nest built either in a nest box, or in the open and constructed of grass blades, hemp teasings, and woollen threads. She also feeds her young unaided until they leave the nest, when the cock takes over. During rearing period canary rearing food, on which the young thrive, may be given; fresh ants' eggs, and hard-boiled egg and a little green food will complete the diet.

The birds must spend the winter indoors, preferably in a moderately heated room.

American Goldfinch (American Siskin) *Spinus tristis*

Origin North America.

4½ in. *Cock:* Crown, wings, and tail black, remainder lemon yellow, bill and legs brown-yellow. *Hen:* Crown olive green. Upper parts brown-yellow and under parts yellow. Cock loses the deep yellow during winter months and also the black on his crown, so that he then resembles the hen. Legs brown.

Birds of this species are seldom imported. They need the same treatment as Black-headed Siskin. No breeding results are available, but crossings with canaries have been reported.

Their song resembles that of the English Goldfinch, to which they are somewhat similar, although they are a true Siskin.

Black-headed Bunting *Emberiza melanocephala*

Origin India.

7½ in. *Cock:* Upper parts chestnut brown and grey with lighter margins and dark striations. Crown and sides of head black, wings blackish. Rump yellow, under parts bright yellow. The cock sings pleasingly. *Hen:* Head dusky brown, breast pale yellow fading to almost white on the belly and without

any striations on the flanks. Under tail coverts bright yellow.

The Black-headed Bunting will breed in a well-planted aviary, provided that insectivorous food in addition to seed is supplied. A cup-shaped nest is built in a thick shrubbery and incubation of the 4–5 green-blue eggs with brown spots, takes 13 days. The young are fed mainly on ants' eggs, meal-worms, and other insects.

One of the hardiest species and can winter in an outdoor aviary provided with a frost-proof shelter at night. It enjoys chickweed, aphis, and spiders, and other small insects.

It will not molest other occupants of the aviary, especially of its own size; but it may be desirable to provide a second feeding table to prevent fights.

Red-headed Bunting (Brown-headed Bunting) *Emberiza m. bruniceps*

Origin India or Persia.

7½ in. *Cock:* Olive brown on upper parts, head, and throat; breast and belly yellow with a brown sheen. Rump yellow, wings and tail coverts have lighter margins. Song is insignificant. *Hen:* Paler in colour, upper parts brown-grey with dark striations, dull yellow-white under parts. Treatment as Black-headed Bunting.

Crested Bunting *Melophus lathami* (*melanicterus*) Pl. 77

Origin India, China.

6½ in. *Cock:* Glossy blue-black, tail coverts cinnamon at base; wings and tail dark cinnamon with dusky tips; beak blackish with flesh colour at base of lower mandible; feet pinkish-brown; eyes dark brown. Prominent pointed black crest. *Hen:* Dusky brown above, feathers with paler edges; wings and tail paler cinnamon than cock. Lores and round eyes whitish; cheeks ashy; throat yellowish white; under parts dull brown with black streaks; under tail coverts reddish with black streaks. Crest less developed than in cock.

Rarely imported but make interesting aviary birds. Cock has a cheerful song. More suitable for well-planted aviary than cage; some protection in winter.

Cinnamon-breasted Rock Bunting
Fringillaria tahapisi

Origin North, East, and West Africa.

4½ in. *Cock:* Upper parts cinnamon coloured striated with dark brown, wings rust coloured and brown-black, head and throat black. White stripes above and below eye. Under parts cinnamon coloured. *Hen:* Browner and duller in colouring.

Although on the market from time to time, they are not in great demand. Their colouring is dull and their song of little consequence, yet they have an appeal of their own. They are sprightly, keep well in view in the aviary among the topmost branches, and have a floating, butterfly flight. They also walk and hop about on the floor of the cage or aviary, hunting for food. They are normally peaceable but sometimes turn aggressive during breeding season. The nest is sometimes built in a nest box, or in a basket placed high up. Outside is constructed with moss and grasses and inside lined with hair and woollen threads. The 4 eggs take 12 days to hatch.

Diet: Canary mixture, oats, millet and hemp, a little insectivorous food, fresh and dried ants' eggs. When feeding the young, canary rearing food and a mixture of hard-boiled egg and rusks should also be given. Germinating grass seeds and other grain and

plenty of weed seed with green food can be offered as variety. These birds enjoy bathing. To keep them in first-class condition, they should be supplied with a bowl of river sand and fresh garden soil.

Indigo Bunting *Passerina cyanea* Pl. 79
Origin America.

5 in. If possible these should be obtained April or May, when the cocks are in beautiful blue plumage and can be picked out from the dull brown hens. After September the cocks change colour, quickly becoming similar to the hens, and it is hard to select a true pair. As these birds are so popular both for their colouring and song they are always in great demand and the supply is limited.

Diet: 'Universal' food, quantities of ants' eggs and meal-worms, green food and fresh leaf buds. Germinated seeds are welcome and essential during breeding season, in addition to a normal seed mixture.

To ensure that the full beauty of the cock's colour is retained as long as possible, liberal supplies of insect food, such as meal-worms, ants' eggs, live insects such as locusts and beetles, fresh fruit—berries and cherries, apples and pears—must be provided. Without these the cocks lose much of their brilliance.

It is not at all easy to breed this species. The birds will nest in a well-planted aviary and may use a box placed not too high up above the ground or build a nest low down in thick shrubbery. The nest is constructed of blades of grass, hemp fibres, and roots.

The cock is aggressive during breeding and it is advisable to keep them with larger species. In the evening and at night he will sing his clear melodious song. Indigo Buntings are migratory and about October they are apt to become very restless.

When first imported, the birds will be found delicate and need special attention and care. But they will grow tougher and can winter in a room kept free from frost. House in the flight with only one pair with other birds, for the cocks always fight those of their own species.

An Indigo Bunting hen can be crossed with a Mexican Nonpareil Bunting cock, but fertility is uncertain. It is doubtful whether hybrids have ever been obtained by crossing with canaries since there is no relationship between the two species.

Lazuli Bunting *Passerina amoena* Pl. 80

Origin Eastern America and Mexico.

4¾ in. *Cock:* Head and rump bright blue, remainder of upper parts bluish grey. Wings slate grey with whitish bar and greater coverts tipped with white. Throat and sides of breast bright blue, upper breast pale, warm brown, rest of under parts white. Beak bluish black; feet black. *Hen:* Mainly dull brown with a blue wash on crown, wings, and tail. Under parts pale buff-brown.

Treat as Indigo Bunting; its song is similar and can be heard throughout the summer.

Little is known of its breeding in captivity, only one case having been recorded, in France. In their natural surroundings the nests of these birds are found about 3 ft above ground in thick shrubbery, made of grass, lined with soft hairs and fibres. Given a large flight with thickly planted shrubs and the richly varied diet prescribed for Indigo Bunting, breeding success should be possible. Meal-worms and grubs must be given as well as canary seed and millet. Good dry accommodation essential, free from frost.

Nonpareil Bunting *Passerina ciris* Pl. 83

Origin Central America.

5 in. *Cock:* Head and shoulders blue, throat and under parts red. Tail, wings and back green. *Hen* has no blue on head and the red is replaced by dull yellow.

Purchase these birds in spring so that the cock can be chosen when in full colour. The young cocks exactly resemble the hens and may be sold for them by mistake as there are only very few hens in each consignment. The birds with the whitest throats and necks are most likely to be the hens.

Although cocks are mostly kept singly for their beautiful colour, I would strongly recommend breeding. Of all species of finches the Nonpareil Bunting is by far the best breeder; sometimes even 3 broods a year are reared. It will soon become tame and remain steady during breeding period. It has often been successfully crossed with the Indigo Bunting.

The young should be fed almost entirely on insects; ants' eggs, flies, grasshoppers, and spiders must be mixed with the 'Universal' food and hard-boiled egg added. Small meal-worms should also be given.

The nest is built in a well-branched shrub, or sometimes in a nest box, in which an artificial nest has been placed. Blades of grass, rope teasings, strips of paper, and moss will be used. The cup is lined with very soft materials. The hen alone will incubate and the eggs hatch in 13 days; the chicks will leave the nest after another 10 days and will be fed by both parents, although the hen will sometimes begin a fresh nest and leave the rearing to the cock.

During the migration period the birds become restless in the evening and at night. They sing very little.

Rainbow Bunting *Passerina leclancheri*
Pl. 81 and 82

Origin America.

5 in. *Cock:* Sky blue above with greenish tinge on mantle. Crown and tail bluish green. Ear-coverts and sides of neck cobalt. Cheeks and underparts bright orange-yellow. *Hen:* Olive green, more yellowish on under parts and with bluish wash on tail.

Much rarer than the Nonpareil and less frequently available. Hens seldom obtainable. In its requirements it closely resembles the preceding species but successful breeding in captivity has not been recorded.

The Rainbow Bunting quickly becomes tame. Its song is soft but melodious and it can very well be kept with other birds in a well-planted outside flight in summer and in a bird room, free from frost, in winter. If given a well-varied diet, it will retain its beautiful pastel coloured plumage after the moult.

This species has one disadvantage. The birds hide in the bushes and rarely show themselves except at the feeding table and occasionally in the grass. Lack of breeding results is probably due to incorrect feeding. Seeds must be regarded as auxiliary food only; live insects and 'Universal' food should form the main diet.

Versicolor Bunting *Passerina versicolor*
Pl. 84

Origin Central America.

4¾ in. *Cock:* Purplish above, back of crown and ring round the eyes scarlet.

Throat purplish, under parts purplish blue and grey. *Hen:* Dull brown, paler on under parts. Flights and tail washed with dull blue; wing coverts edged with pale buff.

A rarely imported bird, seldom known to breed in Europe. Treatment as for other buntings. It must be wintered in a warm bird room.

Diuca Finch *Diuca diuca*

Origin Chile.

7 in. *Cock:* Upper parts grey, black lores, cheeks and throat white, breast and sides light grey, belly white with chestnut spot. Under tail coverts are white with chestnut margins. Wings grey and grey-black. Tail black. Eyes brown, bill black, legs grey. *Hen:* Resembles cock, but is brown with less decisive markings.

These birds have soft voices and will chirrup and chatter. They are seldom offered in pairs and usually only cocks are available. They are simple but charming birds, which soon grow tame and quiet in a cage.

Like the common sparrow, this species of finch will eat anything and everything, and it resembles the sparrow in many other respects. It will breed readily in an aviary or bird room, provided plenty of live food is available for the young. The cup-shaped nest is composed of twigs, blades of grass rootlets, hemp teasings, and feathers and usually built in a nest-box: 3–4 green eggs with brown or blue spots are laid and hatch in 13 days. Both cock and hen feed their young with insects, meal-worms and ants' eggs, small caterpillars, gentles, and egg food. Unless insects are available, however, the parents will not attempt to feed the youngsters. After 16 days the young will leave the nest but they have to be fed for another 10 days by the parents, after which they become completely independent.

Diet: 'Nightingale' food, live insects, much green food, some bread and milk, canary seed, millet, grass and weed seeds, and various fruit should be given as well as titbits, such as mealworms.

Pileated Finch *Coryphospingus pileatus*

Origin South America.

5⅔ in. *Cock:* Grey above, washed grey parts, carmine crest with black edges. *Hen:* Has no crest and is bluish grey above.

Very suitable for a cage or flight as it can be easily tamed. It is lively and not difficult to breed. Best results are obtained in a cage where the pair are on their own or in a small aviary planted with dwarf pines or conifers where, in peaceful surroundings, the nest will be built of thin grass blades, jute threads, and all kinds of teasings and cotton. The hen will build the nest by herself and she will incubate alone. In a communal flight both cock and hen would be aggressive when nesting.

Diet: Seeds, crushed hemp, rape, and a mixture of weed seeds. 'Universal' food, a few meal-worms daily, and egg food are needed to rear the young, together with the usual green food.

These birds can winter in a frost-proof shelter. The hen is imported more rarely than the cock; the latter has a conspicuous red crest which he raises when excited.

Red-crested Finch *Coryphospingus cucullatus*

Origin South America.

5⅔ in. *Cock:* Reddish-brown above, under parts vinous, rump red, tail brown. Carmine crest with black edges. *Hen:* Has no crest, brown above, under parts bright vinous.

Although not very frequently imported, this is very popular because of its brilliant colouring. The cock is used by new-coloured canary fanciers, who cross it with a canary hen. Whether the eventual result will be a red canary is doubtful, although the red is deeper than that of the Hooded Siskin, and the yellow pigment is missing.

Treatment as for the Pileated Finch, but not quite so much food should be given, as it fattens quickly. These birds are best kept in an outside flight with plenty of room for flying. They are peaceable and good breeding results have been obtained.

Black-crested Finch (Pigmy Cardinal) *Lophospingus pusillus* Pl. 86

Origin Bolivia, Argentine, Paraguay.

Nearly 5 in. *Cock:* Grey and white with a black line through eye. Black crown and prominent black crest, and a black spot on throat. *Hen:* Like the cock only without the spot on the throat, and with a dull grey crest.

Only irregularly imported during the last few years.

Diet: Canary seed, millet, some insectivorous food, bread and milk, occasionally ants' eggs and mealworms.

For successful breeding, keep a pair separately in a small aviary. They will make a cup-shaped nest in a canary nest bowl with soft hair and small feathers, or more frequently construct a flimsy nest of twigs and rootlets lined with finer materials on some twiggy branch close to the main stem of a shrub or pine tree. The hen will lay 2–3 greeny-grey eggs, which take 12 days to hatch and the young fly after another 12 days.

Bread and milk and egg food are disdained during the rearing period and insects, especially ants' eggs, form the sole food of the young while in the nest. After they fly the cock alone feeds the young, with any kind of food available, until they become entirely independent, usually about 3 weeks after birth.

When the parents show signs of wishing to start a new nest, remove the first family as soon as possible, or they may be plucked and the feathers used to line the new nest. The young are very much like the hen in colour, but they may be a shade paler. After 5 months the moult is completed, and the difference between cock and hen is clearly visible.

If these birds are to be kept with others it is wise to choose larger birds such as Budgerigars, Weavers, Cut-throats, and similar species as companions.

Virginian Cardinal (Scarlet Cardinal) (Virginian Nightingale) *Richmondena cardinalis* Pl. 89

Origin United States of America.

8–9 in. This bird has in common with other species of Cardinal only its name, which refers to its red plumage. It is one of the most beautiful of its kind and has been successfully bred on a number of occasions.

The *Hen* is brown, with a touch of red on the head. The great difference in colour of the sexes makes it easy to select a true pair. These birds, which are fairly large, must be given an enclosure to themselves if nesting is desired, otherwise there will be continual fighting. The hen builds a nest of grasses and hemp teasings, in a shrub or conifer: 2 or 3 blue-green eggs will be laid and will hatch in 13 days and then both parents will feed the young. The

development of the fledglings is extremely rapid; they will fly after 10 days when they are barely covered with feathers. For rearing they need, almost exclusively, live food, meal-worms, chopped earthworms, fresh ants' eggs, and other insects, such as locusts. Biscuit meal, toast, or rusk crumbs with hard-boiled egg and grated carrots and apples, should be included in the diet. Lack of live food has resulted in the death of many broods. As 2 or 3 broods may be produced in a season it is wise to remove the young birds from the flight as soon as they have grown independent—probably about 2 weeks after they have left the nest.

Normal diet: Besides regular seed, should include sunflower seed and hemp seed, but the latter should be given sparingly, as a captive bird soon gets very fat, becomes lazy, and ceases to sing. These cardinals are best kept in a large flight, not a cage. Their liveliness, the 'flirting' of their tails, and their obvious interest in all that goes on, make them a constant pleasure to watch. Though apt to be retiring at first, they soon recognize their owner and grow adept at catching meal-worms thrown to them.

The nick-name 'Virginian Nightingale', is apt to arouse too great expectations of the birds' singing abilities. The song is certainly melodious and loud and can be heard for hours on a moonlight night, but it does not attain to the variety and richness of sound of the Nightingale. The hen also sings during the breeding season.

Green Cardinal *Gubernatrix cristata* Pl. 93

Origin Brazil and Paraguay.

7–7½ in. *Cock:* Upper parts olive green streaked with dusky black; tail bright yellow with the two centre feathers blackish. Crest, chin, and throat velvety-black; a broad streak over the eyes, and the sides of the throat bright golden yellow; breast greenish yellow, belly and under tail coverts bright yellow. *Hen:* The streak over the eye is pure white as are the sides of throat; breast brownish-grey, and the yellow colouring less vivid. Eyes in both sexes very dark, almost black, and legs are dark grey.

Good breeding birds. In a bird room or aviary they soon begin to nest. It is better for breeding to keep a pair by themselves, otherwise care must be taken to ensure that the other birds in the flight can stand up for themselves, for during breeding season Green Cardinals can be pugnacious. When not breeding or if only one cock is kept, the Green Cardinal can be housed with several other birds, even with smaller finches.

Diet: Oats, berries, 'Universal' food and such green food as lettuce, chickweed, and twigs with young buds on them, also wholemeal bread, mashed potatoes, apples, hemp seed, and sunflower seed. Ants' eggs and live insects must be freely given during breeding and rearing.

They prefer to build their nests in a thick box bush or privet hedge in which artificial nests have been fixed; they will add to these with birch twigs and heather. They will also use a nest box.

This species can be recommended above all others for beginners. They are difficult to spot among thick foliage or grasses for their colour acts as a good camouflage. Quails, Budgerigars, Doves, Starlings and Finches make good companions. They are hardy enough to winter in an outside flight.

Red-crested Cardinal *Paroaria cucullata* Pl. 88

Origin South America.

7½ in. Better known and more obtainable than the Green Cardinal and equally robust. Its colouring is more captivating and it is much more lively. It is, however, aggressive and it is advisable to keep a pair separately, or with larger birds able to defend themselves.

It is difficult to distinguish between *Cock* and *Hen*. The hen is rather smaller and slimmer, and the red on her head is less extensive. The song of the cock, of course, reveals his sex, but the difference is only obvious during the breeding season.

Red-crested Cardinals will soon begin to breed and will build a rather untidy home from heather and grass blades, choosing for preference an artificial nest or willow basket which has been set about 3 ft above ground, in a thick box bush or privet hedge. Both parents will incubate the 4–6 eggs in turn and both will feed the young from the time of hatching almost exclusively with insect food, hard-boiled egg, meal-worms, and fresh ants' eggs. The parents need the same diet as their young.

Pope Cardinal (Dominican Cardinal) *Paroaria dominicana* (*Paroaria larvata*) Pl. 90

Origin Brazil.

7 in. Resembles the Crested Cardinal, but has no crest and is smaller. It is also like it in character but its song is more melodious, although not to be compared with that of the Viriginian Cardinal. There is only a slight difference between *Cock* and *Hen*, and to obtain a pair will present many difficulties for even an experienced fancier. Not

every hen is acceptable to the cock. Nor will a hen accept a cock which is not of her own choice, and this is one reason why efforts to breed this species have so often proved unsuccessful. If possible, the birds should be allowed to select their own partners, and this will mean keeping more than one of each sex to obtain a good breeding combination.

They will breed in a flight and treatment is as for Crested Cardinal. The cock is less dangerous to small birds than the Crested Cardinal, but it is better to keep them separate during breeding season.

Yellow-billed Cardinal *Paroaria capitata* Pl. 91

Origin Argentine, Paraguay, Bolivia.

6½ in. *Cock:* Head intense carmine with black throat mark running down to a point on breast. Nape pure white with small black crescent marks. Remainder of upper surface black, under surface snowy white. Eyes brown, beak and feet yellow. *Hen:* Duller, brick red, and mantle more grey. Immature birds have sandy buff head and brown throat. Their bill is also stained with slate grey.

A delightful aviary bird, less pugnacious than its larger relatives but unfortunately less hardy.

Diet: Mixed seed with small sunflower and a little hemp. Some will take insectivorous food and live insects such as gentles and meal-worms. Green food and twigs of budding hawthorn and fruit trees should be supplied.

The nest is usually placed in a thick bush and is cup-shaped with foundation of thin twigs and coarse grasses, lined with fine grasses and other soft materials. The young are reared largely on insects and require almost unlimited quantities of gentles, meal-worms, and

if possible live ant cocoons. A mixture of rusk crumbs soaked in milk with grated hard-boiled egg would assist in rearing the young; as the chicks progress soaked seed and green weed seeds should be offered.

Black-tailed Hawfinch *Eophona melanura*

Origin China.

7½ in. *Cock:* Head and throat black, upper parts grey-brown. Tail black with bluish gloss. Breast grey running into white, flanks with reddish glow. Wings black with white tips. Eyes brown, legs flesh-coloured; large bill yellow with black tip and blue-grey at base. *Hen:* Grey-brown on upper parts, lighter below with white belly and yellow flanks. Considerably smaller than the cock.

When these birds sing they make a pleasant whistling sound with peculiar, long-sustained notes. They are imported fairly regularly at moderate prices. Hens not always available; this is unfortunate, for a pair can give endless pleasure.

A single bird will adapt itself to a cage and a pair may be kept in a large aviary with other larger birds. They begin to build their nest very early, high up in the aviary, in a dense shrub or ivy. It consists of thin twigs with an inner cup of grasses, fibres, and horsehair. The 4 blue-green eggs will be incubated by the hen alone and hatch in 12 days. The cock will feed the hen on the nest and later on will share in rearing the youngsters. Rearing food consists of meal-worms and ants' eggs, insect food, egg food, and green food. The meal-worm supply should be unlimited. Germinated seeds can be supplied as soon as the birds have left the nest.

Diet: Large and harder seeds— millets, oats, hemp, canary seed, rape, and sunflower seeds. A liberal supply of fruit, such as apples and pears, and various twigs from which the buds will be eaten. Insectivorous food. The birds are inclined to obesity so now and again reduce food supply by cutting out hemp and sunflower and other seeds with high fat content. They become fatter in cage than aviary.

Black-headed Hawfinch (Japanese Hawfinch) *Eophona personata* Pl. 92

Origin Japan and Siberia, ranging into northern and western China.

About 8 in. *Cock:* Crown, lores, base of cheeks, and chin glossy black; ear coverts, throat, breast, and sides pale drab or ash-grey; abdomen, thighs, and under tail coverts almost pure white; back drab, rump washed with rufous-brown; wing coverts glossy steel-blue, greater coverts ash-grey and remaining wing feathers black, the primaries crossed with a white bar; upper tail coverts and middle tail feathers steel-blue tipped with black, remaining tail feathers black; beak yellow with purplish base; feet reddish flesh-colour; eyes light hazel. *Hen:* Generally paler and without black on head which is drab-grey; beak entirely yellow.

This species resembles its near relative, the Black-tailed Hawfinch, in character and behaviour and should have the same food and treatment. In spite of its heavy beak and somewhat aggressive appearance it is said to be a peaceable bird in an aviary and is hardy.

Rose-breasted Grosbeak *Pheucticus ludoviciana*

Origin North America, Canada.

Nearly 7 in. *Cock:* Head, neck, and shoulders black; rump white sometimes with a pink gloss, crop area and breast rose pink, belly white. Wings black with white tips, tail black, outermost feathers tipped white. Beak horn-coloured, eyes brown, legs grey. *Hen:* Upper parts more brown-grey; rump brown, wings brown without white spots. Breast and crop area reddish brown, lacking the brilliant rose pink.

In winter, cock resembles hen but under wing coverts are rose coloured.

The cocks sing a peculiar lamenting song, with some chirruping notes, especially by the moonlight. They may be kept in a large aviary with birds of the same size, and usually prove very peaceable. They can also be kept singly in a cage.

Diet: Should include much fruit, berries, apples, buds on twigs, green peas, insectivorous food, and live insects, including meal-worms. Their strong beak easily cracks oats, sunflower seeds, hemp, millet, canary seed, rape, and maw.

The birds may use a nest box hung high up in the aviary but generally prefer to build in a tall shrub or against a pole or wall in climbing plants. The nest is cup-shaped, carelessly made of grass blades, twigs, and chickweed, and lined inside with coconut fibres and feathers. The 4 eggs are incubated by the hen and hatched in a fortnight. Two broods may be looked for in one season. They can remain in a well-sheltered aviary throughout the year.

Black-headed Grosbeak *Pheucticus melanocephala*

Origin Mexico, West America, and Canada.

Nearly 7 in. *Cock:* Head black, brownish yellow collar round nape, and neck, breast, flanks, and rump dark yellow. Belly paler yellow, under tail coverts white. Wings black with brown-yellow margins and black tips. Tail black and white. Eyes brown, beak brown-yellow, lower mandible somewhat lighter, legs grey-blue. *Hen:* Lacks black on head and on back. Grey-brown on upper parts and yellow-brown to whitish underneath. Less white in wings and tail.

Imported occasionally. Care and feeding similar to Rose-breasted Grosbeak. They have frequently been bred successfully. The birds are nearly always to be found high up in an aviary.

Resembles the Hawfinch, and has the same heavy beak, which enables it to crack nuts and hard seeds. They can be fed with the harder kinds of grain. They sing at night like linnets.

Northern Blue Grosbeak, Chestnut-shouldered Blue Grosbeak *Guiraca caerulea* Pl. 94

Origin Southern portion of the U.S.A., throughout Mexico, and Central America to Nicaragua and Costa Rica, also Cuba.

6½ in. *Cock:* Forehead, chin, and lores black; flights and secondaries blackish, edged with blue; median wing coverts chestnut; remaining upper parts deep, shining cobalt. Under parts softer, greyish-blue. Iris brown; beak, upper mandible almost black, lower greyish-blue; legs and feet greyish-black. *Hen:* Above olive-brown, more rufous on crown and hind neck, faintly streaked with buff; median wing coverts tawny-buff; tail dusky, edged with blue. Under parts paler brownish-buff; chin and throat whitish.

In winter the cock's plumage becomes entirely edged with whitish-buff and yellowish-brown, the blue being almost completely obscured.

This is a charming species which will become quite tame, but unfortunately the cocks particularly are very inclined to bully other birds of their own size or smaller, and are only safe in a mixed collection of species larger than themselves. They are comparatively hardy when once acclimatized, and provided the weather does not become too severe, can remain in an unheated aviary throughout the year if they have a well-built, draught-free shelter to which they can retire at night. Their diet should consist of a seed mixture containing canary seed, white and small yellow millet, sunflower, buckwheat, and a little hemp. They also appreciate apple, from which they will first extract the pips, and will occasionally take rose hips, hawthorn, and elder berries, but display little interest in greenstuff.

They have built in an aviary, but there appears to be no authentic record of young having been reared.

Sometimes offered by dealers as Mexican Blue Bishops.

Brazilian Blue Grosbeak *Cyanocompsa cyanea*

Origin South America.

5–6½ in. *Cock:* Deep blue, lighter towards the tail. Black forehead, chin, and lores. Crown and ear coverts cobalt blue. Abdomen, tail, beak, and legs black. Eyes brown. *Hen:* Upper parts yellowish brown, under parts warm brown, wings and tail brown.

Unfortunately hens are seldom imported. They are strong and quiet and do well in a community aviary, where they are usually peaceable. Breeding successes have often been reported.

Diet: Mainly of seeds, oats, hemp, millet, canary seed, paddy, rape, sunflower seeds, a variety of fruit and insectivorous food, to which mealworms, ants' eggs, and other live insects should be added.

Has a pleasant voice, not too loud. As a cage bird, kept by itself, it shows to advantage but when housed with others in a small space it will fight for control of the seed bowl. One drawback to a cage is that these birds need a lot of exercise to prevent their growing too fat. Food must be rationed at intervals and fatty seeds discontinued. They should have a lot of fruit, buds on twigs, and green peas.

They will start nesting in a dense shrubbery, and build a cup-shaped nest from blades of grass and plant fibres, lining the inside with moss and soft fibres. The 4 eggs are incubated by the hen alone and hatch in 13 days. During nesting season the cock sings continually. The young leave the nest after only 12 days but are fed for a considerable time after by both parents. As rearing food they should be given germinated seed, meal-worms, and canary rearing food.

They like bathing, and may be kept in the aviary throughout the year provided they have an adequate shelter.

White-throated Finch *Sporophila albogularis*

Origin Brazil and Paraguay.

4½ in. *Cock:* Short thick horn-coloured bill. Upper parts grey, forehead and ear coverts black, small white spot in front of eyes. Throat white, extending to back of ear coverts as are the abdomen and the under tail coverts. Remainder of plumage grey. *Hen:* Drab and dull in colour, with red bill.

This bird is unfortunately little known, but lends itself well to cage and aviary life. It is difficult to get a true pair for as a rule only cocks, including young cocks, are imported, and the latter closely resemble the hens. Moreover, hen birds of different species of *Sporophila* resemble each other, and this further complicates matters. Yet many fanciers have succeeded in getting a pair and in rearing the chicks.

They live very peaceably with all other small foreign finches. During breeding period, however, they become very pugnacious and will harass other birds, especially those of their own species, which they do not tolerate too well at any time.

Diet: Finely cut-up fruit. Canary seed mixture, also insects, 'Universal' food and green food, with which they also rear their young.

The song of the cock is shrill, but not unpleasant. These birds have been known to live for more than 10 years in a flight and are one of the most satisfactory species to keep.

Plumbeous Finch *Sporophila plumbea*

Origin Brazil.

4½ in. *Cock:* Ash-grey, lighter on the rump. Lores black, neck and upper breast ash-grey; breast, belly, and under tail coverts white. Wings and tail black with grey margins. Bill black with lighter tip, the strikingly large and thick upper mandible being downcurved. Eyes grey, legs horn-coloured. *Hen:* Light brown with a small white spot on the cheeks, under parts being paler and whiter towards the belly.

Each year a number of *Sporophila* are imported and this species is sometimes included. So far, no great interest has been taken in them and the prices are low. Unlike many other small foreign finches, the cock and hen are never together in the aviary, but are usually at daggers' drawn. The song is pleasant but monotonous.

The birds make a fairly deep nest from plant fibres in which 2 or 3 eggs are laid and both parents incubate, hatching taking 12 days. After a further fortnight the young leave the nest fully fledged. They are then fed for another 3 weeks before becoming completely independent. One pair may raise 3–4 broods in a season.

Diet: Canary seed, millet, rape, maw, and hemp, should be provided—really a canary mixture. Various insects, meal-worms, green food, apples, and pears are also acceptable, as well as insectivorous food and ants' eggs. Germinating seeds during the rearing period in addition to canary rearing food are advisable but not strictly necessary. Bread and milk gives good results.

The birds like bathing. They are peaceable and need not be segregated during the breeding season. They like to build their nest in a pine tree and are not particularly shy of it being inspected from time to time.

These birds are really most agreeable and certainly worth keeping. Successful breeding results are still few and far between, so here is a chance for pioneers.

Bluish Finch *Sporophila caerulescens*

Origin South America.

4½ in. Imported now and again, but hens seldom included in consignments.

Cock: Upper parts grey-blue, upper tail coverts a little more brownish, forehead, lores, ear coverts, and throat black. White moustachial stripes, narrow black crescent on upper breast. Under parts white. Wings grey-brown, bill horn-coloured, legs grey. *Hen:*

Upper parts olive brown, under parts yellowish brown. Belly yellow-white, somewhat browner on the flanks. Wings and tail brown.

Although these attractive birds are quiet and suitable for cage as well as for aviary, very few fanciers like them, possibly because their colouring is somewhat dull. This may be why few breeding results are reported. They make a cup-shaped nest lined with hair. The young cocks do not attain their full colouring for some considerable time, and it is quite possible to purchase them in mistake for hens.

Diet: Canary seed, millet, and hemp. Much green food and apples, especially when they begin breeding, required, as well as meal-worms and ants' eggs. They are very tolerant of other birds, except those of their own species.

They bathe often and thoroughly and are sufficiently hardy to be kept in an outside aviary if there is an adequate shelter. Their song is insignificant.

Lined Finch *Sporophila americana*

Origin Guiana, Tobago.

4½ in. *Cock:* Upper parts black, the head and back being glossy. There is a narrow white line running through the centre of the crown. Cheeks white, throat and chin black, breast and centre of the abdomen, as well as the under tail coverts, white. Base of flights white, but this white is often concealed when the wings are closed. Tail black, tipped with grey. Bill grey, legs blackish. *Hen:* Upper parts olive grey, rump brown. Under parts buff and brown. Bill and legs horn-coloured.

May safely be kept with all kinds of other birds in a roomy cage or aviary. Little is known of their breeding habits as they are infrequently kept and then often singly and not in pairs. Their voice is pleasant. They are quiet birds, which rear their young well, especially when fed with a variety of seed and some insects. Crossing of the various *Sporophila* should certainly be possible.

Frost-proof accommodation during the winter is essential. These birds need the same care and treatment as others of the genus.

Ornamented Finch *Sporophila ornata*

Origin South America, Bahia.

4½ in. *Cock:* Upper parts dark grey-blue, tail shading into brown. Crown and neck glossy black.

One form has a white cheek patch and another a black spot. Under parts white except for a black band across the crop. Bill pale yellow, legs grey, eye brown. *Hen:* Upper parts olive brown, under parts brownish, throat whiter.

Neither form is imported regularly but the black-cheeked is on sale more frequently than the white-cheeked. Fanciers do not show a great interest in these finches, which is regrettable, for they are cheerful, lively birds, make few demands, and are easily catered for.

Diet: Their strong bills enable them to tackle harder types of seeds such as oats; rice is taken readily, as well as canary seeds, millet and hemp, maw and rape. Apples, pears, green food, and even insectivorous food will not be refused. Meal-worms and ants' eggs are delicacies.

The cock's voice is soft but melodious and he sings often. The birds have a chirruping call. They like to nest near the ground in thick shrubs, or in a rose bush. There they make a cup-shaped nest from thin plant fibres, hair, and rootlets. Breeding success has not yet been recorded but it can be assumed that the requirements for breeding and rearing will not be very different from those for the White-throated Finch, *Sporophila albogularis*.

Reddish Finch *Sporophila nigroaurantia*

Origin South Brazil.

4 in. *Cock:* Upper parts cinnamon. Crown, upper tail coverts, and wings black. Bill black, legs dark brown, eyes dark. *Hen:* Brown with under parts yellowish white.

Although their song is not very good, these small birds are most attractive on account of their daintiness and pretty colouring. They need the same care as other *Sporophila*, but details of successful breeding are not available.

Collared Finch *Sporophila collaris*

4½ in. *Cock:* Upper parts black, upper tail coverts and rump cream, throat white with a black band across the upper breast; belly light brown. Bill horn-coloured with a yellow tip, legs light horn-colour. *Hen:* Upper parts brown with olive wash on head and back. Wing and tail feathers dark brown with paler margins. Sides of head and under parts pale tawny-buff, deeper on under tail coverts. Under wing coverts buffish white.

Treat as other *Sporophila*.

Guttural Finch *Sporophila nigricollis*

Origin Brazil.

4 in. *Cock:* Dark olive green above with a lighter rump. Black head and neck, breast and belly yellowish white, flanks greyish with black abdominal band and yellow under-tail coverts, wings and tail greyish brown, beak silver grey. *Hen:* Olive brown, more yellow below with ruddy tinge on breast. Wings and tail blackish. Bill horn-grey, legs brown-grey.

Offered fairly regularly.

It should certainly be possible to breed from this species, which has been successfully hybridized with the White-throated Finch, *Sporophila albogularis*.

Care and feeding do not present any problem, particularly as several species of these finches may be kept together. Many more cocks than hens are imported and it is rather difficult to obtain a pair.

Cuban Finch *Tiaris canora* Pl. 87

Origin Cuba.

3½–4 in. One of the most graceful of all small finches. *Cock* readily recognizable by his black mask, so different from the brown of the *Hen*.

Not only regularly imported, but pairs bred in this country are also regularly offered for sale. Because of its small size and beautiful markings it might be mistaken for a Waxbill on first sight but on closer examination it will be obvious that it is a true Finch. Although it will sometimes steal a Waxbill's nest, it will enlarge it into a dome-shaped structure with a concealed entrance low down at the side. Its eggs are greenish white with red-brown dots.

Unfortunately these birds are not so peaceful as they look, especially in the breeding season. It is advisable to keep one pair only in a flight with other finches, such as Long-tailed Grass Finches, or with a few pairs of Weavers able to defend themselves against aggression.

Their song consists only of an insignificant chirping and twittering. The finches are extremely lively and will soon begin to build a nest, unless they have succeeded in stealing one. Together the cock and hen will build a ball of very fine teasings flax, and hair. The entrance passage is quite 4 in. long.

The hen incubates unaided by the cock and after about 4 weeks the fledglings leave the nest. The hen will probably begin another clutch immediately and the cock will complete the rearing of the young himself. If possible, the birds should be allowed to nest in a quiet corner for they are easily disturbed and many a clutch has been lost in this way. If nesting quietly by themselves in the corner of the cage, breeding will proceed steadily and peacefully.

The young should be reared on soaked and germinated seed, fine 'Universal' food, small or cut up mealworms, and fresh ants' eggs. In addition to the seed used for Waxbills, green food is essential. As soon as the young have grown independent, they must be taken out and placed in a separate cage, for the hen will start chasing the young hens, and the cock will harass his sons. As many as 6 broods may be reared in one season.

The Cuban Finch is well behaved, provided it is not placed in a flight with smaller finches. It is quite a lovely sight to have a small planted flight entirely stocked with Cuban Finches. Once they have started to build their nests they may be allowed to fly at liberty. They will remain in the neighbourhood of the aviary and will soon find the entrance and regularly return to their nest and feeding table. Once the young have hatched, the parents will collect and bring home insects. The advantages of keeping the birds in this way will be obvious, but it needs courage.

Olive Finch *Tiaris olivacea* Pl. 85

Origin Cuba and West Indian Islands, Haiti, and Jamaica.

3½–4 in. *Cock:* Olive above, cheeks black, throat orange-yellow as eyebrow. *Hen:* Much duller colours.

As a breeding bird kept together

with larger birds, in a flight or cage, this species is quieter and rather more dependable than the Cuban Finch but not so pretty and so less popular. The birds will be happy in a flight planted with box bushes and conifers and their young will be reared satisfactorily. The Olive Finch will not agree with the Cuban Finch. Fighting will break out and there will then be little hope of successful breeding. Satisfactory results are usually obtained if a pair are kept separately in a cage.

Diet: Seed mixture, green weed seeds, and seeding grasses and, during breeding season, insect food, small meal-worms, and ants' eggs.

Jacarini Finch *Volatinia jacarini*

Origin Tropical America.

2¾ in. *Cock:* Almost entirely black with dark blue reflection, especially on head and nape. During flight the white underneath wings becomes visible. Eyes are dark and bill black. *Hen:* Earth brown above, ashy on head. Under parts pale brown.

Although very irregularly imported and their song has little to recommend them, these birds are among the most attractive to breed in a flight.

Cock and hen will jointly build a cup-shaped nest in a low shrub or will use an artificial nest, adding hemp teasings and fine grasses. The hen will then incubate alone; the young will be fed by both parents and will fly after 10 days. Although only 2 or 3 young are produced from one clutch of eggs, as many as 6–8 broods in a season have been reported. Insect food and chick-weed, with ants' eggs, are indispensable for rearing the young, in addition to a mixture of small seeds, including weed seeds.

This species of finch is a very tolerant little bird, and will bring liveliness to an aviary by continually singing in a most cheerful manner. It can winter in frost-proof accommodation.

Japanese White-bellied Blue Fly-catcher *Muscicapa cyanomelana*

Origin Japan and Korea.

6 in. *Cock:* Sky blue cap merging into cobalt blue on the back; neck, lores, and sides of head black. Rump ultra-marine blue, the remainder of the under parts white. Wings and tail very dark blue to black. Bill black.

Hen: Upper parts brown, breast grey-brown, belly white, chin and throat light brown. Eyes, legs, and bill brown. The hen may be slightly smaller than the cock.

Examples of this Flycatcher, usually cocks only, are imported now and again, and remain fairly expensive. They are suitable for cages, but less easy to house in aviaries containing a mixed collection. They soon grow tame, and their song is pleasant and sweet. They must always have a chance to bathe.

Diet: 'Nightingale' food, meal-worms, and other live insects.

Verditer Flycatcher *Stoparola melanops Muscicapa thalassina*)

Origin India.

6 in. Pastel greenish blue, under parts lighter, lores black, wings a somewhat darker blue. Eyes brown, bill and legs black. *Hen:* Is smaller in size and duller in colouring.

Cocks are imported fairly frequently, and hens less often. Suitable for a cage and, when acclimatized, become very hardy.

Diet: 'Nightingale' food, meal-worms, ants' eggs, and other insects.

This species seldom alights on the ground, preferring branches and twigs. The birds sing constantly and their song is soft and melodious. It is important for their plumage that they are able to bathe frequently.

Rufous-bellied Niltava *Niltava sundara* Pl. 95

Origin Himalaya and China.

6½ in. *Cock:* Forehead, sides of the head, and throat black, crown and nape, rump and mantle, wing coverts and tail, bright blue. Under parts bright chestnut. *Hen:* Is entirely different, the whole of upper parts being russet and under parts dull brown. There is a white crescent on the throat and a tiny spot of brilliant pale blue on each side of neck. The blue is often concealed except when the bird is alert and with the head raised.

This extraordinarily beautiful little bird is among those of the more delicate and costly species which are imported rather infrequently. It has a very peaceful nature, except with its own kind, and is best kept in a cage or aviary with other small insectivorous birds. Instead of ordinary perches, this bird should be provided with fresh-cut twigs standing in a jar of water, the jar being covered or placed so that the bird cannot get into it. The twigs should be frequently renewed and in this way the bird's legs and feet, which are very apt to become dry and scaly, will be kept in healthy condition.

Absolute cleanliness is essential; the tray at the bottom of the cage should be covered with a sheet of paper which must be changed daily. The bird bathes at least twice a day, and should always have access to a bath.

Diet: The best 'Universal' food obtainable should be given, mixed with a large quantity of dried flies and some cake crumbs, and moistened with a little honey water, so that it is not too dry. Live insects, some meal-worms, and ants' eggs complete the menu.

Although these birds are best kept indoors in a warm room, a conservatory, bird room, or similar accommodation, they are said to be able to withstand the cold. They have wintered in an outside flight, but this seems entirely wrong for our winters are inclined to be foggy and damp and birds cannot survive in such conditions.

If kept in a flight during summer, it is not difficult to obtain enough insects by hanging a piece of cheese, meat, or fish in a butter muslin bag from the top of the netting. This bag will soon become covered with all kinds of crawling flies and the various insect-eaters will pick them off readily.

The birds moult in spring and again during the autumn and extra live food must be supplied at those times. The moult will then be quickly completed. To keep these birds in prime condition, it is advisable to spray them daily with tepid water. This is also recommended for all birds which come from a tropical humid atmosphere. It keeps them clean and encourages them to preen themselves and the feathers then retain their splendid gloss. The Niltava was first bred in England in 1962.

Shama *Copsychus malabaricus indicus* Pl. 96

Origin India and Indonesia.

9½–10 in. *Cock:* Entire head, back, throat, and upper breast glossy black. Flights and long central tail feathers black, the former edged with brown on inner webs. Outer tail feathers and rump, pure white. Under parts deep, rich chestnut. Eyes dark brown, beak black, legs straw-coloured. *Hen:* Those parts which are black in the cock are replaced by dull grey and under parts are warm buff. The white on the rump is less prominent and the legs almost flesh-coloured. Tail decidedly shorter than that of the cock. Young birds of both sexes at first brown, heavily mottled, but later become much like the hen until the first full moult, when their sex becomes apparent.

Probably the finest singer of all foreign birds, but even the best Shama cannot compare with the Nightingale. Its song is infinitely varied and liquid in tone and it quickly learns to imitate the runs and trills of the Blackbird and Nightingale. This talent, however, makes it essential to keep the Shama away from creaking doors, bleating sheep, cackling geese or turkeys, for these noises will also be copied with less desirable effect. However, no foreign bird can give so much pleasure to its fortunate owner. A cock kept separately, if in good health, will soon break into song. Every sound from radio or gramophone record will induce singing. In addition to its magnificent song, interrupted only for a few weeks each year during moulting (usually completed quickly and without difficulty), the Shama possesses practically all the ideal qualities of a cage and aviary bird.

As soon as the newly imported bird has become accustomed to its diet and environment, it will begin to sing and will quickly grow tame. It is particularly elegant and its long tail is jerked rapidly up and down whenever the bird is excited by any unusual sight or sound. This action is accompanied by a sharp 'tek-tek', of alarm. Its plumage is normally kept in immaculate condition and it is a dainty feeder, seldom

scattering or fouling its food. It needs no special care when breeding and frequently the broods are successfully hatched and the young reared.

Diet: 'Universal' food mixed with ants' eggs, and occasionally hard-boiled egg, grated carrot, and small earthworms. A few meal-worms a day, which can be fed by hand, and morsels of raw meat will keep the bird in excellent condition. Small, smooth, green caterpillars, locusts, and other insects are welcome. While the young are being reared, the insect diet should be considerably augmented with quantities of fresh ants' eggs, different varieties of live insects, young meal-worms, and cut-up earthworms. Breeding is more likely to succeed in the aviary, as the birds can pick up small insects from the ground. It is best to keep the breeding pair on their own, although in a very large aviary other species may be tolerated. Pairing is generally rather tempestuous; the cock chases the hen continuously and it is necessary to have a roomy flight with ample cover so that she may escape from her ardent follower, should his attentions become too pressing.

The hen usually builds the nest single handed, preferring a nest box with a half-open front. She fills the box with moss and twigs, lining the cup of the nest with fibrous hemp, fine hair, and other soft material. The cock does not incubate but shares in feeding the young. Within 4 weeks of the laying of the first egg, the fledglings leave the nest and are then fed for a further week or two by both parents. It is advisable to segregate the young as soon as they are independent, so that a second brood can be started.

If the parent birds are allowed to fly out through a trapdoor in the flight, once the eggs have been laid, the hatching will be more easily accomplished by the hen and plenty of insects will be collected and brought back to the aviary. The cock will leave the hen in peace during the incubation and will sing continuously in the garden nearby. A careful watch must be kept against cats and as soon as the fledglings leave the nest, the old birds must again be confined to the aviary, or they might lead the young ones away.

Once the Shama has become acclimatized it can stand the winter quite well and does not need a very warm room, though adequate protection should be provided.

Dhyal Bird (Magpie Robin) *Copsychus saularis*

Origin India, Indonesia, and South China.

7½ in. *Cock:* Black breast, belly and under tail-coverts white. Tail black and white. *Hen:* Greyish brown and some white areas, as cock.

Although a less accomplished songster than the Shama, certainly well worth keeping. Its song is melodious and not over-loud. It is not so easy to tame as the Shama, and moves about restlessly in a cage, in fact it is happier when in a flight.

Diet: A fine grade 'Universal' mixture with a large proportion of ants' eggs and some meal-worms in daily diet keeps the bird fit. As a change, soaked stale bread, grated carrot, minced raw or boiled meat, berries, and hard-boiled egg are recommended; this diet is specially beneficial during the breeding period.

The nest building is similar to that of the Shama. The hen alone incubates but the cock shares in feeding the young. Rearing food should contain a high percentage of live insects and meal-worms.

A well-planted flight is the best place to encourage a pair of these birds to breed. In appearance, they resemble small Magpies, the *Cock* being glossy black and white, and the *Hen* a soft grey and white. They are hardy and in case of necessity can winter in an unheated aviary, but moderate warmth is preferable.

If a cock only is kept, he can be allowed to fly at liberty but naturally must first be accustomed to his cage or aviary and be thoroughly tame. Feeding by hand with meal-worms will help to achieve this. The cock will not leave the vicinity provided he is allowed to return to the flight or shelter at night.

Orange-headed Ground Thrush *Geocichla* (*Zoothera*) *citrina* Pl. 97

Origin India.

About 8 in. *Cock:* Head, breast, and abdomen orange-brown blending into yellowy white. Main colour of upper parts blue-grey. Median wing coverts spotted with white. *Hen:* Upper parts greenish-grey, orange of the head and breast not nearly so bright as in the cock.

Though more gaudily coloured, this bird behaves much like the Song Thrush. It spends much of its time on the ground where it continually searches for worms and insects, turning over the fallen leaves and other debris with its beak. Its song also resembles that of the thrush.

Quiet by nature, it is a suitable subject for a cage where, sitting on one leg, it will sing continuously. It is, however, more suited to aviary life, is tolerant of other species, and does not need a great deal of attention. Breeding habits, about which little is known, probably resemble those of other thrushes.

Diet: 'Universal' mixture, a few small worms, and ants' eggs.

White-throated Ground Thrush *Geocichla* (*Zoothera*) *cyanota*

Origin India.

8½ in. *Cock:* Head, breast, sides, and abdomen rust-coloured. Cheek spots and throat white. Ear coverts white with two wide black-brown bands. Back and tail grey with light blue-grey edges to feathers giving the impression of scales. A white spot on each wing. Bill black, legs flesh-coloured. *Hen:* Similar in colour but much duller.

In general, their care is similar to that for the Orange-headed Ground Thrush, *Geocichla citrina*.

Suitable as a cage bird; can readily be tamed and will sing frequently and melodiously. It thrives if kept in an aviary with other larger birds and will hunt for food on the ground under the bushes and on the grass. If the general food supply is placed on the ground, it is apt to be domineering and keep other birds from feeding. This can be avoided if food intended for the others is placed in a tray suspended from the roof and a separate dish put on the ground where the thrush prefers to feed.

Diet: 'Universal' food, earthworms, meal-worms, and other insects as well as fruit of various kinds; minced meat, hard-boiled egg, and bread and milk may be supplied now and again as a change. Ants' eggs important for rearing the young.

The nest is constructed of leaves, thin twigs, grass, moss, and rootlets, cemented together with mud, which should be available in the flight. The inside is lined with fine grasses or fibres. The 2 or 3 eggs, blue with brown and black spots, are incubated solely by the hen. The cock sings more than the hen and his song is particularly beautiful during the breeding season. Incubation lasts 13 days. As the birds become tame, it is possible to let the parents fly out to collect suitable food when they are rearing young. They will always find the trapdoor entrance to aviary. Two broods a season are normal.

The birds like bathing. They can remain in the flight summer and winter if a good shelter is available.

Cuban Thrush (Red-legged Mocking Thrush) *Turdus plumbeus rubriceps*

Origin Cuba.

10–11 in. General colour above, dark slaty grey. Chin white, throat black, belly chestnut. Long tail black, outer feathers broadly tipped with white. Eyes dark brown with red cere; beak and legs red. *Cock* and *Hen* alike, but hen may be slightly more drab.

Less common than preceding species, but fairly often offered for sale. Its song, though not to be compared with that of thrushes already described, is outstanding and melodious. Readily tamed, it is always actively employed, often on the floor of the cage, searching for insects which it expects to find under stones or other cover, and is likely to tip over its food pot. Treatment as for previous species, but also appreciates a small amount of raw meat.

Hoami (Spectacled Jay Thrush) (Chinese Nightingale) *Garrulax canorus*

Origin China.

8½ in. *Cock* and *Hen* alike. Crown, nape, and back brown, forehead rust-coloured. Sometimes marked with fine black stripes along the nape of neck. Cream line above the eye which is surrounded with white. Abdomen lighter in shade, fading to grey. Bill yellow-horn.

Although rarely imported, this species has become popular on account of the cock's exceptional quality of song. These birds are great favourites in China, and only those of mediocre performance are allowed to be exported. The range of this bird's song is so extensive that it is able to sing both deep and very high notes and thus produce a really wonderful melody.

The bird is very active and must be kept in a cage of at least 4 ft. so that it can take adequate exercise. It may be kept in a flight with other birds, provided the latter are large and of a quiet disposition. It is, however, better to keep the bird by itself in a large cage, as it is apt to display sudden fits of bad temper. If a Shama or a Japanese Nightingale or a second specimen of its own kind is kept within hearing, it is almost certain that a Chinese Nightingale will soon start to sing and imitate the song of these birds and blend it with its own. The Hoamis are trained as 'fighting birds' in China—certainly no recommendation for a communal aviary!

Diet: Oats, hemp, canary seed, with 'Universal' food and numerous insects such as meal-worms, beetles, and locusts, and finely cut-up raw meat. Small mice and small fish are eaten. The bird will hold a fish in its claws and tear it to pieces with its beak, and there is little doubt that small birds might share a similar fate. Fruit and green food are essential.

It is remarkable how frequently this bird bathes. It soon gains confidence in its owner but will always remain shy of strangers. It is hardy and can winter without artificial heat, but is never kept for breeding purposes.

White-crested Jay Thrush *Garrulax leucolophus* Pl. 98

Origin Himalaya.

11½ in. Considerably larger than the preceding bird, this species is rarely met with in private collections although regularly imported. With its graceful white crest, nearly always carried erect, it is one of the most beautiful birds that can be kept with other birds of its own size in a large flight. It is exceedingly active and can easily capture and devour any small birds, but is a cheerful and inquisitive inmate of an aviary, and constantly on the move. Its song, which is powerful, consists of a variety of not unpleasant flute-like tones. Unfortunately, it seldom becomes tame. It likes the same sort of food as does the Hoami, together with much fruit, and is well able to winter in an outside aviary.

It is seldom possible to breed from these birds as they have an unfortunate habit of swallowing their young when these are a week or so old.

To be seen to best advantage, a pair should be kept in a small aviary by themselves. They are among the funniest and most entertaining birds; they sleep huddled together and cover each other with their wings. During the day they play together and tumble over each other with a constant cackling, which sounds much like human laughter, but they are too noisy to be kept in the house.

Golden-eyed Babbler *Chrysomma sinensis*

Origin India.

6½ in. *Cock* and *Hen* alike. Head and neck red brown. Cheeks, area round the eyes, lores, and stripe above the ear coverts white. Ear coverts brown, throat and breast white, abdomen cream coloured. Wings rust brown, tail brown with rust-coloured margins. Eyes yellow and eye cere orange-red. Bill black with yellow nostrils, legs golden yellow.

Not imported with any regularity. They need considerable space on account of their lively nature. They will thrive in a sunny aviary during the summer, but in winter they require a warm room.

Considerable care is needed at first to get them acclimatized; they should be kept warm and given a regular supply of fresh drinking water and bath water, oranges, and other sweet fruit cut up small, together with meal-worms and other insects. To accustom them to 'Nightingale' food, the meal-worms and pieces of fruit can be put on top. The birds will hold the pieces of fruit under their claws when eating. Honey diluted with water is a treat. These Babblers are very peaceable with other birds; their song is pleasant, soft, but very varied.

Yellow-cheeked Crested Tit *Machlolophus xanthogenys aplonotus*

Origin India.

6 in. *Cock* and *Hen* alike. Head, a bar from the beak, passing through eyes and extending to nape, and neck itself are black. Crest black backed with yellow. Eyebrow stripe, sides of head, and spot on the neck also yellow. Upper parts olive grey. Wings black with white spots; tail black, also throat, breast, and abdomen. The remainder of under parts yellow-green. Bill black, eyes brown, and legs grey.

Offered now and again at moderate prices, they are lively, intensely in-quisitive, and readily become tame. They are very agreeable companions for other birds provided they have sufficient room. Their song is insignificant, consisting of soft chirps and twitters.

Diet: Insects and sweet fruit should always be included. Sunflower seeds are a special treat, but should not be given too often as these birds soon become fat. 'Nightingale' food to which crushed hemp seed, grated carrot, and ants' eggs have been added and well mixed in, forms an excellent diet during the summer, while in winter sunflower seeds should be offered. Green food and a number of live insects, meal-worms, and aphis much enjoyed and vary the diet. The birds enjoy a daily bath.

For those experienced in keeping insect-eaters and fruit-eaters this is an attractive bird, which, however, is not considered very hardy. Breeding results are not known.

Chinese White-eye (Chinese Zosterop) *Zosterops palpebrosa simplex*

Origin China.

4¼ in. *Cock* and *Hen* alike. Pale olive green above, lighter on the head and throat. Black lores, circlet of white feathering surrounding eyes. Chin and throat yellow, remainder of under parts greenish grey. Wings and tail olive green with black margins to the flights.

Over 80 species and forms of *Zosterops* are known, but only a few are imported. The best known is *Zosterops palpebrosa*, which is no larger than 4 in. and not so hardy as *Zosterops simplex*.

A pair make good subjects for a good-sized cage. They will tolerate other birds. It is difficult to obtain a true pair; but as a rough guide, one should be dark and the other light in colour. They are most pleasing birds and quickly grow tame. Immediately their cage is opened they will hop out and will return of their own accord.

Diet: They are eaters of small fruits and insects. Their menu needs thought, and must be sufficiently varied; they will then keep themselves in very good trim. Half an orange should always be at hand. They like to eat bread and milk and, if diluted honey and water is not given separately, some honey or even icing sugar could be added to the soaked bread. 'Nightingale' food, to which some soaked, or preferably fresh, ants' eggs have been added is also appreciated. Small live flies (fruit flies are readily cultivated), and occasionally small meal-worms and gentles, are enjoyed, but need not be supplied daily. Hard-boiled egg, grated carrots, canary rearing food, moistened with milk or water, all serve to vary the menu. Pieces of very ripe bananas, cut-up dates, grated apples, and pears are also eaten.

On a simple diet, with frequent variation, these birds will remain in excellent condition for many years. My experience is that the honey drink is so good for them that it should be regarded as an essential part of their diet. A special receptacle should be placed quite near a twig, so that the birds can perch easily reaching the liquid. They appreciate it if their food is not placed on the ground but raised or hung up as they are usually moving among the branches and descend only to bathe and drink. They are very fond of bathing. They are very affectionate to each other and roost huddled together.

Breeding results have been obtained, but great care is needed. The birds like a quiet spot, such as a conservatory or a small sheltered aviary, by themselves or with pairs of quiet finches. A deep cup-shaped nest is made and may be built in a nest basket or in a thick shrub suspended from a forked branch. Fine grasses, hair, coconut fibre, and white woollen threads are used. When the hen is sitting on her blue eggs only her bill, tail, and white eyes are visible. She is constantly on the look-out for danger and during bad weather will pull a large feather or leaf over herself for protection. Young cocks should be removed as soon as the hen commences a second nest, for the old cock will kill any young of his own sex as soon as he imagines them to be rivals for the affection of his mate. An entirely new nest is always made, but the materials of the old one are often used for its construction.

Their high chirping song is more powerful and persistent during breeding season: 3 to 4 eggs are laid, blue-green in colour. The young are reared on live insects, ants' eggs, and aphis.

The birds can remain outside during spring, summer, and autumn as they are accustomed to cold nights in their native country.

Indian White-eye (Indian Zosterop)
Zosterops palpebrosa Pl. 99

Origin India.

4 in. Also a charming little bird, suitable for an indoor aviary or cage. It soon makes itself at home and adapts itself quickly to the *diet* provided, consisting of rusks, crumbled with grated carrot and ants' eggs, fine 'Universal' food, and now and again some crushed hemp. Fresh ants' eggs and various live insects such as greenflies, butterflies, and beetles are much enjoyed. A supply of fresh fruit, oranges, bananas, all

kinds of crushed berries, finely cut-up dates, etc., should always be available.

The birds are readily tamed. They sing sweetly, softly, and continuously. They will clamber along the wires like small tits. If there is a secluded corner in their cage a pair can probably be encouraged to begin breeding. An artificial nest in a nest box can be used as a base to which they will add hemp fibres and woollen threads. If not disturbed, they may well rear a brood. Unlimited quantities of live insects and fresh ants' eggs are needed for the chicks. Sexes alike.

Pekin Robin (Pekin Nightingale, Hill Tit, Red-billed Leiothrix) *Leiothrix lutea* Pl. 100

Origin China.

6 in. One of the most sought-after birds, and also take pride of place as cage birds. The *Cock* has distinctive colouring and can usually be distinguished from the *Hen*, which is much duller. The song of the cock is unmistakable and quite different from the call of the hen. Not more than one cock or one pair of these should be kept together in a flight as they are very intolerant towards others of their own kind although they agree quite well with birds of other species, even with small finches. They cannot be kept with smaller birds that are breeding, however, as they frequently rob their nests and eat the eggs. Although they cannot swallow the eggs whole, they will hold them under one foot and peck them to pieces.

The song of the cock is varied and strong; it is pleasant to listen to and is never disturbingly loud. It makes a good house pet, possessing all the good points of a cage bird: its song is delightful, its plumage is smooth and

colouring beautiful, it is lively, easily tamed, inquisitive, and will readily take meal-worms from the hand. In a flight or in a roomy cage it may sometimes be persuaded to nest. It is not finicky about food, the most suitable *diet* consisting of millet and canary seed, 'Universal' food, green food, and 10 meal-worms per bird per day. Ants' eggs and egg food are necessary during breeding. Elderberry and other berries, bits of figs and peas, are all much enjoyed. Some of these birds eat mainly seed, others mainly insects, but in either case they are not big eaters.

The birds are great bathers, continually jumping in and out of the water. They become very affectionate and build a deep cup-shaped nest of reeds, bark, moss, and fine twigs. They accept artificial linings fixed in nest boxes; the boxes should preferably be out of sight, hidden behind high shrubbery. Although the young will fly 12 days after hatching, they still require feeding by their parents for a considerable time.

These birds can live well in our climate and need not be brought indoors for the winter. The moult is usually completed without difficulty during the autumn.

Silver-eared Mesia *Leiothrix (Mesia) argentauris* Pl. 101

Origin Himalaya and Burma.

6½ in. *Cock:* Head black, ear feathers silver-white, throat and nape orange and red. Olive grey above, under parts bluish grey. *Hen:* Much duller colours.

These birds are regularly obtainable. They may be safely kept with other birds, including a pair of Pekin Robins.

The 5–7 note song of the cock is stronger and sharper than that of the Pekin and too loud for a cage in the room, but the colouring is more varied and beautiful. Its treatment should be as for Pekin Robin. It has often been successfully bred, but not so frequently as the Pekin as it is less freely imported. It will sometimes build its own nest, but it is always advisable to supply an artificial nest placed high up in a thick shrub. Hatching time is 14 days and rearing food should be given as for the Pekin Robin.

Black-headed Sibia *Heterophasia capistrata*

Origin India.

9½ in. *Cock:* Head entirely black, with a black crest. Under parts yellow and red-brown. Back and tail brown-grey, tail feathers being edged with grey-blue with a broad terminal band of blue barred with black. Wings grey-brown with a white strip across shoulders. Legs yellow, eyes brown, bill black. The *Hen* is difficult to distinguish from the *Cock*. She is often, but not always, slightly smaller.

This species is occasionally imported and single birds are offered at moderate prices. They are suitable for a large cage. Thick branches, which must be kept fresh by frequent changing, should be fixed, so that the birds can clamber about hunting between the bark and twigs for beetles and spiders.

Diet: Insectivorous food, finely cut-up fruit, and above all, insects. Finely cut or minced raw meat should be added to the insectivorous food now and again. These birds like beetles of all kinds. Their song is of little significance. Their activity and the beautiful smooth plumage make them very desirable cage birds, and they may be kept together with other large birds. They can stand the British climate well and remain healthy in winter if their homes are kept frost-proof. They look very well in an aviary, but should only be associated with birds of their own size.

Breeding results have not been recorded; this may be partly due to the fact that it is very difficult to distinguish between the sexes, also because the birds are not very commonly kept.

Blue-whiskered Fruit-sucker *Chloropsis cyanopogon*

Origin Malacca.

6½ in. *Cock:* Green to light green above, lores, cheeks, and throat black, moustachial stripes cobalt. A thin yellow band round eyes and throat. Light green and yellow below. Wings green with black flights, tail dark green. Legs dark grey, bill black, eyes brown. *Hen:* Lacks black markings of the cock.

Treatment and care similar to that described for Hardwick's Fruit-sucker (following). Only a very few hens are imported. The cocks are usually taken from the nest as fledglings and reared by hand, and the best singers selected. Fruit-suckers are popular cage birds in India, where they fetch fair prices. Related species should never be kept together; they will not tolerate one another and persistent fighting usually ends in the death of one or both birds.

Hardwick's Fruit-sucker (Hardwick's Green Bulbul) *Chloropsis hardwickei*

Origin India.

8 in. *Cock:* Top green, brighter near rump. The head has a golden sheen on crown. Forehead, orbital stripe, and ear coverts yellow green. Lores, sides of head, and neck black. A wide light blue band runs across cheek. Under parts light green running into orange-yellow towards vent. Primaries and coverts cobalt, remainder of wings

green. Tail green with outer feathers blue. Eye brown, bill black, legs black. *Hen* has less black on throat, no blue on wings, and more yellow-green underneath.

Successful breeding has not been recorded, but if kept alone it makes a delightful cage pet. It seems hardy and its colourful beauty is fascinating. Its song is varied and not too penetrating. It is only when the bird is scared that it utters harsh, unpleasant sounds. A good bird will quickly become tame and reveal great gifts as a mimic. In every way an ideal pet, needing a little extra care in keeping its cage thoroughly clean.

Diet: Fruit, including raisins, finely cut-up dates, pears, oranges and bananas, and currants, 'Nightingale' food, meal-worms, and other insects. This will keep the bird in excellent condition. Finely chopped meat makes a suitable variation. It seldom comes down to the ground and its food should be hung up or placed on a feeding table. Poised above the food tray, it selects what it wants, most carefully carries it to a perch, and there eats it at leisure. Honey and water is a treat.

This Fruit-sucker may be kept with other large fruit-eating birds such as large Tanagers, and also with Japanese Nightingales and similar species. It is very fond of bathing, will jump and climb about the branches all day long, and is well-adapted to a roomy cage. It needs moderate heat in the room during winter.

Golden-fronted Fruit-sucker (Golden-fronted Green Bulbul) *Chloropsis aurifrons* Pl. 102

Origin Himalaya and Burma.

One of the most highly prized both for its song and its exceptional grace-fulness and magnificent colouring of green, blue, and gold.

Fruit-eating birds need special care in regard to the cleanliness of their cages and flights. Although an acclimatized bird will be satisfied with fine-grade 'Universal' food and a fruit mixture, it is not so easy to get a newly imported bird accustomed to this diet. It likes to suck the juice from a cut orange and this may be scooped out a little and filled up with some of the fruit cut up and mixed with insect food. In this way the bird will soon learn to eat this new food. Meal-worms, yolk of egg, and ants' eggs, some finely chopped meat now and again, together with small pieces of fig, banana, and various berries, must vary the diet.

In its natural state it lives almost entirely on nectar and sweet fruit. Honey should be added now and again to a bread-and-milk and fruit mixture. It will soon learn to look for a daily meal-worm, which it will take from the hand.

This species may be kept with all other sorts of birds, except its own kind. The song of the cock is varied, starts softly and gradually rises to a crescendo. The finest songsters are to be found in India, where they are kept chiefly for their song, but among the young birds imported to this country are sure to be some which will become quite good singers. They also imitate the notes of other birds.

This Fruit-sucker will climb and hang suspended from twigs, and hop through branches, but rarely descends to the ground. For those who like a colourful bird which is also an accomplished singer, this is undoubtedly one of the most attractive species.

When the nights begin to get colder these birds must be taken indoors as they cannot stand night frost. A moderately warm room is most suitable for them in winter.

Red-vented Bulbul *Pycnonotus cafer* Pl. 103

Origin India.

8 in. *Cock* and *Hen* alike. Head and front of neck black, remainder of neck and back dark browny-grey with lighter margins. Brown-grey rump, upper tail coverts white. The black of neck merges into dark brown on breast and then into the light brown of abdomen. Under tail coverts carmine. Wings and tail feathers grey-brown with lighter margins. Bill and legs black. *Hen:* Smaller with a longer bill.

Like all Bulbuls they will become tame quickly and eat meal-worms from the hand. Their song is melodious but monotonous. They are strong, hardy, and can be kept with other birds of the same size in an aviary and live happily there. They will even breed. The nest will be made in a nest box, from blades of grass, bark, moss, and coconut fibres. The hen will hatch out her 2 or 3 eggs in about 12 days and the young will fly after another 12 days or so. The cock will diligently share in feeding the family.

Diet: Meal-worms, bread and milk, ants' eggs, raisins, and fruit. The parents will neglect insectivorous food if enough live insects are supplied to meet their wants. Oranges and pears are the favourite fruits.

Himalayan Red-vented Bulbul *Pycnonotus cafer pygaeus*

Origin Himalaya.

8½ in. Black head merging into a dark brown back. Grey breast merging into a grey-white abdomen. Under tail coverts brilliant carmine, and white rump.

A lively bird which can soon be tamed and will eventually take meal-worms from the hand. It cannot be kept with other birds smaller than itself. A pair will sometimes breed. The name 'Bulbul' is Turkish for Nightingale, but its song is not quite like that of the Nightingale, as it consists only of three melodious notes constantly repeated.

A single cock can be kept in a flight or cage with other songsters, but a pair should have an enclosure to themselves. Feeding and treatment similar to that given to the following species.

Red-eared Bulbul (Red-whiskered Bulbul) *Pycnonotus jocosus* Pl. 104

Origin India.

8 in. *Cock:* Black head and crest, white cheek on which a red spot is superimposed. Back brown, white on breast, under tail coverts red. *Hen:* Smaller, colour of back a warmer brown, red ear spot is smaller and under tail coverts a duller red. Bill is longer and finer.

These birds are regularly imported, but the consignments consist chiefly of cocks. They are the most frequently kept cage birds in India.

This species of Bulbul is lively and sprightly, suitable for a cage, but should be allowed some hours of freedom each day. They will become finger-tame, and learn to fly at liberty. A single bird will tolerate others as aviary companions provided they are not of the same species. A pair can be kept in an aviary with other large birds.

Breeding results have been obtained, but for these a quiet aviary with thick cover or a large cage in a quiet room is necessary. The bird's song is strange, and consists of a few quaint flute-like notes, which sound squeaky but not unpleasantly loud.

Diet: Insectivorous food, finely chopped fruit, some grated meat, meal-worms, and other live insects.

Great care must be taken to acclimatize newly imported birds, for they will have become weak and sensitive to cold. Later, when they have recovered their normal condition, they will live well in the aviary for a number of years. They soon lose their initial nervousness, especially if the owner visits them regularly with titbits in the shape of meal-worms.

The nuptial display by the cock consists of a dance with crest erect, tail spread, and wings drooping. The nesting material supplied should consist of coconut fibre and blades of grass. A nest box can be used, though the birds may prefer to build in the open. Any birds likely to disturb the nesting should be removed from the aviary. The 2 or 3 eggs will be incubated chiefly by the hen. The young will be fed almost exclusively on insects, ants' eggs, and meal-worms, although hard-boiled egg and soaked stale bread will also be eaten. Fruit must be supplied regularly, and may vary according to the season. Raisins and currants are special delicacies.

White-cheeked Bulbul *Pycnonotus leucogenys* Pl. 105

Origin India.

8 in. *Cock:* Upper parts grey-brown, head feathers narrow and elongated, those in the centre being particularly long and forming a crest, lores black. Eyebrow stripe white as also ear coverts and cheeks. Dark brown-black spot immediately behind ear coverts. Under tail coverts yellow. Upper tail coverts brown-white, merging into white in the middle. Wings brown-grey with olive margins. Tail brown to black with a white tip. Eyes brown, bill black. Legs grey. *Hen:* A little smaller.

These birds are hardy and except with their own kind are tolerant of other occupants of the aviary, and may even be induced to breed. Care and feeding similar to that for other Bulbuls.

White-eared Bulbul *Pycnonus leucotis*

Origin India and Iran.

7½ in. Head and throat black. Main colour grey-brown, much lighter underneath. Large white patches on cheek and ear coverts. Sexes alike.

A powerful bird with subdued but pleasing markings. The song of the cock is pleasant but tends to become monotonous when too frequently repeated. It can be easily tamed and a pair will show great affection for each other. Left alone in a bird room they may breed, the cock performing the peculiar breeding display dance with its wings hanging down and its tail feathers spread out. The hen will build a cup-shaped nest of fine twigs, blades of grass, and sometimes hemp fibres. The cock will occasionally assist in building.

This species of Bulbul is kept more as a song bird than for breeding purposes and there are few records of successful breeding. The most suitable *diet* is made up of meal-worms and ants' eggs, given with fresh fruit such as tomatoes cut and covered with sugar, raisins, pears, all sorts of berries, and, of course, 'Universal' food.

Bulbuls can winter out of doors provided good shelter is available.

Brown-eared Bulbul (Green-winged Bulbul) *Hypsipetes flavala*

Origin India.

8¼ in. *Cock* and *Hen* alike. Head, grey-brown in colour, with a prominent

K

crest, ear coverts glossy brown. Black lores and moustachal bands. Upper parts grey, throat, centre of abdomen, and under tail coverts white, remainder grey. Wings grey with olive coloured primaries. Slender black bill with strong bristles at the gape. Legs grey, red-brown eyes.

Diet: Consists mainly of insectivorous food mixture with pieces of fruit and meal-worms and other insects.

They are tolerant of other birds. Their song is insignificant: only a chattering sound. They are hardy and can be kept in the aviary summer and winter.

Chinese Bulbul *Pycnonotus sinensis*

Origin South China.

Nearly 9 in. Head with small black crest; above eye runs a wide white eyebrow stripe. Lores grey, cheeks black with a grey spot. Upper parts olive grey, neck white, breast grey, abdomen dirty white. Wings brown with greenish margins. Bill black, legs grey-black. *Hen:* Smaller than cock.

These birds lend themselves to cage life as well as to an aviary, so long as the other occupants are not too small, for there is always a risk that the eggs or fledglings of small birds will be eaten. Kindred species cannot be kept together. They are very lively and sprightly birds, are soon tamed, and will learn to fly freely at liberty. They are easy to keep and cater for. Now and again their song is reminiscent of the linnet, but generally it is less loud and often consists of chattering and chirruping sounds only, which are not very melodious.

Diet: In addition to insectivorous food mixture, finely cut-up fruit, and finely cut or grated raw meat, these birds will eat all kinds of live insects, meal-worms, etc.

With a pair there is a chance of their nesting in a nest box somewhere in a well-sheltered spot high up in the aviary. Grass blades, hemp, and coconut fibres should be supplied as nesting material. The cock will execute a typical bridal dance, displaying a spread tail, trailing wings, and with the head held at an angle. The birds are very shy during the breeding season and should be left alone as much as possible. There should be no interference with the rearing of the young, whose food should consist of hard-boiled egg, soaked rusks, and large quantities of meal-worms and ants' eggs. Once the young have been hatched it is advisable to let the birds out through a small trapdoor; they are certain to remain in the neighbourhood and not to abandon their youngsters.

Various species of doves are suitable as aviary companions; the Bulbuls will not molest birds of this size. If they are allowed to fly about the room occasionally, the Bulbuls can be kept by themselves in a cage, but their lively nature demands room for exercise, and if they cannot fly round at intervals they will soon become dull and sluggish.

Yellow-vented Bulbul *Pycnonotus aurigaster*

Origin Indonesia.

7¾ in. Head black, ear coverts white, neck grey and brown. Rump and upper tail coverts white. Upper parts brown. Chin and throat black. Under tail coverts yellow, remainder of under parts grey-brown with a yellow tinge; tail brown with white spots at the tips. Eyes brown, bill and legs blackish.

This species used to be imported regularly, but now appears only occasionally. They are quite peaceful with species other than their own and so easy to tame that they soon get into the habit of flying about at liberty. They can thus supply their young in a nest built in the aviary, with all necessary live food in addition to the normal diet, which consists of insectivorous food mixture and fruit of all kinds. They have a great liking for honey.

The cock is greatly in demand in Indonesia as a song bird. These Bulbuls are, in fact, among the liveliest and strongest of singing birds. Sexes alike.

Red-eyed Bulbul *Pycnonotus nigricans*

Origin South Africa.

7¼ in. Head and throat black; upper parts brown-grey, brown-white below, merging into white on the lower breast. Eyes and eyelids red. Bill and legs black.

Imported under the trade name of Yellow-rumped Bulbul from South Africa, but do not appear on the market very often. With them the Cape Bulbul, *Pycnonotus capensis*, is sometimes offered. This species is nearly 8 in. long and grey-brown above, being darkest on the head, with red-brown eyes and wine red eyelids. Another very similar species, Layard's Bulbul, *Pycnonotus layardi*, shows less black on the head and throat, has more white on the abdomen, and black eyelids.

Diet: These birds are mainly fruit-eaters but they do not disdain insects and will eat insectivorous food avidly as soon as they have finished the fruit supply. The fruit mixture they like best consists of pears, apples, oranges, berries, boiled raisins, currants, and plums. Large fruit should be cut into small pieces which the birds can easily swallow. Meal-worms are always a treat and will help to tame the birds. Soaked stale bread is also enjoyed. Breeding has been successful, even when insects have been used almost exclusively as rearing food. Nestlings have also been reared on a mixture of finely chopped meat, grated carrots, stale bread, and mulberries, although other soft fruit and berries more easily obtainable may be substituted for the latter.

The birds can winter in a frost-proof room or even in the outside aviary if a good shelter is provided. These birds are lively and easy to tame; they are also good songsters. They can be taught to fly about at liberty in and out of the house and will return at a whistle call.

Blue-throated Barbet *Megalaima asiatica* Pl. 106

Origin India.

Nearly 9 in. *Cock* and *Hen* alike. Crown of head red and a red spot on each side of throat, narrow cross stripe over head which continues along ear coverts, black and yellow. Blue orbital stripe and greeny blue throat and cheeks. Upper parts green, under parts lighter green. Wings green, primaries black with yellow margins. Eyes brown, with orange cere, bill horn-coloured with black tip. Legs blue-green. Notable for its typical 'beard' or tuft of bristles at the base of its beak, which is the origin of its name in French, Dutch, German, and English—'Barbet', meaning bearded.

Barbets are fairly often imported and offered at moderate prices. They must be kept in a very large cage.

The feathers of this colourful and lively Barbet are smooth and glossy. The bird has a peculiar clucking voice which is not often heard. It can be fed with titbits from the hand. As a rule, it will sit quietly on its perch; then, after a while, will jump from perch to perch. It likes to roost in a nest box.

If some soft wood is provided the Barbet will enjoy passing the time by pecking at it with its strong bill. Unsuitable for a community aviary as it is not only pugnacious and destructive but may kill and swallow smaller birds whole. It enjoys an occasional bath, although not a regular bather.

Diet: Insectivorous food, to which has been added various kinds of fruit such as chopped bananas, pears, and cherries. The Barbet also likes mealworms, boiled carrots, and cooked rice, as well as bread soaked with honey and water. Strongly recommended to anyone wishing to keep an unusual species in a cage indoors.

Small Green Barbet (Grey-headed Barbet) *Megalaima viridis*

Origin India.

8 in. *Cock* and *Hen* alike. Head and under parts grey-white; the feathers having brown margins, which are darkest on head, throat, and breast. Nape has a green gloss and brown stripes. Upper parts are grass green, sides with darker margins. Tail green, wings green and black. Eyes brown, bill light brown with black tip, legs greeny-grey.

Suitable only for a cage in which they can be kept alone.

Another species of Barbet which has been imported is the Chinese Green Barbet, *Megalaima virens*, from the south of China. These birds are almost 14 in. long and have beautiful glossy plumage, with golden brown and green on upper parts and a blue head and throat. Breast and belly are also blue, the latter banded with yellowish white. Sides of head are black, remainder of under parts green except for under tail coverts, which are red. Tail is green, bill yellow, and legs grey-green. This is one of the most colourful and most coveted of cage birds.

Diet: Both species eat large quantities of fruit, insectivorous food, and mealworms, with other insects, also finely cut raw meat. Boiled rice, grated or boiled carrots, and various berries must be given to provide variety. The birds often roost in nest boxes. Their voice is indescribably harsh and loud, but is rarely heard. Sometimes on moonlit nights they will be noisy.

The most attractive thing about these birds is their gorgeous plumage. They soon gain complete confidence in anyone who looks after them, and quickly become pets, particularly enjoying a short time of freedom from their cages each day. They enjoy pecking rotting wood, and if this is put in their cages they completely pulverize it with their strong bills.

An interesting bird for those fanciers who like to possess something out of the ordinary.

Black-naped Oriole *Oriolus chinensis indicus*

Origin India and China.

10 in. *Cock:* Back yellow with green sheen. From nostrils and around and above the eye, this bird has a wide black band which joins at the nape. Wings black with yellow and white on the flights. Legs grey, eyes and bill red. *Hen:* Lacks the intensive yellow and is greener than the cock.

This bird is very shy and wild, particularly at first. A cage with a cloth roof is essential, or it is certain to damage itself. A little patience and regular offering of a meal-worm will soon tame it.

Diet: Should consist of 'Universal' food with some finely chopped meat now and again, meal-worms and fresh fruit, cherries, pieces of fig, raisins, and currants.

This species must be kept indoors during the winter. Its song is melodious and powerful with flute-like notes. It will breed in captivity and the young are easily tamed. The cock takes 3 years to attain its full adult colouring.

Golden Oriole (Kundoo) *Oriolus okundoo*

Origin India Himalaya.

10 in. *Cock:* Black wings with white and yellow spots and black lores and a black spot behind eyes. Black tail with yellow tips. Remainder of bird bright yellow. Dark red bill, red eyes, and grey legs. *Hen:* Upper parts grey, rump and upper tail coverts more yellow, chin and throat light grey as is the breast but this has brown markings, with a yellow tone lower down. Belly white, under tail coverts yellow. Wings grey with olive green and yellow-white margins. Bill dark brown, eyes brown. Voice is pleasant and flute-like in tone.

When the birds come into this country usually only cocks are available. They are not very suitable for cages on account of their size. They need ample room, preferably with a plastic or canvas top to the cage as they are very apt to fly upwards and damage their heads. This bird is quite peaceable with others.

Diet: 'Nightingale' food, finely chopped raw meat, hard-boiled egg, and various live insects with fruit as titbits will keep it in good fettle. Bath water must always be available. Breeding results not known.

Racket-tailed Drongo *Dicrurus paradiseus* Pl. 107

Origin India and Indonesia.

14 in. Black with steel-blue gloss and narrow elongated feathers on the crest, nape, and breast. The outer tail feathers extend into long bare quills carrying a tuft of plumage at very tips. Bill and legs black, eyes brown. Sexes alike.

Few fanciers are attracted by these birds, but the species should not be ignored. As a cage bird it is well-liked in its native land, not only for its attractive appearance, but also for its many other good qualities, such as imitative talents, cheerfulness, and tameness. Its song is melodious and flute-like but sometimes mixed with unpleasant harsh screams. These, however, are more than compensated for by the bird's clever imitative ability.

It can be kept quite well with other species of the same size or even bigger. It prefers to sit high up in the branches or on its chosen perch, near which the food bowl and drinking vessel should be placed. It is not fond of bathing and may need to be sprayed now and again. It is adept at catching flying insects.

Diet: Insectivorous food, hard-boiled egg, minced raw meat, meal-worms, and other insects, together with finely cut-up fruit daily.

Although able to withstand coldish nights, it must spend the winter in moderately heated accommodation.

Andaman Mynah *Sturnus erythropygius andamanensis*

Origin Andaman and Nicobar Islands.

8 in. *Cock* and *Hen* alike. Head, neck, and breast white, turning into light grey on abdomen. Back light grey, rump white. Wings black with a green gloss on the outer side, tail similar but with large white tips to outer feathers. Legs and bill yellow. Eyes white.

A single bird or a pair will do well not only in a cage but also in a communal aviary. They soon grow tame and will take meal-worms from the hand. Their general behaviour is similar to that of starlings. They are lively and curious and will imitate various sounds. Their flute-like notes alternate with chattering. They bathe often and eagerly.

Diet: Insectivorous food, sweet fruit, and ants' eggs, with meal-worms as a treat, several kinds of millet and other seed. Turned-over grass turves are much enjoyed.

Breeding results not yet recorded, but it should be possible to breed from this species. Ants' eggs and meal-worms should be made available for the birds while rearing their young. This food should be placed in a bowl mixed with soil and sand, all of which will be appreciated.

Very suitable for our climate and may live in the aviary summer and winter, but adequate shelter must be available.

Pagoda Mynah (Pagoda Starling) *Sturmus pagodarum* Pl. 109

Origin India.

8 in. *Cock:* Black head with a long crest, remainder of bird grey-blue on upper parts and reddish-fawn under parts, tail being black with a white tip. Legs and beak yellow. Cheek striped in white with loosely hanging neck feathers of white and grey. Eyes greenish-white. *Hen:* Like cock but smaller, and crest much shorter.

A companionable bird, readily tamed, and soon imitates various sounds, including the notes of other birds. It is strong and will sometimes start breeding even in a community flight with other big birds. A large nesting box will be needed; this the Pagoda Mynah will fill untidily with all kinds of material at hand. If serious breeding is contemplated, let the old birds fly at liberty as soon as the eggs have been laid. They will stay close to the aviary and will rear their young satisfactorily.

Diet: Meal-worms and ants' eggs, which may be mixed and eaten with soil and sand. Raisins are a favourite food. They love bathing. They are able to winter outside or in an unheated room. Hybridizing with an English starling is possible.

Malabar Mynah *Sturnus malabaricus*

Origin North India.

7½ in. *Cock* and *Hen* alike. Head and neck grey-pink. Back grey, breast and abdomen brown-pink with grey sheen. Wings and tail coverts darker, merging to black with brown tips. Eyes yellow-white. Beak green with yellow tip.

In habits and general behaviour and ability to mimic, they resemble the Pagoda Mynah. They will breed in captivity and are very peaceable. These birds are active and sprightly and are much better in a flight than in a cage. They can winter well outside.

Pied Mynah *Sturnus contra*

Origin India.

Up to 8½ in. *Cock* and *Hen* similar. Head and neck black with a green sheen. Back black-brown, bridle and ear coverts white. Throat black, breast green-black, abdomen beige, under tail coverts white. Upper tail coverts black. Wings black with a green sheen. Beak yellow. Eyes brown with an orange coloured naked orbital patch. Legs yellow. Hen slightly smaller.

Occasionally obtainable and has the reputation of being the best singer in the starling family. It sings persistently with much bowing and scraping, and flapping of wings. It can well be kept in a flight with other birds. If kept singly, will become very tame and can be given the freedom of a living-room. It will, however, leave marks of its presence. It is fond of company, and, if left alone, will whistle until someone comes. Sometimes it will utter a few harsh notes but soon returns to its melodious flute-like song.

The Pied Mynah makes an unholy mess in its cage while feeding or bathing. It is best to keep it in a flight with other birds. Its diet should be the same as that given to the other Mynahs, although meal-worms may sometimes be refused. Breeding results are not known.

Bank Mynah *Acridotheres ginginianus*

Origin India and Southern Asia.

8½ in. *Cock* and *Hen* alike. Black head and naked pink skin around the red eyes. Beak yellow. Back grey. Abdomen grey with a reddish sheen. Wing coverts black with greenish sheen. Tail black with yellow-white tips. Legs orange-yellow.

As cock and hen are similar, it is difficult to select a true pair; the behaviour and song of the cock are the only true signs. The song is a kind of hoarse twittering mixed with flute-like notes and might be described as 'screeching'. Many of these Mynahs are great mimics, and may even learn to say a word or two. They are, therefore, favourite indoor birds, especially as they are cheerful and have sparkling plumage.

They are gourmands and if kept in a cage with insufficient freedom of movement will soon become lazy and fat. The cage must be cleaned out frequently and a mixture of damp peat and sharp sand is ideal as a floor covering. These birds like to bathe frequently. Several of them can be kept in a flight in company with other largish birds.

As their name indicates, Bank Mynahs live by the river. They dig deep holes in the steep banks where they make their nests. To provide similar conditions in an aviary, a dwarf wall can be constructed with a brick left out here and there. The birds will use the cavities as nesting holes. Or they may breed in large nesting boxes, hung high up.

Diet: Mainly 'Universal' food, insects, and fruit. Canary seed, hemp, millet, and oats must be provided, as well as soaked stale bread. If no insects are available, small pieces of raw meat should be given now and again, and some hard-boiled egg and green food. During the breeding season the animal food must be increased considerably by a daily supply of fresh ants' eggs and meal-worms.

These birds are hardy and can winter in a well-sheltered outside aviary or in a bird room.

Common Mynah *Acridotheres tristis* Pl. 108

Origin India, Mauritius.

9½ in. *Cock* and *Hen* alike. The whole head is black. Upper parts brown with a reddish tone. Under tail coverts white. Wings brown with broad black quills. Flank feathers white. Tail black with white tips growing larger towards outside. Eyes brown with a dark ring and yellow cere. Legs and bill yellow.

These birds may be kept together with larger birds. In a cage by itself the Common Mynah is a very pleasant pet, and will soon become completely tame. It hisses, whistles, and chatters. Its imitative talent is great and it will often learn to whistle a short tune and even speak a few words.

When wild, these birds are always near human habitation; they will be found in meadows and on arable land hopping around cattle and hunting for worms and insects. They will sit on trees and roofs with widespread wings and ruffled feathers, singing lustily. They are fond of bathing.

Diet: Insectivorous food, worms, locusts, and other insects. Soaked stale white bread, a variety of seeds, weed seeds, various sweet fruits, and usually green food will be taken eagerly. Now and again some finely chopped raw meat. During rearing time, live food should be in abundant supply.

The presence of a fair-sized nest box will induce breeding. They build a simple nest from grasses, feathers, and hair. The birds are shy and timid while breeding and should not be disturbed.

They can stand our climate and an aviary with a well-protected shelter will be found suitable for both summer and winter.

The scientific name *tristis* presumably refers to the dull colouring of this species, for its liveliness and jollity is a direct contradiction to this name.

Mandarin Mynah (Mandarin Starling) *Sturnus sinensis*

Origin China.

7½ in. *Cock* and *Hen* alike. Front of head cream-coloured running into grey towards back of crown, back grey, rump and topmost of upper tail coverts creamy-white, chin and ear coverts cream, breast and under parts merging into white. Mantle white, remainder of wings black with a steel-green gloss on the outer webs. Tail feathers black with a green gloss and small white spots at the tips, growing larger towards the outer sides. Eyes whitish, bill blue-grey. Legs grey with light horn-coloured nails.

It is difficult to secure a true pair.

Their song is like that of the English starling and consists of an amusing mixture of chattering, fluty, grumbling, and gargling notes. Kept in a cage, these birds rapidly grow tame, but much pleasure will be obtained if they are housed in an aviary; they are gentle, very inquisitive, and lively.

Successful breeding has been recorded. They build in a nest box, their nests being carelessly made with blades of grass, feathers, and hair. When breeding they become very shy and the hen will not go to the nest if anyone is near. As a rule 4 azure blue eggs are laid and incubated by cock and hen alternately. The birds are very fond of meal-worms and earth worms and a liberal supply must be available to meet all needs during the rearing of the young. About 100 of each kind would seem to be necessary per day.

Diet: Insectivorous food, various seeds including millet, canary seed, hemp, and maw. Stale white bread soaked and squeezed dry, chopped raw meat, hard-boiled egg, and sweet fruits are eagerly eaten, while most of these birds also enjoy green food.

They are very fond of bathing. They can be housed in the outside aviary both summer and winter.

Greater Hill Mynah (Javanese Hill Mynah, Northern Hill Mynah) *Gracula r. religiosa* Pl. 110

Origin Indonesia.

10½–13 in. Almost entirely black with a green gloss on back. White spots on flights. Vivid yellow naked folds of skin behind eyes and along ear coverts. Yellow-orange legs. *Hen:* Is more delicate in build than *Cock*, especially about the head. There are various sub-species.

These birds are usually kept singly as they readily learn to imitate speech and other sounds. Housed in a large cage, which must be kept scrupulously clean, they need adequate space for freedom of movement, otherwise they grow lazy and fat. This is due not only to lack of exercise but more often to incorrect feeding.

Diet: 'Universal' food is usually supplied together with some fruit, a few meal-worms, and fresh meat. But the birds can seldom digest the 'Universal' food alone. A liberal and varied fruit menu is needed, together with boiled greens. Dry boiled rice with hard-boiled egg forms the basis of a suitable diet as well as raw finely chopped meat, with some 20 meal-worms. This menu will keep the birds in prime condition and their speech will benefit. As a dainty titbit a young mouse can be offered occasionally.

Some fanciers regard the Hill Mynah as superior to the best of the talking parrots, for this super-intelligent bird can imitate the human voice so well that it is able to repeat parts of a conversation between two human beings without listeners realizing that it is only a bird talking. It will imitate all the noises heard in a home, and will soon grow very tame, responding to special attention and ready to rattle off its repertoire, unlike a parrot which often refuses to do so.

This bird has one disadvantage compared with the parrot. It makes a terrible mess in its cage, for it is a gross feeder. It can be kept in a flight and soon become accustomed to regular visitors; it can also be kept free and learn to come at regular feeding hours but under those conditions it will never learn to talk well.

One reason for keeping these birds separately is that they will kill and devour small birds and if they nest successfully may even eat their own young.

Although the birds can be kept outside in summer they must be brought into a warm room during the winter.

Lesser Hill Mynah (Southern Hill Mynah) *Gracula religiosa indica* Pl. 111

Origin India.

10 in. *Cock* and *Hen* alike. Black with green and purple sheen. Cere, bare patch under eyes and on crown, yellow. Bill orange-yellow, legs yellow.

Imported regularly. In character may be compared with Jackdaws, and soon become household pets. They need a large cage and should be let out now and again. They will learn to talk quite amusingly, and will whistle tunes they have heard.

Diet: Insectivorous food, to which some raw meat or meal-worms have been added, and all kinds of fruit. They are omnivorous, and appreciate scraps from the table as titbits. Menu similar to Greater Hill Mynah. Though they sometimes scream, their voice is usually pleasant and not disturbing. Not only will they imitate the human voice but all manner of domestic noises as well, such as the creaking of door hinges.

Like the Jackdaw, the Hill Mynah will allow itself to be carried about on one's shoulder; it will fly around freely outside and will return at a call or whistle. It is not suitable for a general aviary unless the other inhabitants are also large and able to defend themselves. The cage should be at least 3 ft 6 in. in length and must be cleaned out regularly.

Heated accommodation should be provided in winter.

Yellow-billed Blue Pie *Urocissa flavirostris*

Origin India.

20 in. Sexes are easily recognizable. *Cock:* In full plumage, coloured blue with black wings with white spots, which are entirely yellowish underneath. Under parts pale yellow. Tail very long, dark blue, each feather barred with black and tipped with white. Head almost black with green sheen and white spot on nape. Legs dark red. *Hen:* Dark greenish blue with grey legs. Even if the cock is not in full colour, but resembles the hen, the legs are the determining factor. They may live for 10 or 12 years in captivity.

These very large birds can be kept only in a large flight with birds of a similar type and size, and are seldom met with in private collections. In addition to their very colourful plumage, their liveliness and curiosity, they have the ability to mimic which they quickly learn to do and soon become tame. They are very hardy and can stand all weathers.

Diet: They will eat the scraps from the dining-table, with the addition of raw meat, a dead mouse occasionally, fresh fish, lots of greens, and some fruit. They like sunflower seeds and oats. They require mineral salts, and bone-meal must be mixed with their food occasionally. Care must be taken to ensure that the latter has not been chemically treated for agricultural purposes. During the moult they need cod-liver oil, and extra raw meat in addition to the ordinary menu. Mealworms and ants' eggs are appreciated. Stale bread, soaked and sprinkled with sugar, some hard-boiled egg, a mashed potato with honey, are also good. They need ample variety, and enjoy baby rusks soaked with water and sweetened with sugar and honey. Given such a diet they will keep very fit and will retain their full colouring after the moult which takes place twice a year.

Red-billed Blue Pie *Urocissa erythrorhyncha*

Origin China.

20 in. *Cock:* Head and neck black, feathers of crest with whitish blue tips. White on nape. Mantle brown, upper tail coverts barred with grey and tipped with black. Wings cornflower-blue, tail feathers with black cross bands and white tips. Eyes brown, legs and bill red. *Hen:* Similar but smaller than cock.

Those fanciers with large aviaries who like lively, yet tame, birds, will appreciate this species. They can never be kept with small birds, as they will kill and eat them immediately. They like to sit high up in the aviary and watch with keen interest all that goes on below.

They soon become accustomed to taking meal-worms or a piece of cheese from the hand. When excited they make a most penetrating noise like all the crow tribe, to which their behaviour is similar.

Diet: It is easy to cater for them as they eat greedily all manner of 'leftovers', and relish a piece of raw meat now and again or a young mouse. Bread, greens, boiled potatoes, fruit, grain, especially oats, are enjoyed. They will even eat fish.

They are absolutely hardy and may be kept together with Jays or large Parrakeets.

Occipital Blue Pie *Urocissa e. occipitalis*
Pl. 112

Origin The high plateaus of India.

18½ in. *Cock:* Head, neck, and throat black, light blue sheen on the nape. Back grey-brown, wings and tail deep blue; breast and belly white with a light blue tone merging into grey white on the sides. Wing and tail feathers have white tips. Legs orange, eyes brown-red. Bill red. *Hen:* Is a little smaller than the cock.

Large and lively, they are at their best in a large aviary, not less than 5 ft high. They like to sit high up and watch with curiosity all that goes on below. They are attracted by glittering objects. Once they become accustomed to their environment, they rapidly become tame, and will come to hand to take titbits.

Diet: Besides bread and milk and various seeds, they must have some raw meat chopped into small pieces and meal-worms. They are one of the hardiest species and can stay in the aviary summer and winter, often attaining a ripe old age. They may be taught to speak a word or two; if a young bird is kept alone he will learn to call his name. They are most intelligent, but they cannot be kept together with small birds for the latter would soon be killed and eaten.

Lanceolated Jay *Garrulus lanceolatus*
Pl. 113

Origin India.

12½ in. *Cock* and *Hen:* Head black, throat black striated with white, back grey with dark red tone, under parts dark reddish merging into grey towards throat. Wings grey and black with white tips, tail blue with black cross bands and white tips, margined by wide black bands. Grey legs, greenish horn-coloured bill. *Hen* has a shorter bill.

Suitable for a large aviary with other large birds that are able to protect themselves, as for instance Yellow-billed Blue Pie, *Urocissa flavirostris*.

Diet: In addition to raw meat now and again, which should be cut up into small pieces, and a dead mouse or bird, they will eat various seeds and fruit, also boiled potatoes, stale bread, meal-worms, and a number of other insects. Boiled greens, rice, meat, and table scraps are enjoyed. Vita lime should be given occasionally. During moult extra raw meat is essential. The addition of minerals and vitamins at regular intervals can be recommended. When they have been accustomed to titbits of food they will soon become tame.

Breeding results have been obtained but the young are often devoured by the parents a few days after hatching. This might possibly be prevented by supplying a super-abundance of young mice, insects, and so forth, immediately the young appear.

These are hardy birds and may remain in the aviary summer and winter.

Calandra Lark *Melanocorypha calandra*

Origin Territory around the Mediterranean.

5 in. *Cock* and *Hen* alike. Brown and isabel coloured, markings as a Lark. Feet with extra long hind claws.

This species sings even more beautifully than our skylark. It may be kept in a large cage which must be at least 3 ft long with a cloth covering stretched inside the top, as it has a habit of springing upwards and might damage its head against a wooden- or wire-topped cage. The bird likes to sit on a stone when singing and seldom uses a perch. A fresh turf of grass should be placed on the bottom of the cage every day. The bird likes to scratch about this in search of insects. A bowl of dry sand must also be provided, as this species takes only dust baths.

Diet: Good insectivorous mixture, finely cut-up green stuff, and germinated seeds. During winter months canary seed, rape seed, maw, millet, and crushed oats should be given. Meal-worms are a welcome delicacy, and sometimes these birds will eat soaked stale bread. Various kinds of insects must be given as well as ants' eggs.

The birds make pleasant house pets and live for many years.

Red-billed Lark *Calandrella conirostris*

Origin South Africa.

Nearly 5 in. *Cock* and *Hen* alike. Upper parts brown to rust-brown, the feathers flecked with black. White stripe below lores and eye, throat and chin also white. Under parts yellow-brown, darkest near the crop, spotted with black, particularly in the area of crop. Wings dark brown with light brown and white margins. Tail dark brown. Bill red-brown, legs flesh-coloured. Eyes brown.

Though not often found in our cages and aviaries, it has proved a satisfactory and pleasant house pet, living for many years.

While these Larks can be kept with others in an aviary, their habit of flying suddenly upwards is liable to disturb the other birds. Their plumage may become soiled by other birds which roost above them. They are quiet and spend most of their time on the ground, hirruping while perched on a rock or stump of a tree. They make good ground-floor tenants of a roomy aviary, a part of which should be covered by a thick layer of sharp river sand. Perches should be placed over this and a few sizeable rocks introduced, together with an old tree stump. If this is in a sunny spot, the Lark will sit there and sing to its heart's content. The food dish should be placed on the floor.

Diet: Insectivorous mixture, occasionally some finely chopped raw meat and hard-boiled egg, meal-worms, and ants' eggs. Various kinds of millet, canary seed, and weed seeds. Freshly sprouted oats are a welcome delicacy. Finely cut-up green stuff should be provided daily. A tuft of clover or chickweed is very greatly appreciated. The bird will diligently hunt out all kinds of nourishment, especially green food.

Because this is a ground bird, a cage, if used, need only be a low one. But to provide adequate exercise, its length must be greatly increased. A cage 3 ft 6 in. long with a height of 1 ft provides enough space for a pair of Larks. The lower part of the sides should be boarded for about 4 in. as a 2-in. layer of sand is needed. Fresh garden soil may be added from time to time. The Lark likes dust baths, and a good deal of sand will be scattered about; hence the bowls for food and drink must be placed away from the sand, or hung on the outside of the cage front in which there should be round holes through which the bird can put its head to feed and drink. No bath water is necessary as the lark takes sand baths only.

The sandy bottom of the cage must always be kept clean and given frequent attention. The legs of the birds should be kept clean by washing in tepid water if necessary. Newly imported birds are sometimes full of vermin; this should be got rid of by the use of an insecticide.

The species has never been bred in captivity and a really large aviary would be needed if breeding were attempted. Nests have occasionally been made in a shallow hollow in the ground and eggs have even been laid but these have never been hatched.

With careful treatment they may be kept for many years in an aviary or a large cage. They are hardy and can winter in an outdoor aviary. If frightened, they may suddenly fly upwards, and it is advisable that the top of the cage be made of canvas or plastic so that the bird will not damage its head.

Grey Plantain Eater *Crinifer piscator*

Origin West Africa.

18½ in. *Cock* and *Hen* alike. Head and neck brown, wings grey with brown quill stripes. Elongated feathers on nape of neck have white margins. Tail brown and black. Under parts white with black-brown markings. Bill yellow, legs black.

Not often kept by fanciers, owing to the difficulties of looking after them. Yet they are hardy and once settled down will live for years in a large cage or aviary. Their voice is penetrating and they laugh, bark, and make noises like cats.

Diet: While mainly fruit-eaters, they cannot live without meat and insects. Boiled rice, carrots, and potatoes may be included in their diet, with a small supply of meal-worms, grubs, gentles, berries, and fruit.

The birds like to be in a shrubbery which has grown tall, and a high aviary is the best place for them. If there is plenty of room they can be kept with smaller birds. For fanciers who like to keep unusual birds, this species offers new opportunities for observation and study.

Violaceous Touracou (Violaceous Plantain Eater) *Musophaga violacea* Pl. 114

Origin West Africa.

18½ in. *Cock* and *Hen* alike. Dark glossy blue-black, darkest on the back and under parts. The silky head plumage is purple-red. Below cere and naked red orbital ring runs a white stripe. A green sheen lies over crop area. Eyes golden-brown, legs black. Strong yellow bill has a carmine tip. Hen slightly smaller and shorter in tail. Eyes golden-yellow.

Shy and timid at first, these birds soon become tame. They prefer to perch high up among the foliage. The call of the cock during the mating time resembles that of a cock pheasant. This species may be kept with other large birds.

Diet: As with the Plantain Eater, to which they are closely related, these birds live on fruit, boiled rice, or potatoes, with or without the addition of boiled carrots. A quantity of green food and fruit, such as grapes and bananas, must be given to vary the diet. Live insects are a delicacy.

Suitable for a roomy aviary, these birds are very active and interesting. They should be kept moderately warm in winter.

Cape Robin Chat *Cossypha caffra* Pl. 115

Origin South Africa.

7½ in. *Cock:* Upper plumage olive brown with a grey sheen. Rump red-brown, white eyebrow mark extending behind ears. Cheeks black, throat red-brown edged with white, breast and sides grey. Centre of abdomen white and remainder of abdomen rust-coloured. Wings red-brown and grey, tail brown. Bill black, legs brown. *Hen:* Throat creamy colour, breast red-brown, more white on the abdomen.

Its song is soft and melodious, occasionally marred by a jarring note. This bird is very suitable to keep either in a roomy cage or an aviary with birds of a different species. It is active and will jump from perch to perch and through the branches, or run about on the ground diligently hunting for food. It likes bathing.

Diet: Insectivorous food, to which ants' eggs have been added, fruit cut up small, meal-worms, or other insects. As a change finely minced raw meat may be given as well as hard-boiled egg and bread and milk.

Cape Robin Chat is not imported regularly and has not been known to breed in captivity.

Wattled Starling *Creatophora cinerea carunculata* Pl. 116

Origin East and southern Africa.

8 in. *Cock:* During breeding season has head naked, bright yellow with well-developed black wattles over eyes and at throat. In the non-breeding season wattles are much reduced and apart from a small yellow orbital patch head is covered with pale grey feathers. Grey-brown above with a lighter rump and upper tail coverts. Under parts lighter merging from grey to white. Tail black, wings black and white. Bill yellow, eyes brown, legs flesh-coloured. *Hen:* Darker than the cock, cere part around the eyes and throat greeny-yellow, white rump, brown and white wings.

Very rarely imported. They are interesting, lively, and beautiful and are mainly insect-eaters. In the wild state they can be seen in large flocks, always hunting for locusts and following locust swarms. They also nest where locusts have laid their eggs; usually in large colonies and the young are reared on young locusts.

Diet: Insectivorous food, all sorts of live insects, worms, and some finely cut-up fruit.

No record of breeding in captivity

available. It should be possible to keep Wattled Starlings together with other birds of their own size in an aviary.

Long-tailed Glossy Starling *Lamprotornis caudatus* Pl. 117

Origin West Africa.

20 in. *Cock* and *Hen* alike. Gleaming steely green, more bronze coloured at head and neck, with a blue gloss on the rump and tail, and with black spots on tail as well as on ear coverts and lores. Under parts with a blue gloss bronze coloured on belly. Eyes yellow, bill and legs black.

They cannot be kept with other birds without considerable risk. Everything may seem to run smoothly and then there will be a sudden attack resulting in the death of the victim. Their song is not attractive, and consists of a constant cheeping, hissing, and screeching. They should be removed to a heated conservatory or bird room during winter.

In the sunshine, the sheen and glossy colouring of these birds is a glorious sight. Their initial shyness soon wears off, and they will take meal-worms from the hand, immediately recognizing and coming to meet their owner.

Diet: Insectivorous food, bread and milk, with a hard-boiled egg now and again, grated raw meat, meal-worms, and finely cut-up fruit. They like newly born mice, and germinating seeds will also be eagerly eaten.

They bathe often and thoroughly. It has been found possible to breed from them. They will make their nest in a roomy nest box and their eggs hatch in a fortnight. The rearing food should be similar to the diet just described, but it must be as varied as possible.

Green Glossy Starling *Lamprotornis chalybaeus* Pl. 118

Origin Africa except North.

8 in. *Cock:* Upper parts glossy metallic green, ear coverts, rump, and upper tail coverts blue. Belly deep blue, tail glossy metallic blue-green. Eyes golden-yellow, bill and legs black. *Hen:* Smaller.

Glossy Starlings are not the easiest of birds to keep. The long-tailed variety needs a very large cage, otherwise the birds will soon damage their tails. The short-tailed variety needs a great deal of space on account of its liveliness. Short-tailed Glossy Starlings will not live in constant harmony either with their own kind or with other species even of the same size. Sudden outbursts of temper frequently occur, and may prove fatal. They will, however, not molest the larger parrakeets or such birds as the White-crested Jay Thrush, *Garrulax leucolophus*, not the sweetest tempered of birds themselves. All Glossy Starlings must have a very large aviary at their disposal or a conservatory in which each bird has a corner to itself.

They have been successfully bred in captivity. Both cock and hen will share in building a nest from twigs and grasses in a nest box. The eggs hatch in 14 days, and the young will remain another 4 weeks in the nest. Rearing food should consist of insectivorous food to which must be added ants' eggs, finely chopped raw meat, worms, snails, meal-worms, fruit in season, and also dates, finely cut up. Germinating seeds are enjoyed.

Normal Diet: Must contain insectivorous food and fruit with worms, meal-worms, and chopped raw meat as extras.

These starlings bathe freely and often.

Purple-headed Glossy Starling *Lamprotornis purpureiceps*

Origin West and East Africa.

Cock: 8½ in., inc. tail 3 in. Head black on top with a purple gloss. Sides of head and chest are black with a pink sheen. Remainder black with a blue and green sheen. Eyes yellow, beak and legs black. *Hen:* Is not so glossy, and usually smaller.

These birds must be provided with a large flight if they have to live with other birds of a similar size. Their sharp mandibles can easily kill smaller birds. They will often interfere with the breeding of other birds, rob their nests, and eat their eggs.

Diet: They can be kept in excellent condition with 'Universal' food, a seed menu, some meal-worms, and earthworms, insects, and a few young mice now and again. Finely chopped raw meat and a variety of fresh fruit must be given at intervals. These birds will use a large nest box for breeding and will fill it with all kinds of material. The eggs will hatch after about 2 weeks. Insects, meal-worms, and ants' eggs form the main diet for the rearing of the young chicks.

They need ample bathing facilities, and must have a moderately warm room in winter.

Purple-headed Starlings have hybridized with several of the related species.

Purple Glossy Starling *Lamprotornis purpureus* Pl. 119

Origin Africa except North.

8¾ in. *Cock:* Head and under parts violet-purple, wings and back metallic glossy green and blue, short tail violet. Bill and legs black, eyes golden-yellow.

Hen: Similar, but slightly smaller than cock.

Care and diet as Green Glossy Starlings.

Their colouring is magnificent. Successful breeding and even crossings have been reported. They bathe often and must be kept in moderately heated accommodation in the winter.

Superb Spreo *Spreo superbus* Pl. 120

Origin East Africa.

8¼ in. One of the most beautiful of African Glossy Starlings and so tolerant that it can be safely kept with most other birds in a communal flight. Its voice is rather loud and not particularly beautiful; which makes it unsuitable for a living-room. Sexes alike.

Its gaudiness of plumage and tameness make this species much in demand. Another advantage is that no special diet is needed. 'Universal' food, fruit, and many meal-worms with the addition of finely chopped raw meat once or twice a week is sufficient. The bird soon learns to take the meal-worms from the hand. It is hardy and will breed readily in captivity. A nesting box of the size needed for parrakeets or a little larger will be filled with any materials available. There are usually 2 or 3 chicks in a brood.

During breeding time these birds require a large quantity of ants' eggs and worms, together with other insects, as they will hardly touch the 'Universal' food throughout this period. Large beetles will be eaten eagerly. Hatching takes 13 days.

Guinea Bare-headed Rockfowl (Picathartes) *Picathartes gymnocephalus*

Origin Sierra Leone.

15 in. *Cock:* Whole of under parts white. Back, tail, and wings black. Crown of head, neck, and cheeks bare of feathers and beige in colour. A small tuft of jet black feathers replace ear coverts. Large black bill. Eyes black and large, legs light grey. *Hen:* Similar but slightly smaller.

This species is extremely rare, the first living examples having been brought to the London Zoo, and the Wassenaar Zoo in Holland.

These birds spend nearly all their time on the ground hunting for insects and leaping from place to place on their long powerful legs.

Diet: Such fruit as grapes, bananas, and apples, with some insectivorous food and soaked stale bread, also meal-worms and insects.

Sunbirds *Nectariniidae*

Sunbirds, of which there are very many species, are widely distributed in Africa, southern Asia, and Australasia. They are, as their generic name suggests, all nectar feeders with long curved beaks adapted for thrusting into flowers from which they extract their food, and with tongues which can be easily projected and are provided with a bifid tube at the end.

In addition to nectar, they eat quantities of tiny insects which they find in the flowers. By their method of feeding they play an important part in the fertilization of various plants since pollen sticks to their beaks and is thus transferred from flower to flower.

They do not possess the marvellous powers of hovering flight displayed by Hummingbirds which in other respects they closely resemble, and seldom feed on the wing.

They are very aggressive, especially towards their own kind whether of the same or other species, and it is even difficult to keep a pair together without a serious risk of fighting which often proves fatal. Only during the nesting season, and if cock and hen are in equally good breeding condition, is it reasonably safe to keep them together, in a large aviary which should be well planted with thickly growing shrubs and climbing plants which will afford refuge to either bird should it be persistently chased and persecuted by its mate. It is a wise precaution to supply several feeding places since these birds have a habit of dominating a food tray and preventing any others from approaching to feed.

The plumage of the males of nearly all species is brilliantly coloured and has a rich metallic sheen while that of the female is dull grey or olive, and providing the birds are adult the sexes can usually be readily distinguished.

Young birds of both sexes are like the adult hen in general appearance and the cocks of a few species, such as the Malachite Sunbird, have an eclipse plumage which is assumed during the non-breeding period, when it may prove difficult to recognize their sex.

Unfortunately, those species which have red in their plumage, such as the Scarlet-chested and Double-collared, soon lose the vivid brilliance of that colour when in captivity, especially if confined in cages or under conditions which preclude their being able to obtain an adequate supply of small live insects. With each successive moult, the red tends to become more faded until it is eventually replaced by orange or a dull and rather muddy yellow.

So far no satisfactory method has been discovered to correct this tendency by artificial means but the deterioration may be greatly retarded

and almost checked if the birds are kept in large and well-planted aviaries or at liberty in a tropical planthouse where a maximum of sunlight is admitted and insect life abounds.

If suitable accommodation is limited and it is particularly desired that it should be shared with other birds, it is preferable to associate them with seed-eaters, which will limit competition at the feeding tables. They may be kept with other species of the same genus, providing they are all of one sex, and with Tanagers, Sugar Birds, and other small insectivorous birds, but only if the accommodation is spacious and furnished with plenty of natural cover.

If the aviary or enclosure is completely covered, the plants and shrubs should be frequently sprayed with water as Sunbirds are 'rain bathers', and will keep their plumage in good condition if they are able to bath among the wet foliage but can seldom be induced to descend to a pan of water on the ground.

They should be supplied with artificial nectar in the specially designed glass tubes which are obtainable for this purpose and the mixture can be made up from a teaspoonful of prepared food, such as Mellins or Horlicks, with equal quantities of sweetened condensed milk and honey dissolved in $\frac{1}{2}-\frac{3}{4}$ pint warm water.

The mixture must be allowed to cool before being given to the birds and once a week raw egg should be beaten up and added. It is essential that it should only be available when completely fresh and the supply should be renewed at least twice a day. On no account should the proportion of prepared food or milk be increased or the water reduced, as the mixture is apt to prove too fattening and the birds' condition would suffer.

As an alternative there is now an excellent nectar paste on the market, which is fortified with the essential vitamins and only requires to be diluted with water in accordance with the manufacturer's instructions. This food has the great advantage that it does not sour during the hot weather as will any mixture containing milk.

Sunbirds appreciate sweet oranges and grapes from which they will suck the juice, and will welcome as many small flies, spiders, caterpillars, and fresh ants' eggs as can be supplied. Many will become tame enough to take insects from the hand and some will even take a little finer-grade insectivorous food.

Sunbirds require special care when first imported and when selecting birds from a newly arrived consignment, one should never be tempted to buy a specimen which sits with its head hunched on its shoulders and its tongue protruding, beyond the tip of its beak, for this is a sure sign that it is in a bad way and may well be beyond the ability of the most experienced fancier to restore to health. Once acclimatized, however, they usually prove to be surprisingly hardy and comparatively long-lived.

A considerable number of different species have been imported but it will be sufficient to briefly describe those which are most frequently offered.

Malachite Sunbird *Nectarinia famosa* Pl. 121

Origin East of South Africa.

6¼ in. *Cock:* In breeding plumage entirely shining metallic green. Coppery on back and with wings and tail blackish. The two central tail feathers are considerably lengthened and on the flanks (usually concealed when the wings are folded), are tufts of silky yellow feathers. The beak is long, slender, and curved, and black in colour as also are the legs. *Hen:* Olive grey, lighter underneath, with yellowish eyebrows and facial stripes. She lacks the elongated tail feathers. In eclipse plumage the cock closely resembles her.

This is one of the largest species, a magnificent bird, over 6 in. in length. It has frequently been imported, is hardy when once acclimatized, and a single bird will live well in a large cage. There is a sub-species which has the tufts on the flanks scarlet.

Scarlet-chested Sunbird *Chalcomitra gutturalis* Pl. 122

Origin East and South Africa.

5 in. Another large Sunbird. It is brilliant in colouring when first imported but unfortunately apt to lose much of its beauty when moulted in captivity.

Cock: Is velvety black and dark brown with crown of head and gorget brilliant green. Lower part of throat and breast deep crimson red and there is a spot of violet on the fold of each wing. Black beak is very long and curved. *Hen:* Is grey above, yellowish below with dark grey striations.

Amethyst Sunbird *Cinnyris amethystina*

Origin West of South Africa.

5 in. Similar in size and shape to Scarlet-chested Sunbird. Of intense velvety black with the top of head dark metallic green and throat purple amethyst, so dark that its beauty is only seen to advantage in strong sunlight. *Hen:* Is very similar to the Scarlet-chested hen, and *Cock* resembles her when in eclipse plumage.

Greater Double-collared Sunbird
Cinnyris afer

Origin South Africa.

4½ in. This and Lesser Double-collared Sunbird are the two species which have been most frequently imported.

Cock: Shining green above with the wings and tail dark grey. Rump blue, under parts pale grey with upper part of breast bright red, separated from green throat by a narrow band of dark metallic blue. *Hen:* Is greyish yellow and the cock resembles her when in eclipse plumage.

Lesser Double - collared Sunbird
Cinnyris chalybeus

4 in. Very similar to preceding species except that it is smaller and the breast is less red. It also comes from South Africa.

White-bellied Sunbird *Cinnyris leucogaster* Pl. 123

Origin East Africa.

About 3½ in. *Cock:* In breeding plumage, head, sides of face, and back metallic green with a gold and blue sheen; upper tail coverts more blue; wings black; tail blue-black with metallic green edges and light tips. Neck metallic blue-green, chin dull black; broad band of metallic violet across the chest followed by a narrower band of black. Remainder of under parts white or white slightly tinted with yellow. Yellow tufts of feathers at sides of chest, usually concealed by the wings. Bill and legs blackish. In non-breeding plumage the cock is similar to the adult hen but it retains the blue-black tail, metallic upper tail coverts and wing coverts and a few scattered metallic feathers on the head and mantle. *Hen:* Ashy-brown above

with blue-black tail with metallic green edges and similar edging to the tail coverts. Below dusky white. Immature birds are similar to the hen but are usually more olive brown above and yellowish below.

Mariqua Sunbird (Marico Sunbird)
Cinnyris mariquensis Pl. 124

Origin East Africa.

About 4½ in. *Cock:* Head, throat, and whole of upper parts metallic green with golden wash; wings and tail black with blue-black gloss and some metallic green on edge of wings. Broad violet band across chest followed by a band of maroon with metallic violet tips to the feathers; belly smokey dark grey or blackish. Bill and feet blackish. Unlike many other species of sunbird, the Mariqua has no eclipse plumage. *Hen:* greenish-ash coloured above, darker on the cheeks; tail black with a slight blue wash and whitish tips to all but the centre pair of feathers and whitish edges to the outer feathers. Throat dusky, remainder of under parts yellow with dusky streaks.

Purple Sunbird *Arachnothera asiatica*

Origin India.

4½ in. *Cock:* Entirely black with overlaying metallic sheen of purple and dark green and with orange pectoral tufts. Winter plumage much resembles that of the female, which is yellow olive, but a few dark feathers are usually retained on wings, tail, and throat, thus making it possible to distinguish the sexes at all times.

Red Sunbird (Yellow-backed Sunbird)
Aethopyga seheriae

Origin Far East, Himalaya.

Cock: 5 in. inc. long tail. A small bird with a long graduated tail, the top of head metallic green, and the nape dull green. A band of blue runs from beak to sides of neck, rest of head, upper parts of back and breast being scarlet. Lower back is golden and tail green. *Hen:* Olive with a shading of red on throat.

Unfortunately this is another of the very beautiful species which loses much of its brilliant red colouring in captivity.

Hummingbirds *Trochilidae*

Origin America.

This genus includes the smallest birds known and when in flight they look like butterflies or large dragon-flies. All come from America, where they live in tropical and sub-tropical areas, and subsist on tiny insects and nectar which they sip from tropical jungle flowers. They seldom, if ever, come to the ground, their minute legs and feet being suited only to perching on thin twigs and leaf stems. Much of their time is spent on the wing hovering backwards and forwards round the flowering trees and shrubs from which they obtain their food, and looking like the glittering gems from which they derive their name.

To prepare a suitable habitat for Hummingbirds may well be beyond the means of the ordinary fancier. To be kept alive the bird needs, at the least, a warm conservatory with tropical flowers or a large cage. Steady heat above 60° F (15° C), a daily spraying with tepid water or bathing facilities in dampened leaves, and the greatest possible cleanliness are essentials. Many species, however, have been successfully kept at much lower temperatures than this and some have even lived in outdoor aviaries throughout the year without any artificial heat, and

have remained in perfect health and plumage.

Diet: Consists largely of nectar which should be given in the glass tubes specially supplied for nectar feeding and which have a small, up-turned tube inserted at the base into which the birds can thrust their long beaks as they would into the heart of a flower.

Excellent proprietary brands of nectar are obtainable in a concentrated form and only need to be diluted with water before being given to the birds. These foods do not contain milk in any form and consequently do not tend to turn sour.

As an alternative, the following mixture may be used for the morning feed:

> Approx. 1 teaspoon of Mellins
> food or Horlicks;
> 1 teaspoon honey;
> 1 teaspoon Nestlé's Milk;
> to ¼ pint of boiling water.

Naturally the mixture must be allowed to cool before use and, especially in warm weather, it should be removed at midday and replaced with a solution of honey in the proportion of approx. 2 teaspoons honey to ¼ pint water.

In a wild state they consume quantities of tiny insects and if a supply of fruit flies, *Drosophila*, can be available to them, their condition will be greatly improved.

Though these birds can be kept alive for a long time, they need great care and only the experienced fancier should attempt to keep them. They require a large flight, for they will fight each other ferociously in a small one; ample space is essential and even then only one or two can be kept together. In the wild these birds build beautiful nests but in captivity they seldom attempt to breed.

Ruby Topaz Hummingbird *Chrysolampis mosquitus* Pl. 127

Origin South America.

3½ in. *Cock:* Scale-like feathers of crown brilliant ruby-red; chin, throat, and upper breast metallic gold; hind neck and mantle black; remainder of upper parts olive bronze; tail bright chestnut edged with purple and bronze; flight feathers dusky. Under parts warm brown with tufts of white feathers over legs; beak dull black. *Hen:* Upper parts bronzey-green, greyish on forehead; tail metallic green in centre with dusky tips and with outer feathers chestnut tipped with white. Under parts pale brownish-grey and with a dark stripe on throat.

Pucheran's Emerald Hummingbird *Chlorostilbon aureoventris pucherani* Pl. 125 and 126

Origin Eastern Brazil.

3 in. *Cock:* Upper parts metallic green with coppery sheen; tail dark with bluish sheen. Under parts brilliant green. Beak red with black tip. *Hen:* Less brilliant on back and greyish under parts.

Sugarbirds: *Dacnidinae*

Yellow-winged Sugarbird (Red-legged Honeycreeper) *Cyanerpes cyaneus* Pl. 128

Origin South Mexico and Cuba.

5 in. *Cock:* Crown brilliant turquoise blue, feathers shining and scale-like; a black streak through eyes and across forehead, and a black mark from sides of neck extending back to the centre of the back, remainder of body bright purple-blue with a brilliant sheen. Flight feathers black with inner webs which are concealed when wing is closed, bright canary-yellow; tail black. Beak black; legs and feet red. In eclipse plumage cock is similar to hen but usually retains the red legs although the colour may be less intense. *Hen:* Upper parts olive green, greyish on head and with a dark eye stripe and whitish eyebrow mark; flights and tail brownish, inner webs of flights margined with pale yellow. Under parts, chin, and throat greenish-white blending into yellowish-white on breast and abdomen, all lightly striated with greenish-grey. Beak black, legs and feet pale pinkish-brown.

This graceful and colourful bird is one of the more delicate species, which, however, is not over-difficult to keep. It is offered for sale fairly regularly.

Diet: Fine 'Universal' food and fruit, such as bananas, pears, and oranges suspended near a perch. Real honey diluted with water is essential and must be placed in a drinker in such a way that it can reach it readily without descending to the ground. It also enjoys meal-worms and ants' eggs. As a change soaked stale bread sprinkled with sugar or glucose, hard-boiled egg, a little cooked potato or boiled rice mixed with honey may be given; also rusks mixed to a paste with water and sprinkled with sugar or honey form an acceptable food.

With this menu the bird will remain in excellent condition and moreover will pass through the moult, which occurs twice a year, without difficulty and will retain the full beauty of its natural colouring.

As a covering for the floor of its cage blotting paper is preferable to sawdust and in place of ordinary wood perches, fresh twigs should be used which must be renewed frequently. To maintain the birds in good condition, bathing facilities must always be available. They can then splash about to their hearts' content.

Several may be kept together if they are all cocks but the presence of hens will cause fighting. A single pair may safely be associated with other small birds.

They also make suitable subjects for a large cage. Their food should be suspended near a perch as they dislike being on the floor of the cage.

It has been successfully bred on several occasions both in a cage and in an outdoor aviary. The nest is suspended in the fork of a tall bush and is constructed of fine plant fibres and soft vegetable down.

In addition to the honey mixture and soft fruit, quantities of small live insects such as fruit flies, aphis, and ants' eggs are required to rear the young.

The Yellow-winged Sugarbird has proved to be hardy and can withstand quite low temperatures; it has been known to live for 10–12 years in captivity. They are better kept in a warm room during winter.

Purple Sugarbird (Yellow-legged Honeycreeper) *Cyanerpes caeruleus* Pl. 131

Origin Surinam and British Guiana.

3¼–4½ in. *Cock:* Upper and under parts purple blue. Lores, wings, throat, and tail black. Beak black, legs and feet yellow with black claws. *Hen:* Rich green above, throat chestnut, under parts pale yellowish with dark green striations. A narrow pale violet-blue moustache mark on each side of throat. Lores and feathers round eyes chestnut-

buff. Beak blackish, legs and feet greenish-brown.

The beak of this bird is long and curved, the body stumpy, and tail extremely short, giving it a somewhat wren-like appearance. The birds require a great deal of care, but this does not mean a fancier should not try to keep them.

Diet: As for other Sugarbirds. All food should be hung up.

These birds are very suitable for a cage or indoor aviary, although a sojourn in the outside flight during a warm summer will not harm them. They like sunshine and bathe only occasionally. When outside, spray the plants regularly and the birds will bathe in the wet foliage. They are quite tolerant with birds of a similar type, for instance the Yellow-winged Sugarbird.

A moderate room temperature suits them and they can withstand cool nights. Given a varied diet, they will live for years.

Isthmian Purple Sugarbird *Cyanerpes caeruleus isthmicus* Pl. 129

Origin Central America.

4¾ in. Very slightly larger than the Purple Sugarbird, *C. caeruleus*, from which the *Cock* differs only in body colour which is rather lighter and less violet in shade. *Hen:* Is more distinctive, the feathers of the breast and flanks being fringed with violet which is particularly noticeable on the striations; legs greenish-grey.

Blue Sugarbird (Black-throated or Turquoise Honeycreeper) *Dacnis cayana* Pl. 130

Origin South Mexico to Brazil.

4½ in. *Cock:* Head dark turquoise blue with lores, feathers round eyes, and a large throat patch black as also is mantle, remainder of body plumage turquoise blue with greenish tinge. Wings and tail black, upper coverts and flights being edged with blue. Beak dusky, lighter on lower mandible; legs pinkish-brown. *Hen:* Head turquoise with dusky lores; chin and throat grey; back brilliant green; wings and tail dusky brown, lesser coverts edged with turquoise; under parts apple green shading into yellowish-green on abdomen and indistinctly barred with grey on flanks. Beak dusky, legs pale pinkish-brown.

Scarlet-thighed Sugarbird *Dacnis venusta*

Origin Costa Rica, Panama, Columbia.

4½–5 in. *Cock:* Crown, side of neck, nape, mantle, back, and upper tail coverts brilliant greenish-turquoise; forehead, cheeks, throat, and whole of under parts and also secondaries, flights, and tail dense black and a black bar on shoulders. Thighs a brilliant crimson; legs brown; beak black. *Hen:* A dull edition of the cock, the black being replaced by dark grey and the blue by a dull greyish blue, the demarkation between black and blue areas being very indistinct.

Black-headed Sugarbird (Black-crowned or Green Honeycreeper) *Chlorophanes spiza*

Origin Guatemala to South-East Brazil.

5½–5¾ in. *Cock:* A sharply defined black head and cheeks, remainder entirely shining green varying in shade and darker on upper parts, flights, and tail. Beak, upper mandible black, lower clear yellow; legs blackish. *Hen:* Entirely green, lighter in tone than cock, under parts being yellowish on throat and apple green on the breast. Flights and tail dark brownish-green. Beak as cock but lower mandible a dull yellow.

TANAGERS *Thraupidae*

It is of utmost importance when buying a Tanager to notice its physical condition. The acclimatization and the change over to different food call for the greatest care, for it is then that birds are most frequently lost. Once they have grown accustomed to their new environment and food they are not so delicate as is often assumed. They do not show to advantage in a small cage, and many of them would be too large. A small conservatory or glassed-in loggia containing a varied collection of birds is ideal, for here the Tanagers can display their gorgeous colourings and lively disposition.

Diet: A varied diet is essential. A large variety of soft and sweet fruit must be provided. Figs, dates, raisins, and currants, should be first soaked and cut up into small pieces. This is also the rule for other fruit except apples, oranges and very ripe pears, which may simply be cut in half. Some crumbled rusks should be mixed into this fruit salad, together with ants' eggs either fresh or dried, and small or cut-up meal-worms. An insectivorous mixture is suitable. Grated carrot and crumbs of stale white bread can be given for a change. Bread and milk, with sugar and honey, is very good for them, and they need grit, ground egg shells, and green food.

They eat all day long, so cleanliness is essential especially in a cage. They bathe daily and very thoroughly. Plenty of sunlight is needed to maintain the exquisite colouring of the plumage.

Breeding: Several species have bred in an aviary, and occasionally a pair have bred in a large cage, but they cannot be described as free breeders. They cannot be associated with their own kind during the breeding period, but will leave other species in peace. They can go into the outside aviary about June and need not be brought indoors until October. Breeding takes place during the summer.

Nest boxes should be fixed high up, but if there are any dense bushes growing in the aviary the birds will probably choose to build in these in preference. They use fine twigs and blades of grass for the outside of the cup-shaped nest, which is lined inside with finer grasses, woollen threads, and sometimes with some broad leaves. All Tanagers do not build sturdy nests and it is advisable to insert a piece of wire gauze in the shape of a bowl under the spot where they are building.

As a rule, cocks are imported but frequently there are some hens in the consignment, so with a little patience a pair can usually be obtained. The Scarlet Tanager, *Ramphocelus brasilius* (Pl. 139) and the Maroon Tanager, *Ramphocelus carbo*, certainly tie for first place as successful breeders and hybrids have occurred frequently between them.

The Scarlet Tanager builds a sturdy nest, and often lays 3 eggs, which hatch in 12 days; the Maroon Tanager builds an untidy nest, and seldom lays more than 2 eggs. While young remain in the nest, they are fed almost exclusively on live insects by the hen. A liberal choice has therefore to be provided during that time; it may consist of meal-worms, gentles, ants' eggs, scoured grubs, spiders, flies, locusts, and everything which can be swept with a butterfly net from the tall meadow grass on a warm summer's day. Sometimes the young have been fed exclusively on meal-worms, but more often the hen has refused to feed these only after the third day. The youngsters leave the nest after 12 days and remain hidden in the undergrowth as they are unable to fly properly. From the 12th day the cock and hen begin to feed them on insectivorous food, bread and milk, and bananas in addition to live insects. The young resemble the hen. Three weeks after leaving the nest they become independent and must be transferred to other quarters because a new nest will be started and the young from the first nest will then be persecuted ferociously and killed.

Generally, the cocks only assume full colouring after a year, and in some species not until after 16 to 20 months. Only in an outside aviary do the birds retain their brilliant colouring, and an extensive and varied menu assists them to do so.

The birds will soon become tame if given careful treatment and will take meal-worms from the hand. It has been stated that Red Tanagers can remain in the aviary during the winter, but I prefer to see them in a frost-proof room, or, better still, in a room moderately heated. It is not what they can stand, but how they will feel most comfortable, that is important.

Violet Tanager *Tanagra violacea*

Origin Guiana and Brazil.

Nearly 4 in. *Cock:* Above, the plumage is entirely of a rich violet black except for an orange-yellow spot on forehead. Below, it is entirely orange-yellow. Beak and legs black. *Hen:* Entirely olive green, paler under parts.

Diet: As for Tanagers generally. Some meal-worms and finely grated boiled meat (liver or heart) can be added now and again. Berries need not be crushed as they have strong beaks.

The cage must be kept scrupulously clean. Clean blotting paper for the floor covering and fresh water in the bath should be provided every day.

During the breeding season the cock sings sweetly and well; at other times only a plaintive call note is heard. The song is not very varied. Sometimes they will imitate a few notes from the song of another bird.

They are lively and more at home in a larger flight. They soon become tame. They are heavy eaters, and need considerable space to exercise, or they will grow over-fat.

Blue and Black Tanager *Tanagrella velia cyanomelana*

Origin South-East Brazil.

5½ in. *Cock:* Forehead bright blue, crown, and lower back silvery green, upper tail coverts, wing and tail feathers deep blue. Sides of head and throat bright blue, remainder of head and collar velvety black. Under surface greyish-blue with centre of abdomen and under tail coverts chestnut. Under wing coverts white. *Hen:* Very similar but a distinct greenish tone to blue of head and upper parts.

Not suited to cage life, being of a very active disposition, and best housed in a large flight affording ample opportunity for exercise.

Treatment should be similar to that given to the Violet Tanager, *Tanagra violacea*. It can be associated with other birds of its own size.

Three-coloured Tanager *Tangara seledon*

Origin South-West Brazil.

5½ in. *Cock:* Above shining green, bluish tone on crown, otherwise with a golden sheen. Forehead and upper back velvety black; lower back golden yellow; wings black, coverts edged with deep blue, primaries edged with bluish green and secondaries with golden green. Tail black edged with bluish green. Chin bluish green, a broad black patch on throat extending to join black on back. Breast and upper abdomen dark blue, flanks, belly, and under tail coverts golden green. Beak black, feet blackish. *Hen:* Colouring not so brilliant and with a more bluish tone generally, the black of the back being more of less spotted with green.

These birds should, if possible, be kept in a large aviary or cage where they will have an opportunity to show off to full advantage the beautiful and varied colours of their plumage. This shimmers and shines in the sun, and is a delight to behold.

Wrong feeding is the reason these birds have acquired a reputation for being 'difficult'. A varied diet, as in the case of the Violet Tanager, makes for healthy birds which can enjoy a long life. Spraying and fresh bath water are always essential. These birds are very tolerant, and can be kept with others of their species.

Their song is of no consequence, but they will quite readily become tame.

Superb Tanager *Tangara fastuosa* Pl. 132

Origin Brazil.

5½ in. *Cock:* Head and neck shining emerald green, forehead black. Upper back velvety black, lower back brilliant deep orange. Lesser wing coverts green, outer coverts purple, wings and tail black edged with purple. Chin black followed by a narrow band of green. Broad black crescent on upper breast. Breast and abdomen silvery blue deepening on belly and under tail coverts to deep ultramarine. Beak black, feet blackish. *Hen:* The green of head with a bluish tone and the feathers on the nape showing some black at the base. Lower back and rump less golden.

Similar treatment to that for the Three-coloured Tanager. They are peaceable, although sometimes they will squabble over roosting perches, but without serious consequences. They cannot be kept with small breeding birds, as they have a tendency to rob the nests of eggs and young.

Normal diet: They enjoy soaked bread with sugar and honey.

It is of utmost importance to purchase healthy birds, as should they be suffering from digestive trouble upon arrival it is almost hopeless to try to get them into good condition again.

Emerald-spotted Tanager *Tangara chrysophrys* Pl. 134

Origin North of South America.

5 in. *Cock:* Upper parts bright green, feathers of head, back, and wing coverts spangled with black; forehead and round the eyes pale golden-yellow;

lores black; wings dusky, the feathers edged with green; tail blackish edged with green. Under parts mainly greyish-white; flanks tinted green and the under tail coverts yellowish; sides of throat and upper breast conspicuously spotted with black. Beak blackish, legs dark brown. *Hen:* Like the cock but more grey in tone and lacking the yellow on forehead and round eyes. Green of a slightly more bluish tone. Often slightly larger than cock.

Silver-throated Tanager *Tangara icterocephala* Pl. 136

Origin South America.

5½ in. *Cock:* Forehead and crown golden with faint greenish markings on centre of crown, and greenish tone on nape; mantle, back, and rump greenish-gold with black markings on mantle; wings and tail blackish with golden-green edges to the feathers. A black moustache mark running from gape, below eyes to base of nape; throat silvery-grey; whole of under parts yellow, rather greenish on sides of breast and flanks; beak blackish-brown, legs and feet yellowish-brown. *Hen:* Upper parts less golden, with olive-green wash; throat dull greenish-grey, less distinctly divided from yellow of breast; stripes below the eyes greyish-black.

Paradise Tanager *Tangara chilensis*

Origin Netherlands Antilles.

5½ in. *Cock:* Nape, sides of the neck, back, and shoulders velvety black; forehead and crown shining yellow green, the feathers having the appearance of scales. Throat cobalt blue, lower part of back and rump orange-red running into golden-yellow, lower parts turquoise blue, under tail coverts black. Wings showing blue, tail black, eyes brown, bill and legs black. *Hen:* Similar to cock but smaller and colours less vivid.

Very seldom imported and consequently always expensive.

Desmarest's Tanager *Tangara gyrola desmaresti*

Origin Venezuela.

5½ in. *Cock:* Brilliant grass green. Under parts lighter. Sides of head and crown chestnut red-brown divided from nape by a narrow band of golden yellow. Wings grass green, flights with black margins and tail green, outer feathers being black on the inner webs. Eyes very dark brown almost black, bill and legs brown horn-coloured. *Hen:* A little less brightly coloured, and narrow golden collar at base of chestnut head is dull and less defined.

Like *Tangara seledon* and *Tangara fastuosa*, these birds are said to be delicate, but this erroneous idea is due to the fact that great care is necessary during acclimatization. Although the small Tanagers of the *Tangara* group may be more difficult to keep than the larger species of other groups, with normal care and with no undue trouble they will live in an aviary or cage for 10 years or more.

As a rule they do not arrive in good condition. They need to be kept warm and provided with fresh bath water several times a day. They should also be housed in a sunny spot.

Diet: As for Tanagers generally. 'Nightingale' food can be used and honey mixed with milk is particularly useful.

May be kept with other birds, preferably with other fruit- and insect-eaters. It is essential to keep the cages scrupulously clean. The birds look at their best in a conservatory where their colourful beauty will glitter in the sunshine. There they have ample room and will be active all day; in a small cage their activity is hampered. They will remain in grand condition, but should be kept in a warm room in winter.

Bay-headed Tanager *Tangara gyrola* Pl. 135

Origin Northern South America.

5½ in. There are 8 forms of the Chestnut-headed Tanager all of which differ only in minor details of colouring. *Cock:* Is mainly a bright green with a golden wash on the upper parts and more or less blue shading on the under parts. The head is golden-brown to reddish-chestnut and in most forms this colour is divided, on the nape, from the green of the back by a collar of gold, which is narrow and in some cases almost, or completely, inconspicuous. The flights are blackish; tail dark green on outer edges of feathers, more brown in centres. Beak and legs blackish. *Hen:* Is said to be less brilliant in colouring and the collar of a pale yellowish-buff.

Desmarest's Tanager, also described, is another of the forms of *Tangara gyrola*.

Mrs. Wilson's Tanager (Masked or Golden-masked Tanager) *Tangara nigrocincta franciscae* Pl. 133

Origin Mexico and northern South America.

5½ in. *Cock:* Forehead and cheeks bright violet-purple fading into turquoise; a narrow black line running across beak, through eye and on chin; crown, nape, sides of neck, and throat shining golden-buff with deep golden-buff in centre of throat. Mantle, scapulars, tail, and breast velvety black; wing coverts shining turquoise, secondaries and flights black, edged with golden green and turquoise; rump, upper tail coverts, and flanks bright blue with cobalt and violet wash and some black flecks; abdomen and under tail coverts pure white; beak and legs black. *Hen:* Very similar to cock but rump and flanks are said to be clear, light blue without violet wash or black flecks. Crown, nape, and throat less golden.

There are several races of this Tanager, varying slightly in size and intensity of colouring, especially on the head which in some is pale, pinkish-buff with a very pronounced reddish-gold throat spot.

Pretre's Tanager *Spindalis zena pretrei*

Origin Cuba.

5¼ in. *Cock:* Olive above, nape and rump orange-yellow. Head black with wide white stripe above the eye running to neck. Chin and wide malar stripe white. Under tail coverts white, abdomen orange, divided from throat by a black band. Wings black with brown and white marking. Tail black with white stripes. The various races all vary slightly in colouring. *Hen:* Is olive grey on head, throat, and upper parts. Wing feathers darker brownish-grey with pale or white margins. Under parts vary from dull grey to olive yellow.

Diet: Very easily catered for and satisfied with fine-quality 'Universal' food, soaked stale bread with sugar or rusk mixed with ants' eggs and grated carrot, with a few drops of honey.

They may be kept with the Paradise Tanager. They, too, like bathing and should also be sprayed. They keep mainly in the bushes and only descend to the ground to eat and drink. It is preferable, therefore, to fix their feeding table high up.

Their song consists only of a soft chirruping sound.

Maroon Tanager *Ramphocelus carbo*

Origin Surinam, South America.

6½ in. *Cock:* Dark wine red, back almost black, breast red but towards belly blue-white, legs dark brown. *Hen:* Pinkish-brown; rump and breast have a red glow. Wings and tail brown-black, bill brown.

Imported regularly but the consignments usually contain only cocks. Their acclimatization needs great care. They should be kept in a cage and fed with ripe apples and pears, bananas, and oranges, with meal-worms as a daily treat. They will become tame quite readily and eat meal-worms from the hand.

Diet: Canary seed, maw, and millet are liked, and insectivorous food may be mixed with the seeds. Bread and milk, sweetened with sugar or honey, is usually the basis of the daily menu. Ants' eggs, finely divided hard-boiled egg yolk, and all manner of insects will add variety.

The Maroon Tanager is said to be less hardy than the Scarlet Tanager, with which hybrids have been obtained. It must be kept in a moderately warm room during the winter.

Scarlet-rumped Tanager *Ramphocelus passerini* Pl. 140

Origin Central America.

6¾ in. *Cock:* Velvety black with rump and upper tail coverts brilliant scarlet. Beak silvery grey; legs blackish. *Hen:* Head and neck brownish-grey, otherwise brownish-olive, brighter on rump. Flights and tail sooty.

There are two other very closely related species, *R. chrysonotus*, the Orange-rumped Tanager, and R. *icteronotus*, the Yellow-rumped Tanager, which differ only in the colour of rump and upper tail coverts as indicated by their common names.

Scarlet Tanager *Ramphocelus brasilius* Pl. 139

Origin Brazil.

7 in One of the most freely imported of larger Tanagers, and often obtainable in pairs. The hen is dull brown.

Newly imported birds must be acclimatized very carefully. During that period they should be given some stale white bread soaked in milk, and mixed with fine-grade insect food and orange cut up into small pieces and sprinkled with icing sugar.

The floor of their cage should be covered with sawdust. Bathing is necessary to keep them in good condition. A hanging bird table is recommended for feeding. The birds can be kept out of doors, from May to the end of August, but they must be in a shelter at night. The remainder of the year they should be kept indoors in a moderately heated room.

This species is a reasonably free breeder in captivity. The cock assists the hen to rear the chicks. The nest will be rather carelessly constructed in a nest box with an artificial nest lining or in an old nest. The chicks are fed mainly on insects and fruit. In addition to the fine-grade insectivorous food, a quantity of ants' eggs and finely chopped meal-worms must be given, mixed with hard-boiled egg. Finely chopped fruit and berries should always be on the menu. These birds must, as a rule, be kept by themselves as they prey on chicks from other nests and also steal the eggs. A single bird

may perhaps be kept with other large birds of a similar type. They soon grow tame.

Black Tanager *Tachyphonus rufus* Pl. 137

Origin Brazil.

6½ in. *Cock:* Glossy blue-black, wings and tail dull black, secondary wing coverts white. Eyes brown, bill black, with grey-white mark at the base of the mandibles. Legs black. *Hen:* Rusty brown, the under parts more yellow-brown, wings dark brown with light margins.

Diet: Once they become accustomed to a menu of Canary seed, millet, and oats, on which they can live for quite a while, together with insectivorous food and lots of fruit such as bananas, oranges, pears and apples, bread and milk sweetened with sugar or honey, they do well. They have been known to reach an age of at least 20 years and are very hardy. They can even winter out of doors if a good shelter is available. They like hard-boiled egg which has been chopped; fresh spinach and thistles as green food; meal-worms, locusts, and other insects.

A very varied menu is essential to get them into good condition for breeding. If other birds are to be kept in the same aviary they must be the larger types of parrakeets or the larger weavers, who will not be intimidated by the stormy temperament of the Tanagers.

The nest is constructed from coarse grasses and leaves such as the withered foliage of narcissus and other bulbous plants, and some feathers. The birds prefer to build in a dense bush but will sometimes use a nest box or baskets.

The 2 or 3 eggs are incubated solely

by the hen and hatch in 12 days. The young leave the nest after another 12 days, but they cannot fly properly and will remain hidden in the branches. During rearing unlimited quantities of insects should be supplied; variety is most essential. After the birds have left the nest, the parents will begin to feed them with insectivorous food and bread and milk. The youngsters resemble the hen, though paler in colour. When the hen starts to nest again and it is time for the second clutch to come out, the first family must immediately be housed separately.

Palm Tanager *Thraupis palmarum*

Origin Brazil.

7¾ in. *Cock* and *Hen* similar. Olive green above, blue-grey on under parts. Wings brown-black, as is the tail with olive green margins. Eyes dark, bill dark horn-coloured, legs brown. In selecting a pair, a bird of slighter build and paler colouring should be chosen as a likely hen.

Diet: As for Tanagers generally.

Their song is insignificant but their colour and gloss compensate for all other failings. They are lively and show to better advantage in an aviary than a cage.

If a nest box or basket is hung up high in the aviary, they will build in it. Grasses, hemp teasings, roots of plants, and mosses will be used to form the nest. The young may remain in the nest for as long as a month after they have been hatched, and the parents will feed them for a considerable time longer.

These Tanagers bathe frequently and thoroughly. The cage and the aviary must be kept scrupulously clean. The birds should be kept indoors, or in a frost-proof room, during winter.

Silver-blue Tanager *Thraupis virens*
Pl. 138

Origin Central and South America.

6½–7 in. *Cock:* Head pale ashy-blue, deeper on back and more blue on rump and breast; wings and tail dark greyish blue with a greenish sheen on edges of flights and upper wing coverts glittering pale blue. Beak dark greyish-horn; legs black. *Hen:* Similar but duller in general tone and slightly more greenish. This is a hardy species when once acclimatized, and provided the aviary has a frost-proof shelter, may be safely kept outdoors throughout the year. Like all the larger Tanagers, it is inclined to be spiteful and should not be associated with smaller birds which are not capable of defending themselves.

Sayaca Tanager *Thraupis sayaca*

Origin Brazil.

6 in. *Cock* and *Hen* alike. The colour is light grey-blue, under parts somewhat lighter. Green-blue on the wings, along the tail and upper tail coverts, the flights and tail feathers having green margins.

These birds do not show to the best advantage in a cage. They need at least a bird room, still better an outside aviary, in order to display their full beauty. They are nearly always peaceable with other birds. They build a cup-shaped nest in dense shrubbery, constructed of stems of plants, rootlets, hay and moss, all of which they will blend together.

Diet: Insectivorous food, live insects, and a regular supply of fresh fruit cut into small pieces; on this fare they will remain in good health for many years.

They bathe freely several times a day. They must be kept in a frost-proof room during the winter or, better still, a moderately warm room.

Toco Toucan (Giant Toucan) *Ramphastos toco* Pl. 142

Origin Guiana, Brazil, Paraguay, and Argentina.

22 in., of which the beak measures nearly 9 in. *Cock:* Upper parts velvety black except rump which is pure white; cheeks, throat, and upper breast white, more or less tinged with reddish-orange at edges; under tail coverts crimson; remainder of under parts black. Bill orange, stained on culmen and cutting edges with red, a broad black band across base of both mandibles and a large circular black mark at tip of upper mandible. Naked orbital patch orange and the dark hazel eyes surrounded by a ring of rich cobalt. Legs and feet blue-grey.

No difference in colouring of sexes but bill of hen is deeper, shorter, and more bluntly terminated.

This is the largest of the Toucans and only suitable for a large aviary where it can take plenty of exercise. It can stand quite low temperatures but dislikes damp, cold winter nights and should be provided with a well-protected and frost-proof shelter in which some heat can be supplied during severe weather conditions.

Diet: It subsists mainly on fruit and should be supplied with a mixture of dates, dried figs, and apple cut into small cubes and well sprinkled with a dry insectivorous mixture to prevent the fruit from becoming too moist or sticky. Wet fruits such as banana, pear, and grapes or other soft fruits should only be given occasionally, as a change of diet, as they are not sufficiently sustaining for such an active bird.

Individual birds can become delightfully tame and confiding, and make splendid pets, but they are pugnacious and will fight savagely between themselves, often causing severe injury to their beaks which, in spite of their massive appearance, are almost hollow apart from a network of fibrous nerves, and very frail. It is seldom possible to keep even a true pair together, once they become fully adult, as they will almost certainly attack each other sooner or later.

There is a southern race, R. *toco albogularis*, which differs only in having the throat snowy white without any tinge of orange.

Toco Toucans have never been bred in captivity although a pair did have eggs which the hen incubated for some time but which proved to be infertile. In common with all species of Toucans, they nest in holes in trees, usually at a considerable height from the ground, and the young are given a certain amount of animal food in addition to fruit.

Green-billed Toucan *Ramphastos dicolorus* Pl. 141

Origin Brazil, Paraguay, and Argentina

20 in. *Cock:* Upper parts entirely black. Cheeks, chin, and throat yellow. Breast orange. Abdomen red. Round the grey-green eye there is a red naked orbital patch. Beak green with red cutting edges and a black basal band. Legs grey. *Hen:* Similar colouring but distinguished by shape of bill which is deeper and more arched on clumen, and upper mandible ends with a more pronounced down-curved 'tooth', whereas bill of cock is narrower and tapers more gradually to a forward pointing tip. Though these interesting birds are rarely found in private collections, I want to draw attention to their suitability as house pets. The Toucan chicks are usually taken from the nest

when quite young and then reared by hand. As a result the birds are quite tame as a rule, and readily accept a new home and master. Their voices are loud and very harsh, but they also make a purring sound. It is advisable to keep them in a very large flight or to give them the freedom of the room. They soon learn to take food from the hand and will also perch on one's shoulder.

Diet: Toucans are chiefly fruit-eaters. Macaroni boiled until soft, potatoes, rice, soaked bread, and boiled maize mixed and covered with sugar make suitable food if given with cut-up pears, sections of orange, pieces of apple, banana, and various berries. The birds appreciate hens' eggs, hard-boiled, or raw birds' eggs, and pieces of raw meat. A dead sparrow is eaten, also mealworms and all kinds of beetles.

These birds must be given opportunities to bathe. During the summer they enjoy sand baths.

There are various smaller Toucanets and Aracaris.

Chestnut-billed Emerald Toucanet *Aulacorhynchus haematopygus* Pl. 144

Origin Colombia and Venezuela.

About 14 in. *Cock:* Plumage entirely green except for crimson rump. A golden sheen on nape, wings rather a dull brownish-green, tail bluish-green with chestnut tips to the central feathers; under parts more apple green which tends to turn bluish when the birds moult in captivity.

Bill is long, rather straight, and tapering to a slightly hooked tip and black with chestnut running down the centre of each mandible, with a broad white band across base. The naked orbital patch is dark reddish-purple, eyes dark hazel, and legs and feet bluish-grey. *Hen:* Very similar but

distinctly smaller and with smaller bill. This species comes from a comparatively high altitude in the Andes and is fairly hardy when once acclimatized but it needs some protection in winter as it is subject to frostbite. It is less pugnacious than the large toucans and a pair will usually live in harmony, but should not be associated with species smaller than themselves as they will kill and swallow small birds.

Diet: They require the same form of fruit mixture as described for the Toco Toucan although it should be of a rather smaller grade. They, and in fact most of the toucans, are very fond of cherries and these may be given whole as the birds will have no difficulty in disposing of the stones. They also appreciate live insects and an occasional mouse or small amount of minced beef, but the latter should not be given more than once a week.

They have never been bred.

Spot-billed Toucanet *Selenidera maculirostris* Pl. 143

Origin Southern Brazil.

About 11 in. *Cock:* Head, nape, throat, and breast glossy black, a tuft of orange and yellow feathers on cheeks and ear coverts. A half collar of orange at base of hind neck; remainder of upper parts glossy dark bottle-green, the tail being tipped with chestnut; abdomen greenish-brown, flanks golden-brown; under tail coverts scarlet. Orbital patch is bright greenish-blue, eye orange and bill greenish-grey with black markings on both upper and lower mandibles which shade into dull yellow at the tips. Legs and feet blue-grey. *Hen:* Those parts which are black in the cock are dark, warm brown and the tufts on ear coverts greenish-yellow. Collar at back of neck dull, less conspicuous, and sometimes entirely absent.

This species once succeeded in hatching a chick at the London Zoo but unfortunately failed to rear it. This is the only record of any of the Toucans having bred in captivity.

Feeding and general management should be as described for the Emerald Toucanet but the Spot-bill is less hardy and needs artificial heat in winter.

American Mocking Bird *Mimus polyglottus*

Origin North America.

Nearly 10 in. *Cock:* Above greybrown, the feathers having darker centres. Eyebrow streak pale greyishwhite, lores dusky. Wings very dark brown with two white bars. Tail blackish with outer feathers white. Beak and legs black. *Hen:* Similar, but marking less prominent.

Attractive sóngsters and reasonably free breeders, these are best kept in pairs. When first imported they must be carefully acclimatized, but once they become accustomed to artificial food and our climatic conditions they will prove hardy and can even winter out of doors.

Being active, they need plenty of space; they bathe frequently. They can be readily reared in an aviary but are somewhat erratic nesters. The hen is often fiercely pursued by the cock and if she is allowed no rest at all, it is better to catch the male and only allow him to be with the hen occasionally until a successful mating has been observed. After that it is, as a rule, safe to leave them together.

Diet: Similar to that of the thrushes, and should include quantities of living insects, on which the young are almost entirely reared.

The cock must be watched for the first few days after hatching to see that he does not kill the young. If he starts to feed them there need be no more cause for anxiety. When the young have grown to be independent, they must be placed in a separate aviary, so that the parents can begin further breeding operations in peace.

Mountain Bluebird *Sialia currucoides* Pl. 145

Origin Canada, North America.

6 in. *Cock:* Entirely light sky-blue, metallic on upper parts paling on throat and abdomen; flight and tail feathers with an almost cobalt sheen; under tail coverts white. Eye very dark brown, beak and legs blackish. *Hen:* Upper parts dull brown with only a wash of blue; flights and tail dull, deep blue. Under parts pale ash-brown. Beak and legs brownish-black. Immature birds much like hen but the breast is spotted with pearl-white.

There are two other species of American Bluebird, Western Bluebird, *Sialia mexicana*, the cock of which has the back dark chestnut-brown across the shoulders and saddle, the remainder of the upper parts including the face, throat, and tail deep purplish blue; breast and flanks rich chestnut; abdomen dull blue; under tail coverts white. Beak and legs black. Eastern Bluebird, *Sialia sialis*, which differs in having the whole of the upper parts, including the face, deep sky-blue and the under parts chestnut-red.

Hens of all three species are much alike but may be distinguished by the shade of blue on wings and tail which corresponds with that of the cocks.

All three species are comparatively hardy, although they are migratory within the American continent, moving south for the winter months, and therefore appreciate some protection during the worst of our winter. They will do well in an outdoor aviary and will breed readily, using any type of nest box of suitable size providing it is in a secluded position, and building therein a cup-shaped nest of grasses and moss, lined with finer grass. The eggs, pale blue and usually 4 in number, hatch in 14 days. Cock and hen share the task of rearing the young which are fed entirely on live food such as gentles, meal-worms, and other grubs, and ants' cocoons if available.

When adult they will live on any fine-grade insectivorous mixture, with the addition of a few gentles or meal-worms daily. In a wild state they are said also to eat berries but in captivity they seldom show much interest in any form of fruit.

Unfortunately they are all of a quarrelsome nature and pairs are best kept in an aviary on their own. During the non-breeding season it may even be necessary to separate the sexes, as a pair which have lived contentedly together during the summer months may suddenly start to bicker when their nesting activities are over and occasionally may fight really viciously with fatal results. The Mountain Bluebirds appear to be the most aggressive of the three species and need careful watching at all times.

Yellow-headed Marshbird *Agelaius icterocephalus*

Origin South America.

Nearly 7 in. *Cock:* Entirely glossy black except for neck and head which are bright yellow. Eyes brown, legs brown-black. *Hen:* Upper parts black, under parts yellowish, head olive coloured.

Only cocks are imported, and these but seldom. They may be kept with other large birds in an aviary.

Diet: Mainly in seeds, canary seed and millet, and insectivorous food in moderation. They are very fond of meal-worms and when offered these, soon become tame.

Their song is insignificant and rather harsh; hence they are not suitable for a cage. In an aviary, the vivid yellow of the head shows up to the best advantage against the glossy black colouring.

Details of breeding from these birds are not yet available. The young are reared entirely on insects.

Red-winged Blackbird (Red-shouldered Marshbird) *Agelaius phoeniceus* Pl. 146

Origin Canada and North America.

Nearly 9 in. *Cock:* Black with dull green sheen. Lesser upper wing coverts orange-red and vivid red. Bill and legs black. *Hen:* Considerably smaller. Entirely dull brown heavily striated, with lighter eyebrow stripes.

Diet: As well as insectivorous food, they require canary seed, rice (paddy), and occasionally half-ripe corn on the cob; also insects, such as meal-worms, daily. To prevent them from becoming over-fat, they must be given fruit regularly and need ample freedom for exercise.

Their song is rather sharp and chirrupy, but not disturbing. They can be kept with other large birds so long as these are not of the same species, but the cock becomes exceedingly aggressive during breeding season and the pair are then best kept on their own.

As the hens are so rarely imported, breeding results are seldom reported, but the species has been bred on numerous occasions. In their natural state the young are reared mainly on insects. The birds can safely remain in the outside aviary summer and winter.

Yellow-headed Blackbird *Xanthocephalus xanthocephalus*

Origin North America and into North Mexico.

9½ in. *Cock:* Head and neck orange-yellow, black lores, and remainder of body black. Eyes brown, legs and bill black. A white spot is seen on wing. *Hen:* Smaller, grey-brown, eyebrow stripe and cheeks yellowy-white. Side of the breast striped with white, upper breast yellow. Sings with metallic flute notes, mixed with a creaking and cheeping sound.

These birds live amicably with larger species in a roomy aviary. During the nest-building and breeding time, however, they become aggressive and are dangerous to small birds.

Diet: Insectivorous food and canary seed with millet; meal-worms and various insects. The birds spend much time on the ground where they hunt diligently for food and will work hard on upturned sods of turf. They build their nest in slovenly fashion in a pine tree or nest box from blades of grass, feathers, and fibres.

They like sand baths and also bathe frequently. They can stand our climate well and can even winter outside. It is remarkable that during the winter months the yellow colour on their head will turn to brown.

Black Cowbird *Molothrus ater*

Origin Mexico and U.S.A.

6½ in. *Cock* and *Hen:* Head and neck brown. Underneath greenish-black, above shining violet-black. Beak and legs black, eyes brown. These birds are available fairly regularly, sometimes even in pairs. Their song is not especially beautiful.

Diet: Consists of canary seed, grass seed, weed seed, and millet, 'Universal' food, meal-worms, some green food and fruit.

Not always suitable companions for small birds. This species is parasitic and has not yet been successfully bred in captivity. Incubation is said to last 12 days.

The Brown and Silky Cowbirds are also imported sometimes. Their treatment should be similar.

Military Starling *Pezites (Trupialis) militaris*

Origin South America.

Nearly 10 in. *Cock:* Brown, heavily striated, with buff eyebrow stripes and a touch of red in front of eyes. Chest and abdomen red, legs grey. Beak dark horn-colour and eyes brown. *Hen:* Less red on breast, and her tail feathers are barred with brown.

Not obtainable regularly, but easy to keep and, because of its inquisitive nature, can be quickly tamed.

Diet: Insects and seeds, 'Universal' food, cut-up fruit, and green food.

These birds sing pleasantly although their voice is not powerful. They are strong and spend much of their time on the ground searching for food. They must be kept separately or with other large birds as they are inclined to be aggressive and their sharp beaks may easily cause serious injury to smaller birds which are less able to defend themselves. These starlings like to sleep on the floor of their cage or aviary, where they will hide beneath tufts of grass.

They are most attractive birds to

keep, but in winter need protection in an unheated room. They can be out in the flight on sunny days.

Common Hangnest (Brazilian Hangnest) *Icterus icterus*

Origin South America.

Nearly 9 in. Head, throat, nape, and tail feathers black. Wing coverts orange and black with white bar on flights. Underneath breast is orange merging into yellow. Around yellow eyes is a naked bluish orbital patch. Nape feathers are long and somewhat loose. *Hen* smaller.

They are active, and, as they are very inquisitive, can be quickly tamed. Their song is pleasant and flute-like, although they have not a wide range of notes.

Diet: In addition to 'Universal' food a liberal supply of meal-worms must be provided, beetles, locusts, etc. Soaked stale bread or biscuit and a little raw meat may be given now and again. All kinds of fruit such as bananas, oranges, pears, and grapes, cut into pieces, and elderberries are essential. Dried fruit, if cut-up finely and soaked, is appreciated, and as a special treat currants, raisins, pieces of date, and fig can be given. Infinite variety is advisable. If a young skinned mouse is offered as a change, this will also be eaten with avidity.

This diet is suitable for all species of Hangnest.

Although these birds are hardy and feel the cold but little, they must be kept indoors during the winter, preferably in a warm room.

Baltimore Hangnest (Baltimore Oriole) *Icterus galbula* Pl. 147

Origin North America.

7 in. *Cock:* Orange-yellow in colour with black head, throat, and back. Tail and wings black, wings with white markings. Beak and legs black. *Hen:* Greyer on the upper parts and pale yellow underneath.

Supplies of these birds are irregular but they are most desirable both for cage and aviary, and are not difficult to feed or to associate with other birds. They are satisfied with 'Universal' food and seed, meal-worms, and cut-up fruit.

They can be very quickly tamed and are most amusing pets. They may be allowed to fly at liberty now and again. Other species of Hangnests are more suitable for aviaries, but are nearly all rather larger than the Baltimore, and may prove dangerous companions for other smaller occupants. They are also inclined to interfere with other birds' nests.

Baltimore Hangnests will build beautiful nests in captivity and have been successfully bred. Their song is varied and pleasant. To keep them fit they need adequate flight space; they are always active and must be able to take plenty of exercise among the branches. They will seldom be found on the ground but they are fond of bathing. As all Hangnests are mainly yellow, black, and white in colour, it is not at all easy to distinguish different species.

APPENDIX A

THE ZEBRA FINCH AND ITS MUTATIONS

Taeniopygia guttata castanotis and its various domesticated forms

The hobby of breeding Zebra Finches has increased so much, and will continue to attract so many more fanciers, that a thorough discussion is necessary.

Readers may be more familiar with the scientific names used by Gould. In his *Synops. Birds of Australia*, 1837 he named it *Amadina castanotis* and later amended this to *Taeniopygia castanotis*. Later it became *Poephila guttata* but it was then discovered that this name applied to a sub-species in the islands of Flores and Timor. To distinguish the Australian form the name was adjusted to *Poephila guttata castanotis*. Recently the name has again been altered to *Taeniopygia guttata castanotis*.

It might have been expected that the colour varieties now generally seen would all be bred in Europe, but nothing could be further from the truth. Much colour breeding has taken place in Japan and Australia and regular consignments of birds have been sent to Europe from those countries. But breeders in Europe now specialize in the newest varieties and, attracted by the high prices offered, carry on a profitable spare-time business. This unfortunately results in misleading names being given to some varieties and high prices being paid for birds which derive their value only by reason of an expensive 'label'. When the bird societies have fixed a standard for each variety and have decided on a standard name, this regrettable practice will cease automatically. In fact, this has already been done in England by the Zebra Finch Society, which was formed some years ago specially to foster interest in the breeding of this Finch.

CARE AND BREEDING OF THE ZEBRA FINCH

In their natural surroundings these birds breed in colonies. Owing to their virility and strong breeding instincts, there is apt to be considerable bickering and disturbance if only 2 or 3 pairs are kept together in a roomy cage or aviary, but if 10 or more pairs are kept there is a better chance of peace and tranquillity. Care must be taken to see that there are many more nest boxes than there are pairs of birds.

The feeding of Zebra Finches presents no difficulty. A mixture of small panicum millet and canary seed is sufficient to keep them in prime condition. The best method is to supply these seeds unmixed and separately in seed pots or in separate compartments of the automatic seed hopper. It is, of course, essential that the seed be of first-class quality.

Green food, such as lettuce and chickweed, must be supplied in ample quantities and suspended in a small rack. The floor of the cage or aviary must be covered with fine oyster grit or ground sea shells. Finely ground charcoal mixed with this is also beneficial. A few drops of cod-liver oil should be sprinkled on the seed during the winter months. This prevents difficulties with the moult and especially reduces the risk of egg binding. The breeding time usually runs smoothly, and although the parent birds can rear their young quite well on the seed and green food mentioned, the favourable development of the youngsters can be stimulated by giving them germinated seed and stale bread soaked in milk, during this period. Unripe grass seed on the stalk as well as millet sprays are a treat, and are at the same time excellent food. Cuttlefish should also be supplied. The hen should be given a lot of lime.

Wherever Zebra Finches are kept, in a small breeding pen in the attic, the living-room, or in a large flight together with kindred or other foreign finches, they will start nesting. They incubate diligently and are seldom disturbed by periodical inspection of the nest. They become terribly fussy once the young have been hatched.

When the nest boxes have been hung up, they must be filled immediately for the greater part with hay, moss, and blades of grass. These birds prefer to build their nest right up to the top of the box. If they begin with an empty nest box, the hen will lay her 4 to 6 eggs on the foundation layer of nesting material. Then another nest will be built on top of the eggs and a further clutch will be laid, sometimes even 3 layers one on top of the other. The top layer will then be hatched, but often something goes wrong, for the hen has become completely exhausted after the laying of a dozen or more eggs. The boxes must therefore be filled up beforehand, and after the eggs have been laid no more nesting material should be supplied. This trouble will then be avoided.

The best nest boxes are those which have a partially open front. They should be filled up to just under this opening, and then left to the birds themselves. It is better not to let them incubate more than half a dozen eggs, or the nest gets too full and the old birds cannot provide enough food. The young would receive insufficient nourishment and this would affect their physical condition later in life. It is very unwise to breed with birds which are not at least 8 months old. They will not be fully developed and this will result in the production of inferior young.

After 12 days' incubation (both birds sit alternately) the young hatch and leave the nest after only 20 days. Although they learn to eat by themselves quite quickly, they allow themselves to be fed for some time by the cock. Once they have grown independent they should be transferred to a large flight where they can exercise to their hearts' content. They will then develop well.

No nesting facility should be available in such a flight or these young birds might begin to nest after about 3 months. This must be prevented at all costs. Not more than 4 nests of young should be bred and reared per pair per season. This must be watched, especially if the birds are kept indoors. If not prevented from doing so, they will go on and on, summer and winter, and then one morning it will be found that the hen, which outwardly has looked quite healthy, has become completely exhausted and has died.

Birds which have been bred in Europe will be fully acclimatized. If they are kept outside, they can stay there summer and winter, provided there is adequate shelter. During severe frost the drinking water must be watched, but no bath need be provided. If the birds are taken indoors for the winter there is a risk of sickness and even death in the spring; the birds will become weak and unable to stand the change from the warmth of a room to an outdoor aviary.

Zebra Finches not only breed in nest boxes but also roost in them all the year round; therefore these boxes should not be taken away during the winter. To prevent breeding during the winter, the cocks should be separated from the hens. Indoors the nest boxes may be removed, as the birds can roost quite well on perches if the room be kept at a correct, even temperature.

If it is desired to keep the birds in a heated room during the winter, they can also be allowed to breed. In that case they must be given a few months' rest during the summer. It is quite pleasant to have young birds in the nest during the dark winter months. An even temperature is essential, but during the nights it may be allowed to drop a little.

Naturally, the birds must be caged in a light position in the house, say on top of a book case; not in the kitchen above the range. It is well to repeat that one pair of birds only should be kept in a cage. Special consideration must be given to the fact that any odd cock or hen will be persecuted to death.

In considering the various colours to be found in bird shops as a rule, cock and hen can be readily distinguished. But this is more difficult with the white variety, where the lacquer-red bill of the cock and the slightly less bright bill of the hen is the only obvious difference.

For serious colour breeding with Zebra Finches it is essential to house each pair separately in breeding pens, thereby avoiding the risk of undesired matings; the birds remain quiet and the breeding can be properly controlled. The colour breeder should keep an accurate record book and should see that a card is fixed on every cage, stating hereditary factors and pedigree. Often he will have to determine by experiment whether a certain bird has one or other recessive or sex-linked factors; this may be of the utmost importance for future breeding. The outward appearance of the birds in most instances conceals one or more other colour factors.

If a pair of fawn-coloured birds were owned and these were split for white, a fact which could not be detected from their outward appearance, this would become evident with an experimental brood, since not all of the youngsters would be fawn. Probably the greater part, say, 75%, would be, but the remaining 25% would turn out white. Of this 75% only one third would be homotype fawn, *i.e.* pure fawn colour. This is almost impossible to detect by looking at the birds, but the remaining two-thirds which might appear pale in colour are actually a dilute fawn merging in to beige.

THE COLOUR VARIATIONS

White

The first mutation which appeared, apart from variation in shades of grey, was white. Not an albino type, although this also exists, but a recessive white, of which the heredity is as follows:

white × normal = 100% normal split for white;
white × normal/white = 50% white and 50% normal/white;
white × white = 100% white.

The normal/white birds cannot be distinguished from the normal. From different combinations normal as well as normal/white appear. Unless the pedigree is known and guaranteed, there is no certainty that birds carrying the white factor have been bought.

Variegated (pied)

The grey birds show white spots in the grey feathering. The more regular these spots are, the better. Symmetry must be aimed at. It is difficult to build up a handsome pedigree stock; the cock and hen must be practically equal in markings and colour. Variegated is also recessive to normal grey; the heredity runs therefore as follows:

variegated × normal = 100% normal/variegated;
variegated × normal/variegated = 50% variegated and 50% normal/variegated;
variegated × variegated = 100% variegated.

If we now combine the two recessive colours we again obtain grey, *viz.* variegated × white = normal/white and variegated.

The variegated may be produced in other colours as well as grey.

Fawn

In place of grey, a fawn hen has appeared. The heredity factor is quite different here, *viz.* sex-linked. From a fawn cock only his daughters will inherit the fawn colour. *As hens can never be 'split' for another colour, at the beginning of a sex-linked hereditary series hens only of this colour will appear.*

M

This is clearly shown by the following rules:

> normal/fawn × normal = 25% normal/fawn, 25% normal cocks and 25% normal, 25% fawn hens;
>
> normal/fawn × fawn = 25% normal/fawn, 25% fawn cocks and 25% normal, 25% fawn hens;
>
> normal × fawn = 50% normal/fawn cocks and 50% normal hens;
>
> fawn × normal = 50% normal/fawn cocks and 50% fawn hens;
>
> fawn × fawn = 100% fawn for cocks and hens.

It must always be borne in mind that: *The percentages are calculated for 100 young birds when it is also assumed that cocks and hens are produced in equal proportions.*

The above figures are therefore no more than theoretical expectations. In a nest of 4 to 6 birds it is quite possible that they will be all cocks, or on the other hand, all hens, and hence the percentages for that nest are entirely different from the above expectations.

In the grey as well as in the fawn series, mutations appear, as for instance, variegated and white, while in both the fading factor may be active. As a result a large number of shades appear. The fawn which has appeared in place of the grey really points to a colour weakening, and it follows that the white which has appeared from the fawn is less forceful than the white which has materialized from the grey.

Silver (wrongly named Pastel Blue)

The silver factor is a dilute of the grey and may show itself as a single (I) or double (II) factor, which makes no difference to the outward appearance, but will become evident by experiments on a hereditary basis. The silver factor is passed on differently *viz.* it is dominant to the normal grey.

The intensity of the bluey-silver gloss varies a great deal and the colour may be divided into three groups, dark, medium, and light. The heredity runs as follows:

> silver I × normal = 50% silver I and 50% normal;
>
> silver I × silver I = 25% silver II, and 50% silver I, and 25% normal;
>
> silver I × silver II = 50% silver I and 50% silver II.

*To all rules on heredity, with the exception of sex-linked rules, the expecta-
tions for hens and cocks may be equally divided.*

White-throated (nomenclature—Peter A. Pope)

Now renamed Penguin and has also been known as Silver-winged.

The most important characteristics of this variety are the pure
white chest and abdomen, the white cheeks, the almost white tail,
and especially the lack of the barring on throat and breast. The grey
is silver-grey on the back, head, and wings.

The colour is recessive to the grey. It is possible to breed various
shades of this colour and a number of new variations are created by
this means.

The White-throated Zebra Finches have entirely black eyes. On
the whole, they are somewhat smaller than the other varieties. By
the transference of the recessive factor the young in the nest have the
outward appearance of dominants, but they are all 'split' for the
recessive properties of the parent bird. When youngsters are crossed
back with their recessive parents, 50% of them resemble the parent
birds. It is immaterial whether the cock or the hen was the bearer of
the recessive factor. This is quite different in the case of the heredity
of the sex-linked factors, such as fawn, cream, and marked
cream.

A combination of two recessive factors produces in the first
generation normal birds, *i.e.* grey or fawn, which are 'split' for both
recessive factors. Fawn birds can only come into existence if the parent
cock was 'split' for fawn. All fawn youngsters will then be hens (see
under heading *Fawn*).

It may be expected that nearly all fawn, grey, white, and cream
Zebra Finches which are offered for sale possess a number of unknown factors, which may appear only in the course of future genera-
tions. The presence of this hidden factor explains why breeding results
do not always conform to recognized rules of heredity or expectations.

But the fault lies with the fancier, who forgets that these rules can
only be applied if breeding is carried out solely with absolutely
pure stock birds of known pedigree. Only when the breeder buys
birds with a guarantee of pure pedigree may the rules be relied upon;
otherwise pure stock has to be built up by corrective matings.

Cream

This is one of the most attractive colours developed from the combination silver × fawn. Here there exist combined hereditary rules, *viz.* the dominant and the sex-linked.

The following are examples:

fawn × silver = silver/fawn cocks and cream hens;
silver × fawn = cream cocks and cream hens.

It should be noted: *With all matings the cock is named in the first place.*

To breed a beautiful light cream bird, lightly tinted silvers and lightly tinted fawns should be paired together. The silver factor can appear twice and by this means cream may have a double silver factor from which the most beautiful birds can be produced.

If a start is made with two cream birds, there should be some double silver factors among the young provided none of the brood are lost. Unfortunately reliable pedigrees of such birds are rare.

Following are the results of a number of matings—*expectations*, not inevitable results. Abbreviations are:

SS single factor silver, DS double factor silver,
SC single factor cream, DC double factor cream.
♂ = cock; ♀ = hen; f = fawn; n = normal.

I. SC × SC = DC, SC, and f. SC × DC = SC and DC. DC × DC = DC.
SC × f = f ♂ and SC ♂ and f ♀ and SC ♀.
II. f ♂ × SS = n/f and SS/f ♂ and f ♀ and SC ♀.
f ♂ × DS = SS/f ♂ and SC ♀.
III. SS × f = n/f ♂ and SS/f ♀ and n ♀ and SS ♀.
DS × f = SS/f ♂ and SS ♀.
IV. SS/f × f = n/f ♂ and SS/f ♂ and f ♂ and SC ♂, n ♀ and SS ♀, f ♀ and SC ♀.
DS/f × f = SS/f ♂ and SC ♂ and SS ♀ and SC ♀.

In practice double factor birds will appear seldom or not at all.

If birds of a normal colour come from a mating, then the parent birds are always single factor specimens.

If one of the parents has the dominant factor double then all the youngsters will inherit that factor and hence will be recognizable by their appearance.

Marked White (nomenclature—Rutgers) (chestnut-flanked)

One of the last mutations, in which the cocks and the hens are creamy white but show distinctly the black markings as well, while the cocks have the typical orange brown flanks with white spots. The colour is hereditary sex-linked.

When it is realized that the most important new mutations which have been described show a great difference in their depth of shading indicating a corresponding number of variations, and that the parents of these birds may themselves be the products of a cross between different colours, resulting in the cocks being 'split', for more than one variety, it will be understood that it is vital for a colour specialist breeder first and foremost to ensure that he has accurate pedigree of his stock birds.

When acquiring birds, the following rule should always be remembered: *There are no grey birds which can pass on the silver factor* (except by mutation) *and there are no fawn birds which can pass on the cream factor.*

Advertisements unfortunately often offer birds with fixed colour propensities; sometimes the advertisers act in good faith because they are not conversant with the laws of heredity and only intend to state that the birds to be sold have come from parents of a certain colour.

The best plan is to buy exclusively those birds which proclaim their colour by their outward appearance. The guarantee of purity of stock heightens their market value considerably. The Zebra Finches have now reached the same standard attained years ago by Canaries and Budgerigars. Many people lack the courage and patience to take up this interesting breeding seriously and will be quite content with casual results from widely divergent birds, or will restrict their interests to one special colour and endeavour to produce the most beautiful type of bird possible in that particular variety.

In any case it is an interesting experiment to start breeding Zebra Finches. Their charm and liveliness will be worth all the trouble involved.

INDEX OF ENGLISH NAMES

Illustration numbers are in bold figures. The other numbers refer to text pages

INDEX OF LATIN NAMES

Illustration numbers are in bold figures.   The other numbers refer to text pages